With admiration,

Mark

Measuring Judicial Independence

A volume in the series

STUDIES IN LAW AND ECONOMICS
EDITED BY *William M. Landes and J. Mark Ramseyer*

Also in this series

Pervasive Prejudice? Unconventional Evidence of
Race and Gender Discrimination
BY *Ian Ayres*

Politics and Property Rights: The Closing of the Open Range
in the Postbellum South
BY *Shawn Everett Kantor*

Are Predatory Commitments Credible? Who Should the Courts Believe?
BY *John R. Lott Jr.*

More Guns, Less Crime: Understanding Crime and Gun Control Laws,
Second Edition
BY *John R. Lott Jr.*

Japanese Law: An Economic Approach
BY *J. Mark Ramseyer and Minoru Nakazato*

When Rules Change: An Economic and Political Analysis of
Transition Relief and Retroactivity
BY *Daniel Shaviro*

Smoke-Filled Rooms: A Postmortem on the Tobacco Deal
BY *W. Kip Viscusi*

Measuring Judicial Independence

The Political Economy
of Judging in Japan

J. Mark Ramseyer
and
Eric B. Rasmusen

The University of Chicago Press
Chicago & London

J. MARK RAMSEYER is the Mitsubishi Professor of Japanese Legal Studies at Harvard Law School. He is the coauthor of *Japanese Law: An Economic Approach.* ERIC B. RASMUSEN is the Indiana University Foundation Professor of Business Economics and Public Policy at Indiana University. He is the author of *Games and Information.*

The University of Chicago Press, Chicago 60637
The University of Chicago Press, Ltd., London
© 2003 by The University of Chicago
All rights reserved. Published 2003
Printed in the United States of America

12 11 10 09 08 07 06 05 04 03   1 2 3 4 5

ISBN: 0-226-70388-6 (cloth)

Library of Congress Cataloging-in-Publication Data

Ramseyer, J. Mark, 1954–
    Measuring judicial independence : the political economy of judging in Japan / J. Mark Ramseyer and Eric B. Rasmusen.
    p.   cm. — (Studies in law and economics)
Includes bibliographical references and index.
ISBN 0-226-70388-6 (cloth : alk. paper)
    1. Judges—Japan.   2. Judicial process—Japan.   3. Political questions and judicial power—Japan.   4. Courts—Japan.   I. Rasmusen, Eric.   II. Title.   III. Studies in law and economics (Chicago, Ill.)

KNX1610 .R36 2003
347.52′014—dc21

                                                                        2002072081

For Jenny and Geoffrey;
Amelia, Elizabeth, and Benjamin

Contents

Preface

In modern democracies, the shape of judicial independence depends on the electoral market. After all, once a constitution is fixed, choices about when and how to try to control the courts are choices that sitting politicians make. Necessarily, they will tend to make the choices in ways that maximize their odds of winning reelection. "Necessarily" because an elected official who consistently flouts voter preferences will likely return to the status of *aspiring* politician. Subjectively, politicians may act for reasons other than self-conscious vote-maximization, but objectively they face an electoral market constraint. If voters like judicial independence, the politicians who survive electoral challenges will tend to be those who supply it; if voters prefer that their judges respond to the popular will, the politicians who survive will be those who supply that responsiveness instead.

In this book we explore when and how real-world politicians keep judges independent, and when and how they try to control them instead. As such, the book is an exercise in positive science, not normative science. We do not purport to say when and how independent courts would be a "good thing." Yet precisely because many intellectuals do heap plaudits on independent courts, modern politicians who intervene in judicial affairs prefer to cover their tracks. Thus, even when politicians do not find it advantageous to leave judges alone, they apparently like to *seem* to have done so, by coercing them privately rather than publicly. Of course, some politicians actually do leave judges alone, and it is this observational equivalence between the seeming and the actual that creates the empirical problem we attack in this book.

Given the difficulty involved in unraveling the independence of judges in modern democracies, we choose not to survey a broad swath of countries.

Instead, we focus more narrowly on the independence of judges in one country—Japan. We think the resulting comparison between Japan and the United States helps us develop a positive theory of real-world judicial independence. At the very least, we hope it encourages others to begin to assemble similar data from other countries as well. Ideally, we hope it helps clarify some of the comparative dimensions to existing patterns of judicial independence.

Acknowledgments

In carrying out the component projects on which we based this book, we received invaluable suggestions and criticisms from a wide variety of extraordinarily helpful friends and colleagues. Without their advice, this book could never have reached this stage. We thanked them individually in the several articles that we published separately, but are happy to repeat our thanks to them here: Gregory Caldeira, John Coates, Ada Finifter, John Haley, Bruce Johnsen, David Johnson, Christine Jolls, Louis Kaplow, Dennis Karjala, Daniel Klerman, Masaru Kohno, Richard Lempert, Mark Levin, John Lott, Mathew McCubbins, Curtis Milhaupt, Yoshiro Miwa, Setsuo Miyazawa, Randal Picker, Eric Posner, Steve Reed, Roberta Romano, Frances Rosenbluth, Arthur Rosett, Tokuo Sakaguchi, Richard Samuels, Gary Saxonhouse, Stewart Schwab, Gary Schwartz, Pablo Spiller, Michael Thies, Eiji Tsukahara, Detlev Vagts, Kip Viscusi, Mark West, and participants at workshops at the University of California–Berkeley, the University of Chicago, George Mason University, Georgetown University, Harvard University, Hitotsubashi University, IIT Chicago-Kent, Indiana University, Kyushu University, the University of Michigan, Ohio State University, Osaka University, the University of Tokyo, the University of Virginia, Waseda University, the University of Washington, Washington University in St. Louis, Yale University, the American Law and Economics Association, the Midwest Law and Economics Association, the Comparative Law and Economics Forum, the Japan Behavioral Statistics Association, the Law and Society Association, and the National Bureau of Economic Research. As is evident, half the world has given us comments, something for which we are grateful—and we haven't even included the anonymous referees.

We received generous financial and logistical help from the John M. Olin Center for Law, Economics and Business of the Harvard Law School, the Indiana University Kelley School of Business, the Lynde and Harry Bradley Foundation, the Sarah Scaife Foundation, the John M. Olin Foundation, the University of Tokyo's Center for International Research on the Japanese Economy, and the University of Chicago Law School Committee on Japanese Studies. We gratefully acknowledge this assistance.

Some of the empirical work on which this book is based appeared in an earlier form in the following publications: "Why Are Japanese Judges So Conservative in Politically Charged Cases?" 95 *American Political Science Review* 331–34 (June 2001), © American Political Science Association; "Why Is the Japanese Conviction Rate So High?" 30 *Journal of Legal Studies* 53–88 (January 2001), © The University of Chicago; "Skewed Incentives: Paying for Politics as a Japanese Judge," 83 *Judicature* 190–95 (January–February 2000), © American Judicature Society; "Why the Japanese Taxpayer Always Loses," 72 *Southern California Law Review* 571–96 (January/March 1999), © The Law School, the University of Southern California; "Judicial Independence in a Civil Law Regime: The Evidence from Japan," 13 *Journal of Law, Economics, and Organization* 259–86 (October 1997), © Oxford University Press; and J. Mark Ramseyer, "The Puzzling (In)dependence of Courts: A Comparative Approach," 23 *Journal of Legal Studies* 721–48 (June 1994), © The University of Chicago. We use the results of these studies with permission of the publishers.

Our data and STATA regression programs are available at the website http://pacioli.bus.indiana.edu/erasmuse/jbook/jbook.htm. Please note that since publication of the articles on which we have based this book, STATA has published a new release that calculates the marginal effects of tobit coefficients. In this book, the tobit tables will differ from the tables included in our original articles. This is because we have used new statistical software to generate easier-to-understand marginal effects, and displayed these rather than the tobit coefficients themselves.

Introduction: 1968

I. Japan

Nineteen sixty-eight. The best of times, the worst of times—probably it all depended on what one wanted to do, much as it had for Therese Defarge and Sydney Carton two centuries before. For those with sufficiently libertine preferences, they were at least amusing times. *Hair* and *I Am Curious (Yellow)* made standing in line for pornography respectable. LSD was a new miracle drug. And in that narrow window between the discovery of penicillin and the emergence of AIDS, anonymous sex almost seemed safe.

But they were grim times too. Already in 1967 the Red Guards had sacked the British compound in Peking. Come 1968, the Vietcong launched the Tet offensive, American troops massacred civilians in My Lai, and the Soviets trashed Czechoslovakia. James Earl Ray killed Martin Luther King Jr., and the state and federal governments called out fifty-five thousand National Guard troops to quiet the riots that followed. Students sacked Columbia University and shut down the city of Paris. They took over the streets of Chicago and Berkeley. And when young instructors at San Francisco State told their students to bring guns to class, the university president just quit and went home.

Nineteen sixty-nine brought more of the same, and with a more sour tinge besides. In Chicago, federal judge Julius Hoffman ordered defendant Bobby Seale bound and gagged. Students brought machine guns to Cornell, commandeered Harvard, and struck or closed another four hundred universities. And in Vietnam, the death toll climbed to forty thousand Americans and more than half a million Vietnamese.

Life in Japan paralleled much of this upheaval. Over the course of 1968, New Left radicals staged riot after riot. They took over the prestigious University of Tokyo. They fought off the police with bricks and Molotov cocktails. Time and again, they took to the streets. On October 21 they organized a mob 800,000 strong to pour through town. And with true Jacobin panache, they saved the worst for their best friends: in just one year, their internecine brawls left eleven hundred injured and two dead.

It was in this mad, mad world of late-1960s Japan that judicial independence hit the evening news. According to Article 76 of the Constitution, all judges were to be "independent in the exercise of their conscience and bound only by this Constitution and the laws." Paper promises, scoffed the radicals. Sure, judges had independence—until they did something the ruling conservatives did not like. As cases tied to the disputes of the day passed through the courts, radicals began to tell tales of leftist judges punished with derailed careers in the judicial outback. Again and again, they told of judges who flouted the ruling conservative Liberal Democratic Party (LDP), only to fall into professional disgrace.

In this book, we ask whether this really happened—whether Japanese judges did face career incentives with a political bias. Our answer: yes. The radical left was wrong about many things, but they were right about the courts. Japanese judges did need to worry about the views of the politicians in the Cabinet. They did not face skewed incentives in most litigation, for most litigation carried no political import, and it was not the capitalists but the politicians who could hurt judicial careers. Capitalists, in fact, were no doubt happier with a level playing field for their contract disputes and corporate litigation anyway, and would have let their politician friends know this. In politically charged disputes, however, judges who flouted the majority party paid with their careers.

II. The Comparative Enterprise

A. Easy Questions

In the study of judicial independence, the normative questions are superficially the easiest: surely, independence is a good thing, and the more independence the better. In private disputes, the normative issues probably are indeed as easy as they seem. If parties to a dispute could buy judicial bias (in the context of such private disputes, corruption is part of judicial independence), judicial services would cease to have distinctive use. Where selling favors to the highest bidder resulted in the side winning that cared the most, this might be a good thing (though even then, the passionate side could always have paid off the other side privately rather than going to court). More often, the auction would help no one but the judge. In any case, if judges are just as pliable as the other branches of government, it is not clear what use it is to maintain the special dignity and talent that judges have—expensive features that the private sector seems to find unnecessary even among auctioneers of old furniture or art.

Intervention by politicians in private judicial disputes is as unattractive as bribery by the parties themselves. It merely shifts the bribery up a level. Rather than competing to bribe the judge, the parties compete to bribe the politician who pulls the strings. The function of the judge has vanished; by eliminating him, the disputants and politicians could achieve the same results at lower cost.

Because preventing corruption is costly, the level of judicial corruption in private disputes will turn on the costs and benefits of monitoring judges and on the time horizons of the people involved. The more cheaply rulers (whether politicians or autocrats) can monitor their judges, the less the judges will take bribes. The longer the rulers' horizons, the greater their incentives to operate the economy efficiently, resisting the temptation to take bribes themselves to intervene in private disputes, and the more effectively they will prevent their judges from taking bribes.

B. HARDER QUESTIONS

The harder questions concern the independence of judges in public, politically charged disputes. To be sure, most observers argue that independence in these cases is just as good a thing as in cases between private parties. But why? If voters elected the incumbent politicians to deliver a given portfolio of policies and services, why should a judge be able to stymie their ability to deliver it? Judges who were truly independent would not even face incentives to work assiduously or without bias. They would be free to inject their personal prejudices into their rulings, to take bribes, or even not to work at all. Granted, intellectuals typically argue that independent judges protect assorted minorities from the majority. But absent a theory to explain why or evidence to show how judges would or do protect politically powerless minorities (not ethnic minorities that form a significant part of the coalition behind a major party), this claim heads nowhere fast.

Will real-world politicians keep judges independent from themselves? Some voters may have a preference for independent judges, but that preference is one among many. Even voters who like the idea of judicial independence expect politicians to provide a broad portfolio of policies and services. Yet the more independent the judges, the harder politicians will find it to deliver the policies and services for which the voters elected them.

Hence the fundamental positive question: Under what circumstances will politicians maintain judges who are independent from themselves? The question has two dimensions. First, under what electoral conditions are politicians more likely to keep judges independent? Modern democracies offer a variety of electoral environments and their details might well affect the costs and benefits to politicians of intervening in the courts. Second, in what disputes are politicians most likely to keep judges independent? Governments are party to a wide variety of disputes, and their incentives to intervene may also depend on the nature of the dispute.

III. The Project

In this book, we do not ask the normative questions. Instead, we explore the positive issues by focusing on empirical data regarding judicial independence in Japan. We focus on one country because of the difficulty of ferreting out the appropriate numbers. This difficulty stems from two factors. First, when politicians intervene in the courts, they usually try to disguise their tactics. As a result, to study the impact of political pressure on courts, scholars cannot rely on the more obvious, direct measures. Yet academic specialization being what it is, few will know enough about more than a handful of foreign countries to locate any but the most obvious data. Second, if a judge anticipates that a politician is apt to intervene, he may well choose to forestall intervention by deciding the case the way the politician wants. The politician will not have intervened—yet will obtain exactly the decision he wants. For both of these reasons, the seemingly most independent judiciary may simply be the best at concealing political pressure. Surprisingly, this appears not to be well understood, and any attempt to rely on data compiled by others on other countries risks concluding that the most politicized judiciaries are the most independent, since they may show the fewest signs of dissension between politicians and judges. To mitigate these problems, we compiled the data ourselves on one country only, which we then analyzed in view of the country's particular institutional structure.

To be sure, we try to discuss Japan in a way that invites the reader to return regularly to the broader comparative questions. If Japanese politicians intervene in some disputes, will they intervene in all? If politicians in Japan intervene in disputes of a certain type, will politicians elsewhere intervene in that same kind of dispute?

We begin in chapter 1 by showing how Japanese politicians could shape judicial careers if they chose. We outline the institutional structure of the courts and recount some of the tales the Left told about political bias. Having the institutional potential to introduce politically biased incentives for judges, however, is not the same as actually introducing such incentives, and so the rest of the book tries to determine whether politicians actually use the incentives. Thus, in chapter 2 we turn from anecdotes to social science: to econometric tests. For our non–economically inclined readers we explain the methods we use to test for biased incentives. We then assemble data on several hundred judges. We ask whether membership in a leftist organization affected judicial pay (yes); whether it affected a judge's posting at the outset of his career (no); whether it affected the cities to which he was later assigned (yes); and whether it affected the range of responsibilities he later received (yes).

In chapter 3 we discuss a still more controversial issue, one that is at the heart of this book: Does the political orientation of the opinions a judge writes affect the assignments he receives? Preliminarily, we find that it can—and it is this issue that we explore extensively in later chapters. In what types of disputes do Japanese judges face skewed incentives? In the politically most sensitive cases? In all cases raising constitutional issues? In criminal cases? In routine administrative cases?

To begin to answer these questions, in chapter 4 we focus on the politically most charged disputes, the ones in which politicians would be most tempted to intervene. Using data on several groups of cases, we compare the careers of judges who decided against the government with those who took more orthodox positions. Holding constant a variety of proxies for a judge's abilities and work habits, we find that the heterodox suffered.

In chapter 5, we ask whether judges face similarly biased incentives in more ordinary public-law cases. We first explain why politicians might rationally want to keep judges unbiased in these cases. Our example of the routine administrative case is the tax dispute, of which we have a large sample. Holding constant our usual control variables, we find that judges do not hurt their careers by favoring taxpayers, but do suffer for being reversed. In routine administrative cases they apparently do not jeopardize their careers by second-guessing lower-level bureaucrats. They do jeopardize them by getting the law wrong.

In chapter 6, we examine criminal cases. In Japan, criminal defendants face extraordinarily high conviction rates. We ask whether this might reflect skewed incentives: Do judges convict because hanging judges face better careers than lenient ones? At first glance, the data seem to make just that point. Importantly, however, the first glance misleads. To be sure, judges who acquit have worse careers. Yet a judge who acquits in a mundane case (for example, a judge who decides that the prosecutors nailed the wrong man) does not incur a professional penalty. Instead, the dynamic again involves politics and accuracy: a judge incurs the penalty either when he acquits defendants in sensitive prosecutions involving political activities, or if he misconstrues the law.

In chapter 7, we return to the broader implications of the relation between judicial independence and democratic politics. Toward that end, we trace the conditions under which rational politicians will most likely keep their judges independent. As already discussed, judicial independence is not an unambiguous good for politicians facing competitive elections. Accordingly, we trace the political benefits and costs to judicial independence, and explore the conditions under which politicians would most likely provide it. We apply the theory in the context of three very different regimes: imperial Japan, postwar Japan, and the United States.

1

The Setting

In the aftermath of 1968, leftists and centrists traded a wide variety of insults over the courts. To unravel what actually happened, we turn first to the courts' institutional structure. We then ask how that structure affects judicial outcomes. In chapters 2–4, we explore the effect of structure on outcome in disputes stemming (in part) from the 1960s chaos. In chapters 5 and 6, we explore that relation in disputes that have arisen since. In this chapter, we first outline the organization of the courts and the personnel structure within it (section I). We discuss the implications of the theory of public choice for why Japanese politicians might choose to manipulate judicial incentives (section II.A). Finally, we recount some of the tales told by the Left about politically biased judicial incentives (section II.B).

I. The Career Judiciary

A. COURT STRUCTURE

Japan maintains one national court system and no prefectural (i.e., state) courts. It has eight High Courts and a widely dispersed array of District and Family Courts (Courts Act, §§ 2, 15–52; Family Courts deal with disputes such as contested divorces).[1] Attached to these courts are branch offices. About two thousand judges work within this system. Another eight hundred serve in Summary Courts (i.e., small claims courts). As the latter judges face less stringent hiring criteria and are not part of the career judiciary, we will not discuss them further. The Supreme Court has fifteen justices, appointed differently from other judges, as we detail in subsection G.

1. Saibansho ho, Law No. 59 of 1947.

Judges in the lower courts face mandatory retirement at age sixty-five (Courts Act, § 50). Formally, they serve a series of ten-year terms (Courts Act, § 40). In practice, they work continuously. Only twice since World War II has the Cabinet formally refused to reappoint a judge at the end of a ten-year term. Of those two, claim critics, one was denied reappointment because of his liberal politics (a debate detailed in section II.B.3). The other was turned down shortly after he refused to accept a transfer to a court in another city (subsection D.1). Critics do argue that several judges have resigned in anticipation of not being reappointed (subsection II.B.3).

Note three additional points. First, Japanese courts do not use juries. All trials are bench trials, the judges deciding questions of fact as well as questions of law. Second, most trials are conducted by three-judge panels. Routine non-serious criminal trials are the exception. Third, lower-court opinions (though not Supreme Court ones) are signed by the entire panel. Even if a judge dissents, he does not publicly disclose that fact.

B. EDUCATION

A would-be judge begins his legal education while still a college undergraduate.[2] Usually, he majors in law. During his last year, he takes the entrance exam to the one national law school, the Legal Research and Training Institute (LRTI). Until its recent expansion, the LRTI admitted only about five hundred students each year. A would-be judge passed the entrance exam on his first try if he was very lucky or very smart. Not many did. Given that the pass rate usually ranged from 1 to 4 percent, a rate that included not just first-time test-takers but those who had tried repeatedly, he more likely flunked. He then retook the exam once a year until he passed it four or five years later or despaired and chose a different career.

Students stay at the LRTI for two years (recently cut to one and a half years). There they attend lectures on legal practice and serve clinical assignments at various private and public offices. Toward the end of their stay, they select a career. Most became lawyers in private practice. Some apply to become prosecutors. Still others apply to become judges. Traditionally, the courts have included a disproportionate number of students from the top of the class, but because of the increase in the financial returns to international corporate practice in recent years the best have tended to join the bar.

2. For details on this educational system, see Ramseyer and Nakazato 1999: ch. 1.

C. HIRING PRACTICES

Formally, the Cabinet chooses which judges to appoint to the lower courts (Courts Act, § 40). Typically, it delegates that power to the Supreme Court Secretariat, the administrative office of the courts. The Secretariat in turn hires almost all LRTI graduates who apply to be a judge. From time to time, defenders of the courts cited this administrative delegation as evidence that the Cabinet does not try to influence the courts. From time to time, they cited the Secretariat's willingness to hire all comers as evidence of political openness. Would that it were so simple.

That the Cabinet did not intervene might indeed reflect judicial independence. But there are other possibilities. First, the Cabinet's acquiescence in the decisions of the Secretariat might just reflect the fact that it could veto appointees with heterodox political views; that the Secretariat knew the Cabinet could veto such appointees; and that the Secretariat therefore maintained personnel policies that tracked the preferences of the long-time ruling Liberal Democratic Party (LDP).

Second, that the Secretariat accepted most applicants and appointed them as judges could reflect the effect that a politically biased set of career incentives had on the quality of those who applied. Suppose the Secretariat did penalize judges who indulged their leftist preferences (the issue at the heart of this book), and everyone knew that. If so, leftist LRTI graduates would disproportionately have opted to work in the private sector. Disproportionately, those who applied would have been those who shared LDP preferences.

The problem, which we revisit in more detail in section II.A, is that in equilibrium a completely independent court looks very much like a completely dependent one. The differences show up mainly when people make mistakes. If the Secretariat appointed a few troublesome judges, for example, the Cabinet might limit its discretion; if left-wing judges started promoting communist policies in court, the Secretariat might begin screening applicants more rigorously.

The problem has bedeviled students of corporate governance and government bureaucracies for years. If shareholders rarely intervene in corporate affairs, can corporate officers do as they please, running the business for their own purposes rather than to make profits for the shareholders? Or do those officers, because they know they could be fired if shareholders were to intervene or to sell to a hostile bidder, maximize profits to forestall the loss of their jobs? From several decades of work in finance, we now know that the answer is the latter: both in the United States and in Japan, corporate officers largely promote shareholder interests (on Japan, see Kaplan 1994; Kaplan and Minton 1994; Kaplan and Ramseyer 1996).

Similarly, if politicians rarely intervene in a government bureaucracy, is that because bureaucrats can do as they please? Or do bureaucrats, knowing the incumbent politicians could intervene at any time, implement policies that promote the reelection of incumbents? From several decades of work in political science, we now know that here too it is the latter: both in the United States and in Japan, bureaucrats largely promote the interests of key politicians (on Japan, see McCubbins and Noble 1995; McCubbins and Thies 1997; Ramseyer and Rosenbluth 1997).

Our question is whether judges similarly answer to the Cabinet. Untangling this could be tricky. Ask a judge and he will likely reply, "Of course we're independent." But he might add, "We carefully protect that independence. Whenever we're tempted to do something the Cabinet wouldn't like, we restrain ourselves. By avoiding asserting our personal views, we maintain our independence." Or, if leftists have disproportionately opted for jobs in the private sector, the issue would seldom even arise: disproportionately, the people who chose to become judges would have been those who shared LDP views anyway.

D. POSTINGS
1. Incentive Structures

The crucial institutional incentive in the Japanese judicial structure is not the renewal of ten-year terms, a decidedly blunt and public instrument. Rather, it is the triannual transfer. About every three years, the Secretariat moves judges around the country and up and down the judicial hierarchy. To track those moves, we use the *Zen saibankan keireki soran* (the ZSKS, which details all posts held by all judges educated since World War II; unless otherwise noted, we rely on this volume for all judicial career data in this book). Table 1.1 shows the possible appointments a judge might face. When he joins the judiciary, the Secretariat names him to a specific court for two or three years. At the end of that term, it moves him to another. Some cities (such as Tokyo) are more desirable than others (see subsection 3 below), just as some duties (such as a Secretariat posting; see subsection 4) are more prestigious than others (such as branch office assignments; see subsection 2). As a result, by controlling these periodic assignments, potentially the Secretariat could reward and punish judges based on their performance, their politics, or whatever else it might care about.

Nominally, a judge can refuse any posting he dislikes. In fact, he refuses at his peril. By 1969, Judge Shigeharu Hasegawa had worked in Hiroshima

Table 1.1 Aggregate Judicial Postings, 1990

By Court Hierarchy		By Geography	
High Court	295	Tokyo	537
District Court	1,101	Osaka	231
Family Court	541	Other metropolitan	416
Secretariat	45	Nonmetropolitan	1,742
Other nonjudicial	96	Branch offices	848
Sokatsu	353		

NOTE: Some categories (e.g., *sokatsu* and District Court) overlap. *Sokatsu* appointments add modest administrative (e.g., personnel) duties to a judge's trial work.

for seventeen years. The Secretariat then assigned him to an out-of-town position, formally a promotion. Hasegawa, however, had a sick wife and did not want it. He declined the promotion, and when the time came for his next ten-year appointment he found himself out of work (Ramseyer and Rosenbluth 1997: 156).

2. Branch Offices

Almost uniformly, judges consider branch office assignments the worst posts in the system. In part this is a function of geography, since the branch offices tend to be in smaller cities. In part, it is a function of prestige, since they tend to be considered less important.

Despised as branch offices may be, even most successful judges usually spend some time there. In table 1.2 below we give the number of years as of 1990 spent in branch offices for all judges who began their careers in 1965. Most spend at least at least one three-year stint in branch offices; a few spend more than half their career there.

3. Geography

Like most Japanese professionals, judges generally prefer to work in Tokyo if possible and in one of the other metropolitan centers if not. This is a preference American readers often find hard to understand. To many Americans in Japan, Tokyo is the last place they want to be. An over-priced Manhattan, it seems the least interesting place in the country. Far better, they reason, to live in exotic shrine cities like Izumo or luscious mountain villages like Takachiho.

Japanese professionals are not looking for ancient architecture or scenic beauty, however, and judges are the quintessential fast-track professionals. For the sake of their careers, most Japanese professionals want to be near the hub of the system, and Tokyo is the ultimate hub. It houses not just the central government, but the headquarters for the incumbent and opposition political parties, the media, and most of the major corporations.

For their children's sake, Japanese judges want the best schools. As educationally obsessed as professionals anywhere—especially those who have entered their profession via one of the most restrictive merit examinations in the country—they want their children in the most selective schools. Tokyo contains not just the famed University of Tokyo (attended by one-sixth of the judges), but at least one other top-five national university, most of the best private universities, and most of the best preparatory schools. For exactly those reasons, when assigned to courts in smaller cities many judges (like their peers in business) leave their families in Tokyo and spend the work-week alone. Whether a judge favors career or family, in other words, he will likely to want to be in Tokyo, and if not in Tokyo at least in some other large city.

4. Administrative Duties

Some posts involve prestigious administrative duties. The most successful judges eventually become one of eight High Court presidents. Modestly successful ones become District or Family Court chief judges. Almost all judges spend some time as a district judge with internal personnel responsibilities (a *sokatsu* assignment), and a few judges work several years in the Secretariat or the Ministry of Justice. The Secretariat itself selects the judges who staff it, and apparently negotiates the Ministry of Justice postings with the ministry's own personnel office. Visibility and influence do not completely overlap: a staff position within the Secretariat can be highly influential, even if less visible than a seat on a High Court.

5. Pay

Can the Secretariat manipulate judicial pay? Although it cannot lower a judge's salary (Constitution, Art. 79), it can vary the pace at which it promotes judges up the salary scale. Pay data is not public, but place on the pay scale does correlate with some observable indices—notably, *sokatsu* assignments. We explore this issue in chapter 2, section II.

E. University Cliques

Critics argue that the courts have long been under the control of a clique of University of Tokyo and University of Kyoto graduates, a charge they routinely make of the elite bureaucracies as well. These graduates, they claim, dominate the personnel office in the Secretariat and manipulate it in ways that let them look out for their own. They route the best jobs to younger alumni from their schools, and promote them more quickly than anyone else.

The Universities of Tokyo and Kyoto do supply the largest number of judges. Of all judges hired from 1961 to 1965, 16 percent were from the University of Tokyo and 19 percent from the University of Kyoto (see table 3.2). The problem, of course, is that the Universities of Tokyo and Kyoto graduates are also disproportionately the most able. These are the schools with the most selective entrance examinations. Overall, University of Tokyo and Kyoto alumni routinely score among the highest in the LRTI entrance examinations (passage rates of 8.2 and 7.8, respectively, in 1995, compared to the overall average of 3.0; Ramseyer and Nakazato 1999: 7–8), and among judges the Tokyo and Kyoto alumni tend to fail the exam the fewest times (table 2.7, regression C). Inconvenient as the fact may be for some populist academics, exam performance does correlate with intelligence and hard work—and both qualities matter crucially to professional success. The old school tie might still matter, but merely looking at the numbers appointed from the old school tells us nothing about it if the old school is a selective old school.

F. TRACKING

The Secretariat does not assign new hires randomly to their first postings. Instead, it distinguishes among the new recruits and posts those judges it believes most talented to the Tokyo District Court. During their career, these fast-track judges will rotate out of Tokyo and serve some time in less desirable posts—recall that most judges do spend time in branch offices at some point in their careers. In general, however, fast-track judges will spend less time in branch offices, spend more time in Tokyo and other metropolitan areas, and earn higher pay (as we show in various regressions in later chapters).

To illustrate the career track, see table 1.2, which compares fast-track and ordinary judges on several dimensions. For the sample of fast-track judges, we take all judges in the ZSKS who had by 1990 obtained postings either to the Supreme Court or to High Court presidencies. For the sample of ordinary judges, we take all judges hired in 1965 who had not retired or left the judiciary before 1990.

Table 1.2 shows that the most successful judges (i) started their careers at a younger age (they flunked the LRTI exam fewer times); (ii) were disproportionately University of Tokyo or Kyoto graduates (especially the former); (iii) published more opinions per year (see table 3.1 for a definition of this variable; the numbers will seem low to American reader—whether Japanese judges write fewer opinions than U.S. judges or publish a smaller fraction of the opinions they write is unclear); (iv) spent more time in Tokyo and Osaka; (v) spent more time in the Secretariat and other administrative posts; and (vi) spent less time in branch offices.

Table 1.2 Successful and Ordinary Judges

	I. Successful Judges ($n = 25$)			II. Class of 1965 ($n = 55$)		
	Minimum	Mean	Maximum	Minimum	Mean	Maximum
A. Personal data						
Starting age	23	26.84	32	24	29.85	38
Male	0	.96	1	0	.91	1
Tokyo U	0	.76	1	0	.2	1
Kyoto U	0	.12	1	0	.036	1
Opinions/year	0	4.02	16.5	.16	1.75	7.82
B. Fraction of career in various posts as of 1990 (not mutually exclusive)						
Tokyo	0	.52	.89	0	.23	.88
Osaka	0	.14	.73	0	.068	.56
Secretariat	0	.17	.58	0	.007	.12
Other nonjudicial	0	.12	.78	0	.083	.56
Branch offices	0	.043	.19	0	.15	.58

NOTE: "Successful judges" are those eventually named either to the Supreme Court or to the presidency of a High Court and whose career records appear in the ZSKS. This rules out those appointed to these positions early in the postwar era, as they would have begun their careers prior to 1948 and thus would not appear in the ZSKS.

For purposes of deriving these figures, the time of appointment to the Supreme Court is treated as the time of retirement.

Panel B gives the fraction of career, as of 1990, spent in the various positions

For a sense of what this means in specific cases, compare two judges hired in 1953—one who was eminently successful, and one who had a more ordinary career:

Katsuya Onishi, an exceptional judge. Born in 1928. Kyoto University graduate. 1953: Kyoto District Court (DC). 1958: Secretariat. 1961: Hakodate DC. 1964: Secretariat. 1968: Tokyo DC. 1970: Osaka High Court (HC). 1971: Osaka DC, *sokatsu*. 1974: Tokyo DC. 1974: Tokyo DC, *sokatsu*. 1975: Secretariat. 1985: Kofu DC (Chief Judge). 1986: Tokyo HC, *sokatsu*. 1986: Secretariat (Secretary General). 1989: Tokyo HC (President). 1991: Supreme Court.

Masakazu Kuwamori, a typical judge. Born in 1926. No university information. 1953: Yamaguchi DC Branch Office. 1957: Osaka DC. 1960: Sendai HC. 1962: Sendai DC. 1963: Nagasaki Family Court. 1968: Osaka Family Court. 1970: Osaka DC, *sokatsu*. 1971: Fukuoka DC, *sokatsu*. 1974: Fukuoka HC. 1977: Osaka HC. 1979: Fukuoka DC Branch Office (Chief). 1985: Tokushima DC (Chief Judge). 1986: retired (notary public).

The comparison highlights several points. First, even Onishi, who rose to the top of the organization, had postings that went down as well as up. Indeed, at certain points—for example, in 1961, eight years into their careers—Kuwamori held a more prestigious post than Onishi. Second, elite as Onishi was, he did not start at the Tokyo District Court. The advantages enjoyed by judges who start there do not entirely preclude opportunities for others.

Still, the comparison also illustrates several typical features of judicial careers: Onishi was a University of Kyoto graduate, and apparently was two years younger than Kuwamori had been when he passed the LRTI exam; within twenty years Onishi had spent two stints in the Secretariat while Kuwamori had spent none; and within twenty years Kuwamori had served two stints in Family Courts and one in a branch office while Onishi had served in neither. At any given time an observer might not be able to predict the more successful judicial career by the quality of their current posts. Over the course of a decade or two, one would have no trouble doing so.

G. THE SUPREME COURT

The Supreme Court stands apart from this system. The Cabinet and Prime Minister appoint Supreme Court justices to serve until mandatory retirement at age seventy, rather than the sixty-five years of lower-court judges (Courts Act, § 50). The justices are subject neither to ten-year terms nor to periodic reassignment by the Secretariat. Nominally, voters can remove them by election (Constitution, Art. 79), though in fact they never have. As of 1990 the highest disapproval vote a Supreme Court justice ever received was 15.17 percent (ZSKS 1990: 468–74).

Supreme Court justices typically take their job in their early sixties: for the last twenty justices appointed as of 1990, the mean age of appointment was sixty-four (Ramseyer and Rosenbluth 1997; ZSKS 1990: 468–74). A plurality serve as career lower-court judges before their appointment (Courts Act, § 41). As in the United States, a lower-court judge's appointment to the Supreme Court depends not just on talent but also on luck, and lots of it. Table 1.3 shows the make-up of the Court in 2001, after the period of our study and the political events of the 1990s that shook up LDP dominance, but still not atypical of postwar Supreme Courts. For the fifteen justices on the Supreme Court in 2001, the mean age of appointment was sixty-three. Seven of them were University of Tokyo alumni, six went to Kyoto, one to Nagoya, and one to Chuo. Three were former bureaucrats, three were appointed from the private bar, one was a professor, and the remaining eight—just over half—were lower-court judges.

Japanese prime ministers appointed justices late in life during the period of our study for a straightforward political reason. For most of the postwar years, the LDP faced very high odds (though less than 1, as it discovered in 1993) of winning elections. As such, the Prime Minister had no need to try to extend his influence past the next few elections by appointing relatively young justices. Instead, by appointing justices late in life he could alleviate what is called the "Harry Blackmun problem"—the risk that a politically friendly justice would, over the course of a long career, end his life by sleeping with the enemy. As

Table 1.3 Members of the Supreme Court in 2001

Judge	Year of Appointment	Year of Birth	Age at Appointment	University	Background
Chikusa	1993	1932	61	Tokyo	Judge
Kawai	1994	1932	62	Kyoto	Judge
Ijima	1995	1932	62	Kyoto	Bureaucrat
Fukuda	1995	1935	60	Tokyo	Bureaucrat
Fujii	1995	1932	63	Kyoto	Judge
Ohde	1997	1932	65	Tokyo	Bureaucrat
Kanatani	1997	1935	62	Kyoto	Judge
Yamaguchi (chief justice)	1997	1932	64	Kyoto	Judge
Kitagawa	1998	1934	63	Nagoya	Judge
Kameyama	1998	1934	64	Tokyo	Judge
Okuda	1999	1932	66	Kyoto	Professor
Kajitani	1999	1935	64	Tokyo	Bar
Machida	2000	1936	63	Tokyo	Judge
Fukazawa	2000	1934	66	Chuo	Bar
Hamada	2001	1936	64	Tokyo	Bar

SOURCE: http://www.courts.go.jp/english/ehome.html (August 2, 2001).

of 1990, a justice with nearly the longest time served by any was Matasuke Kawamura. He was appointed at age fifty-four, but not by the LDP. Instead, he was appointed by the Socialist Prime Minister Katayama who briefly held power in the late 1940s (ZSKS 1998: II-272; Justice Iriye named by successor Prime Minister Yoshida served slightly longer).

Of the fifteen Supreme Court justices, one works as the Chief Justice (Constitution, Art. 79). As such, he is the administrative head of the entire lower-court system. Crucially, in that capacity he supervises the Secretariat. In this role he is not the titular head of a bureaucracy he does not understand. Rather, he usually is someone who ran the Secretariat as Secretary General before joining the Supreme Court, and who spent a greater-than-average part of his judicial career in administrative postings. He knows where the bodies are buried. In fact, he probably buried more than a few of them himself.

H. THE LIBERAL DEMOCRATIC PARTY

Throughout the period we study, the LDP controlled the Japanese Cabinet. Although occasionally accused of being fringe-right (ideology is relative, after all, and Japanese newspapers have traditionally been socialist), the LDP was in fact a moderately conservative capitalist party. Formed in 1955 through the merger of two conservative parties, during the 1950s and 1960s it kept strong roots among rural voters. In the 1970s and 1980s, it self-consciously repositioned itself as the party of the urban consumers. Consistently, it maintained the support of the business community, whether of the large firms listed on the Tokyo Stock Exchange or of the smaller provincial enterprises.

Internally, the LDP organized itself through several shifting factions. These factions were not ideological. Rather, they were fund-raising and fund-dispensing organizations keyed to the multimember electoral districts in Japan. Elsewhere, Ramseyer and Rosenbluth (1997) explain the ties among the internal party organization, the electoral district structure, and the long-standing dominance of the party.

For present purposes, suffice it to say that the LDP maintained extremely high odds of remaining in power during the period at issue. Although it lost control in 1993, the defeat was a surprise even to the LDP, largely a result of brinksmanship among rival LDP legislators (Ramseyer and Rosenbluth 1997: preface). For the story we tell, however, the expected longevity is crucial—as we explain in section II.

II. Principal and Agent

A. THE THEORY

Given the structure of the judiciary, the LDP could indeed have controlled Japanese courts had it wanted to do so. If it did, outsiders would not readily have noticed. As Randall Calvert, Mark Moran, and Barry Weingast put it in the bureaucratic context (1987: 501), the process of policy administration by autonomous ministries is "observationally equivalent" to that under strict legislative control.

Suppose legislators can cheaply and effectively monitor and discipline bureaucrats. If bureaucrats try to flout what legislators want, legislators can intervene and punish the miscreant bureaucrats. Because legislators can do so, bureaucrats will have an incentive to give them what they want in advance. If bureaucrats give legislators what they want, legislators will have no reason to punish—bureaucrats will regulate as legislators want them to, and legislators will largely leave them alone. This would be true for any person, but perhaps especially true for bureaucrats who care more about the smooth running of their bureaucracies and their careers than about particular policy outcomes or newspaper publicity.

Recall the world of Kazuo Ishiguro's novel *The Remains of the Day*. James Stevens (played by Anthony Hopkins in the film) is a butler, and the son of a butler. His family has long worked for the Darlington family. The heir to the Darlington estate rarely tells Stevens what to do. Instead, Stevens goes about his business on his own, with scarcely a word of instruction from his titular master.

Yet Stevens is not independent. Lord Darlington leaves him alone only because Stevens knows what Darlington wants done and does it. Precisely because Darlington could discipline him and Stevens knows that Darlington could, Stevens unquestioningly fulfills Darlington's wishes. Precisely because Stevens correctly anticipates Darlington's wishes, Darlington never intervenes.

This makes for bedeviling research. Suppose we observe bureaucrats whom politicians leave alone. Do we conclude, as Chalmers Johnson famously did of the Japanese Ministry of International Trade and Industry, that the bureaucrats "make most major decisions, draft virtually all legislation, control the national budget, and [are] the source of all major policy innovations in the system" (1982: 20–21)? Or do we instead conclude that they are latter-day Stevenses who anticipate their political masters' every wish?

In circumstances such as these, the key usually lies in the institutional details. As Mathew McCubbins and Gregory Noble (1995) put it, the answer depends on how much information the politicians have, what they can learn about the bureaucrats' activities, and whether the bureaucrats control the agenda. In the context of the Japanese bureaucracy, others have shown that the bureaucrats do indeed answer to legislative masters. Ramseyer and Rosenbluth (1997: ch. 7), for example, show that Japanese bureaucratic policymaking generally promotes the electoral returns of the LDP. McCubbins and Noble (1995) show that the LDP collects information on the political implications of bureaucratic policy, and controls key aspects of the policy-making agenda. And McCubbins and Thies (1997) show that even shifts in LDP factional strength cause bureaucratic policy shifts.

In Japan, the structure of the courts similarly points to the potential for political control. During the period at issue, the LDP controlled the institutional apparatus it needed to maintain control over the courts. Through the Cabinet, it hired the Supreme Court justices. It named them late enough in life that they would not shift their political preferences before retirement at seventy. It gave those justices control over the personnel office of the courts. And it gave that office power to reward and punish judges as it saw fit. Did it exercise that potential?

B. The Stories
1. Japanese Military

According to the anecdotes the Left tells, the LDP did indeed present judges with politically biased incentives. Turn first to the most famous Japanese judicial dispute of all: the constitutionality of the military. Back in 1947,

Douglas MacArthur imposed on Japan a Constitution that explicitly banned all military force through its Article 9.[3] By 1955, conservative politicians had formed the LDP and solidified their control over the Diet. Eager to reassert national independence, they tried to remove Article 9. The Socialists and Communists responded by making opposition to constitutional revision the cause of the day.

The LDP did not wait for a constitutional amendment to rearm. Instead, it announced that Article 9 banned only offensive force. Defensive weapons were constitutional, and there was no reason why Japan could not organize a Self-Defense Force (SDF). Other than lacking nuclear weapons, ICBMs, and aircraft carriers, the SDF looked much like any other ultrasophisticated modern military machine. Whether it would survive turned on what judges thought of the LDP's theory that "it's ok as long as it's defensive."

In the 1960s, nearly two hundred locals in the northern island of Hokkaido sued under Article 9 to enjoin a planned SDF missile base.[4] Case assignment in Japanese District Courts varies by court, but in order to prevent corruption most use a variant of random assignment. By the exigencies of that assignment process, the SDF case went to Judge Shigeo Fukushima.

Fukushima was a member of the Young Jurists League (YJL). By its own constitution, the YJL was dedicated to preserving the Constitution of Japan. As the discussion above should make clear, this did not make the YJL the Japanese analogue to the Daughters of the American Revolution. Instead, it was by many accounts a Communist Party affiliate fighting the LDP's attempts to amend the Constitution and delete Article 9.

The local chief judge was Kenta Hiraga. When Hiraga realized that the SDF case had gone to a YJL member, he apparently panicked. He wrote Fukushima a long memo (reproduced in Fukase 1971: 59–60) explaining why, if he were deciding the case, he would not enjoin the base. The reasons were sensible enough, and went to issues of justiciability and the like. The memo also made it clear that Hiraga was merely offering advice, and did not pretend to tell Fukushima what he had to do.

Fukushima roundly ignored the memo and enjoined the base. As Hiraga noted, he could have picked any number of administrative-law doctrines to duck the issue. He did not. Instead, he aggressively reached out and confronted the substantive question. The case went up to the High Court, which promptly

3. "[L]and, sea, and air forces, as well as other war potential, will never be maintained."
4. The following account is taken from Ramseyer and Rosenbluth 1997: 162–64.

reversed and sent it back to Fukushima. On remand, Fukushima forthrightly declared the SDF unconstitutional.[5]

Meanwhile, Fukushima sent copies of the memo to his friends in the YJL. They, in turn, sent copies to the press. All hell broke loose, and the press accused Hiraga of subverting judicial independence. The Diet soon launched impeachment proceedings. Hiraga emerged without serious damage to his career. The impeachment committee reprimanded him and went no further, dismissing the charges. After additional reprimands from the court system, he was promoted to the Tokyo High Court.

Fukushima fared worse. He, too, faced impeachment proceedings. But where the committee had dismissed the charges against Hiraga, it declared that Fukushima had violated judicial ethics by leaking the memo to his friends. Not that Fukushima seemed to care. He continued to rail against the judiciary, and soon issued his opinion that the SDF was unconstitutional, flatly contradicting Supreme Court precedent.

After his Hokkaido posting, Fukushima went to the Tokyo District Court, but that signaled nothing. The Secretariat maintains a long-standing rule that judges stationed to either Hokkaido or Okinawa (the two points farthest from Tokyo) will spend their next post in Tokyo. With Fukushima, it simply followed that rule. After that stint, though, it sent him to provincial cities in the northeast. There it kept him. By 1989, he was fifty-nine years old and had served in provincial Family Courts for twelve years running. After writing an op-ed for a national newspaper complaining that the Secretariat had sandbagged his career, he quit.

2. Campaign Restrictions

Several other disputes raised issues of judicial independence in the turmoil of the late 1960s and early 1970s. Among the more prominent were cases involving campaign restrictions. The Public Offices Elections Act bans a variety of campaigning tactics.[6] Most critically, § 138 bans door-to-door canvassing. Incumbents enjoy free publicity by virtue of their being incumbents, of course, while challengers need ways to make themselves known. As a result, campaign restrictions generally increase the incumbency advantage. As the LDP has more incumbents than its rivals, the restrictions generally favor the LDP.

---

5. Ito v. Hasegawa, 565 Hanrei jiho 23 (Sapporo D. Ct. Aug. 22, 1969), *rev'd sub nom.* Kuraishi v. Ito, 581 Hanrei jiho 5 (Sapporo High Ct. Jan. 23, 1970); Ito v. Kakuraichi, 712 Hanrei jiho 24 (Sapporo D. Ct. Sept. 7, 1973), *rev'd,* 821 Hanrei jiho 23 (Sapporo High Ct. Aug. 5, 1976), *aff'd,* 26 Saihan minshu 1679 (Sup. Ct. Sept. 9, 1982).

6. Koshoku senkyo ho (Public Offices Elections Act), Law No. 100 of Apr. 1950. The following account is taken from Ramseyer and Rosenbluth 1997: 170–72.

The Japan Communist Party was perhaps the most determined opponent of the campaign restrictions. From time to time, its candidates flatly ignored them and went door to door. When they did, prosecutors filed criminal charges. In defense, the communists contested the constitutionality of the restrictions: the § 138 ban violated, they claimed, their right to free speech (Constitution, Art. 21). The Supreme Court consistently upheld the statute. Already in 1950 it had held a predecessor statute constitutional.[7] But facing new constitutional challenges, a 1967 Tokyo District Court gingerly suggested that the statute might be unconstitutional.[8] The Supreme Court responded quickly: § 138 was indeed constitutional.[9]

That did not satisfy all the judges in the system. Haruhiko Abe was a star— a University of Tokyo graduate who began his career at the Tokyo District Court. Both factors conduce to fast-track status, as our regressions in later chapters show. Not only was he one of the most talented members of the YJL, however, he was also one of the most outspoken. In 1971, for instance, he declared:

> Trials must also be fair politically. To make them politically fair, some people claim that we judges should be politically neutral. . . . But suppose we interpret this to mean that we should be neutral toward all political ideologies, and should not let our political value judgments affect our work. Given these tumultuous days, is this possible? Clearly, to avoid political value judgments would cause us uncritically to support and blindly to follow the preferences of the establishment. Clearly, to avoid political value judgments would cause us to abandon our quest for fairness. (Abe 1971: 194)

When one of us attended law school in the United States in the late 1970s, several professors of the New Left delivered much the same harangue. As bizarre as his statement may seem today, Abe was nothing if not in touch with his time.

In 1968, sitting temporarily in Summary Court with less than five years of experience, Abe held § 138 unconstitutional. Barely months before, the Supreme Court had upheld the statute against constitutional challenge. Not to worry; Abe was not going to avoid "political value judgments."

Abe's ten-year term came up for renewal in 1972, and observers worried that the Secretariat might not reappoint him. It did, but into oblivion. In 1973 it sent him to a Family Court, and in 1979 to a branch office. And in branch offices the former fast-tracker stayed, even as of 1997 (ZSKS 1998: I-102-3).

---

7. Japan v. Masako, 4 Saihan keishu 1799 (Sup. Ct. Sept. 27, 1950).
8. [No names given], 493 Hanrei jiho 72 (Tokyo D. Ct. Mar. 27, 1967).
9. Japan v. Taniguchi, 21 Saihan keishu 1245 (Sup Ct. Nov. 21, 1967).

Since 1967, the Supreme Court has held the canvassing ban constitutional at least another seven times. The ban's political importance is obvious, yet—maybe for that very reason—lower-court judges persist in fighting it. When they do, they suffer. Holding politics constant, one would not expect the Secretariat to quickly promote judges who ignore precedent (an issue to which we return in later chapters). But politics are not constant, and the punishments judges suffered here seem severe.

For example, former YJL member Tetsuro So held § 138 unconstitutional in 1978. From 1981 to 1997, he spent four years in Family Court and ten years in branch offices (ZSKS, 1998: I-122–23). Kunio Ogawa held the ban unconstitutional in 1979. From 1979 until the time he retired in 1993, he never left branch offices (ZSKS, 1998: I-120–21). And Masato Hirayu held the ban unconstitutional in 1979. Like Abe, he was a University of Tokyo recruit who started his career at the Tokyo District Court. Until he retired in 1991, he spent his entire career in either branch offices or Family Courts (ZSKS 1998: I-142–43).

3. Young Jurists League

One effect of the Fukushima fracas was to call attention to the YJL itself.[10] During the 1960s, the Right had largely left the League alone. As a low-profile organization, it had published a newsletter and organized separate chapters for lawyers, judges, and law professors.

Soon after the Fukushima debacle, the LDP decided to act. Seeing over two hundred judges on the YJL rolls, it flatly declared that Japan, "as a constitutional nation, could never allow" its judges to join the League (quoted in Ushiomi 1971: 3). The judges got the message. The Secretary General of the Secretariat declared that judges should not join political organizations, and the Chief Justice of the Supreme Court announced that the judiciary should exclude political extremists (quoted in Zadankai 1971: 69). Most YJL members promptly resigned from the League and sent copies of those resignation letters to the Secretariat.

In April 1971, however, the Secretariat refused to reappoint League member Yasuaki Miyamoto. Critics accused the LDP of politicizing the court. Miyamoto had been an assistant judge on the Kumamoto District Court, and had served on judicial panels that had written several mildly left-leaning opinions. They hardly seem so aberrant as to warrant the unprecedented punishment, and where other League members argued political bias, Secretariat supporters hinted that Miyamoto was simply unproductive.

10. The following account is taken from Ramseyer and Rosenbluth 1997: 164–70.

Officially, the Supreme Court and its Secretariat refused to comment. Given that the Court would not explain why it did not reappoint Miyamoto, observers could only speculate. The Court insisted that ten-year contracts were just that—contracts for ten years. It could offer judges additional terms or it could let their contracts expire. In either case it owed no one a reason for its decision. And so it has remained to this day.

The next year, 1972, assistant judge and YJL member Toshio Konno heard that the Secretariat would not reappoint him either. Among other things, Konno had published an opinion holding that the state could not constitutionally require drivers involved in traffic accidents to report their accidents to the police. If ever there were a reason not to reappoint, one might have thought this was it. In any event, Konno did not wait to find out. Rather than risk Miyamoto's fate, he preemptorily resigned.

Did the Secretariat continue to discriminate against former YJL members after the resignations and the high-profile cases? On the one hand, several prominent members had unusually bad careers. Take Masamichi Hanada, appointed to the bench in 1957. Like so many others, he had begun his career as a star—a University of Tokyo graduate assigned at the outset to the Tokyo District Court. Yet Hanada was a leader in the Young Jurists League, and when the Secretariat refused to reappoint Miyamoto, Hanada took up his cause. He petitioned the Court over the Miyamoto affair, and contributed an article to a 1972 book on the Miyamoto affair titled *Security of Status for Judges.*

Soon thereafter, Hanada's career took a turn for the worse. In 1972, the Secretariat transferred him to a branch office, in 1976 to a Family Court, and in 1979 back to a branch office. By 1987, he was fifty-six years old and had spent the last fifteen years in branch offices and Family Courts. "Enough already," he apparently concluded, and he quit.

So too with the men around Hanada. Minoru Takeda was Hanada's principal co-signatory of the petition. In 1972, the Secretariat moved him to a branch office, where he remained for eleven years. Several other judges contributed with Hanada to the book about the Miyamoto affair. Katsuhiko Moriya soon found himself in a northern Family Court. By 1990, he had been spending eleven consecutive years on family disputes, with four of them in a branch office. Tsuneo Suzuki went to a branch office after the book appeared. So did Masahiro Tanaka, and there he stayed—for seventeen years straight, as of 1990.

On the other hand, some former members of the YJL landed in exceptionally prestigious and sensitive posts. Kozo Tanaka headed the Ministry of Justice's litigation bureaus for Fukuoka and Osaka. Naoyuki Kuroda did the

Table 1.4 Highest Judicial Positions Attained as of 1989
by Classes of 1960 and 1961 (Percentages in Parentheses)

Position	Non-YJL Judge	YJL Judge
High Court president	1 (1.27)	1 (2.63)
District Court (or Family Court) chief judge	6 (7.59)	4 (10.5)
High Court judge	48 (60.8)	24 (63.2)
District Court judge	22 (27.8)	7 (18.4)
Family Court judge	2 (2.53)	2 (5.26)
Total	79 (100)	38 (100)

same for Hiroshima and Nagoya. Akira Machida served on the Cabinet's Legal Affairs Bureau. Yoshio Osaka went on to the presidency of the Osaka High Court. More generally, table 1.4 compares the highest positions attained by the judges hired in 1960 and 1961 according to whether they were members of the YJL in 1969. At least at this level, the numbers suggests no real difference; if anything, YJL judges did better than the others.

III. Conclusion

The charges and countercharges we have considered in this chapter raise two empirical puzzles. First, what actually did happen in Japan? Second, what do the events in Japan, whatever they turn out to have been, imply more generally for someone constructing a positive theory of judicial independence?

On the first question, the puzzle is whether the anecdotes hold up statistically. Fukushima held the SDF unconstitutional, and had an unsuccessful career. Abe held the ban on door-to-door canvassing unconstitutional, and had an unsuccessful career. Miyamoto was a member of the Communist-affiliated YJL, and found himself out on the streets. Several judges who took his side in the ensuing quarrel fell into serbonian bogs where judges whole have sunk.

There seems to be a pattern, but it is hard to be sure. These judges may have been punished for their politics. But they also might have been slow or lazy or unlucky. As we show later, the Secretariat does reward the smart and the hard-working, and these particular judges may just have tried to cover their mediocrity with political charges. The Secretariat also moves judges with a degree of randomness, and these judges may simply have drawn the short straw. Somebody has to serve in the branch offices, after all.

Although the Left worked hard to keep the issue of judicial independence in the news, it was often its own worst enemy. When the Secretariat declined to hire several leftist LRTI graduates, they publicly accused the Secretariat of "gestapo" tactics. When the Secretariat continued to hire LRTI graduates selectively, leftists declared that judicial independence required it to hire all comers, bright or not, hardworking or not, sensible or not (Ramseyer and Rosenbluth 1997: 164–65).

Absent an approach that tests for political bias while holding constant various indices of intelligence and hard work, we simply cannot tell whether the Secretariat punished judges for their politics. Unfortunately, it is an approach the Japanese Left has not tried to use. Without it, table 1.4 refutes the left-wing claims; maybe a few YJL judges seem to have had bad careers, but in the big picture, YJL judges did better, not worse, than their colleagues.

In the chapters that follow, we both look at the big picture, and adjust for the many other things besides politics that influence a judge's career. In essence, we use econometrics to test whether the anecdotes the court critics recount apply generally, or whether there might be an equal number of less-publicized anecdotes on the other side—LRTI judges whose careers went well, or non-LRTI judges whose careers took nosedives—if anyone bothered to look. Generally, we confirm the accusations of the Left: politics matters, and a judge who inserts "political value judgments" into his decisions suffers, at least if they involve anti-LDP political value judgments. We then move to more mundane disputes (routine criminal and administrative cases) and explore the effect of these opinions on judicial careers as well. We find little or no evidence of politics there.

Throughout, we integrate this empirical analysis into modern principal–agent theory—that is, the science of how someone who employs someone else to work for him copes with the inherent divergence between their interests. In business, the theory helps explain when and how shareholders control the directors they vote for and the executives they indirectly hire. In politics, it helps explain when and how voters control the politicians they elect, and how those politicians control the bureaucrats they hire. In the courts—we will argue—it helps explain when and how those same politicians control the judges. It is through this theory, we suggest, that we can begin to build a more general positive theory of judicial independence, and begin to understand when judges will be more independent and when less, and how judges may be induced to do what voters ultimately want them to do.

2

Preliminary Empirics: Methodology
and Communist Judges

What with frenzied battles over Fukushima, Miyamoto, and the Young Jurists League (YJL), the Japanese Left assembled no end of anecdotes about the lack of judicial independence. Judge after judge was sentenced to years in the boondocks for daring to vote his conscience. Or so the stories ran.

As rhetorically effective as these anecdotes were, in the end they settled very little. Anecdotes seldom do. A critic of the Japanese government could point out that Judge X spent nine years in a branch office and was a vigorous Marxist. But the critic could never show that Judge X was posted to the branch office *because* he was a Marxist. Whatever the tale, government supporters could always reply that X was injudicious, dumb, lazy—or just plain unlucky. Some judge has to get that branch office posting, after all, and why not X? Or even if government supporters admitted that the case of Judge X was political, they might still deny that it represented any systematic persecution. Maybe an oddball in the Secretariat just got out of control himself. And how do we know it didn't happen to ordinary judges too? The press in Japan is generally to the left, and so might not report other examples.

On the other hand, the anti-Marxist middle will not win debates with anecdotes either. A government supporter could try to refute tales of persecution by citing the career of Judge Y, who wrote left-wing opinions and still became a District Court chief judge. But Judge Y might also have been judicious, brilliant, and a workaholic besides. Absent his political heterodoxy, might he not have become chief judge six years earlier? Might he not have become a High Court president? If Y had the brains and energy to be a star, the very normalcy of his career could reflect political discrimination.

A few observers have collected data on larger samples of judges (e.g., Kashimura 1991), but to date even they have simply compared averages.

26

Although averages will answer whether leftists had worse careers than centrists, or whether judges who wrote opinions favoring labor unions did worse than those who favored management, the answers can badly mislead. Simple averages do not hold constant judicial ability and effort. That left-wing judges on average had careers as good as mainstream judges does not tell us whether they were punished for being leftists. We also need to know whether they had average abilities.

Adjusting for judicial ability and effort is crucial, for a post that is a reward for the lazy and dull may yet be a punishment for the industrious and bright. To know whether the Secretariat punished Japanese judges for their politics, we need to measure the effect of judicial politics *holding all else constant.* What we need is an approach that measures the effect of multiple factors simultaneously.

Econometrics gives us the tools to measure simultaneous effects. In this book, we first assemble a variety of data on Japanese judges. We then use econometric regression analysis to untangle the effects of politics, ability, and background on various segments of judges' careers before and after the events that might generate politically biased incentives.

In this chapter, we explain the method and illustrate it with some preliminary substantive results on salaries and job postings for members of the YJL. We begin by explaining econometric regression analysis for those who are unfamiliar with it (section I). We then use the simplest of regression models—ordinary least squares (OLS)—to ask whether the Secretariat promoted leftist judges up the pay scale as quickly as other judges. We find that it did not. Holding constant proxies for judicial ability, we find that leftists earned lower pay than their peers (section II). Finally, we pause to outline the format of the regressions we will use for the rest of the book, and discuss what constitutes a successful career for a judge (section III).

I. Regression Analysis for the Nonmathematical

A. INTRODUCTION

Judge Abe of chapter 1 clearly had a bad career. So did Fukushima and Miyamoto and Konno. The question is whether the careers were so bad that we cannot explain them by some combination of talent, effort, and luck. To answer it, we need both a database covering a wide variety of judges and a multivariate test. More specifically, we need a way to test whether they did worse in their careers because of their politics, at the same time that we hold constant their seniority, IQ, work habits, and anything else that might otherwise have affected their careers.

Although we do not teach students how to run these statistical tests in law school, they are basic to social science and crucial to our inquiry here. Stripped of their mathematical derivation, they also present a straightforward intuition. To show that simple intuition, we begin with the logic of regression analysis. We stress "simple." This section is meant for those mathematically challenged verbal whizzes who spent their university careers talking and writing their way out of their SAT and GRE math scores. Professional economists and political scientists can skip the section, and proceed to section II.

B. The Basic Framework: Ordinary Least Squares

Suppose we wanted to know whether a particular law firm discriminated against female associates in pay. We would not want to know simply whether the average woman earned the same as the average man. After all, if the firm had only started hiring women recently, they would have less experience than the men. Because lawyer earnings tend to rise with experience, their low pay might just reflect that inexperience. Alternatively, even if they earned the same pay as the men, if the firm's partners had hired run-of-the-mill men but only (given their bias) superstar women, then that very equality could reflect pay discrimination.

The simple way to test for bias is to estimate associate pay (the "dependent variable" or, by custom, the "left-hand-side variable") as resulting from several other factors. These would certainly include *Male,* a variable equal to 1 if the associate is male, 0 if female. Such a variable that only takes 0-1 values is called a "dummy variable," even outside our present context, and allows us to incorporate nonnumeric dimensions of a problem. The several factors would also include assorted "control variables": the usual determinants of associate pay. These variables are not directly relevant to the question of sex bias, but we control for them because they may cause a sex-based pay differential if men and women happen to differ along any of those dimensions. The control variables would include things like IQ (if we knew it), hours billed, and seniority. The entire group of variables we use to estimate associate pay—the male variable of central interest and the control variables—are called the "independent" or "right-hand-side variables," for reasons we will shortly see.

Suppose we compiled the data on the associates of the law firm as shown in table 2.1. Using this data, we would try to estimate the coefficients ($a, b_1, b_2, b_3,$ and b_4) in the following equation, which has the left-hand-side variable on the (surprise) left, so that it depends on the right-hand-side variables on the right.

$$\text{Pay}_i = a + b_1 * \text{Sex}_i + b_2 * \text{IQ}_i + b_3 * \text{Hours}_i + b_4 * \text{Seniority}_i + e_i,$$

Table 2.1 Hypothetical Law Firm—Raw Data

Lawyer	Pay	Sex	IQ	Hours	Seniority
Adams	86,000	1	118	2,100	1
Bailey	100,000	1	120	2,200	4
Casey	105,000	1	115	2,100	5
Davis	95,000	0	134	2,400	2
Epstein	98,000	1	118	1,700	5
Fahey	120,000	1	135	2,200	5
Giller	105,000	1	129	2,100	4
Haley	86,000	1	130	2,200	1
Isaacson	96,000	0	140	2,500	2
Jacobs	100,000	0	135	2,300	3
Klein	98,000	0	125	2,200	3
Lawlor	118,000	1	125	2,100	6
Mason	102,000	1	120	2,000	4
North	115,000	1	133	2,000	6
O'Neill	93,000	1	129	1,650	3
Peterson	90,000	1	105	2,100	4
Quinn	90,000	0	130	1,800	2
Ralph	86,000	1	125	2,100	1
Saltzer	105,000	0	140	2,700	4
Toomey	104,000	1	117	2,000	5
Unumb	99,000	1	121	2,400	2
Valentine	92,000	1	122	1,600	3
Walker	124,000	0	145	2,600	6
Xu	98,000	1	120	1,900	5
Yaffee	106,000	1	125	2,100	5
Zimmerman	90,000	1	118	1,650	4

Because the *Sex* term drops out of the equation when it takes the value of 0 (for female) but stays in if 1 (for male), the calculated value of the co-efficient will give the difference in pay between equally qualified men and women.

The last term, e_i, indicates that our equation describes the data with error. This error is a "miscellaneous" term for the equation, covering the effects of any other variables affecting pay that are not correlated with sex, IQ, hours, or seniority, including simple luck, so that the left-hand side of the equation equals the right-hand side. The subscript i indicates lawyer i, for whom each of the variables is measured, where we let i range from 1 to 26 for the twenty-six associates in table 2.1. Alone of the variables, the error is not measured. It represents what is unobservable about that lawyer but relevant to his or her pay. Note that the coefficients a, b_1, b_2, b_3, and b_4 do not have the i subscript. That is because our underlying assumption is that those things affect each lawyer the same way, and lawyer i no differently than any other lawyer. Another way of thinking about this is that we are just looking for the average effect of being female on a lawyer, rather than attempting the impossible task of finding for each lawyer an individual effect of being female.

If we were to pick values for the coefficients a, b_1, b_2, b_3, and b_4 and plug them into the equation using the data, we would have an estimate of e_i for each of the lawyers, for i from 1 to 26. The better our values fit the data, the smaller the resulting error e_i will be. We could pick the values by guesswork, or by hiring teams of graduate students with slide rules, as was done in the 1950s. What the computer does for us in regression analysis is to calculate the values of a, b_1, b_2, b_3, and b_4 that best fit the data. It does so by finding the values that minimize the sum over all the lawyers of the squares of the error estimates (hence the term "ordinary least squares," or OLS).[1]

If, as seems likely, pay rises with IQ, hours billed, and seniority, then the coefficients b_2, b_3, and b_4 will all be positive. If the firm pays men higher wages than women (holding constant IQ, hours, and seniority), the coefficient b_1 will be positive too. If it pays men and women the same, b_1 will be 0.

We are not done, though. Any data set like this will have considerable noise—those e_i terms, which even the computer estimates cannot rid us of, since some noise is an inherent part of the data. As a result, we need to know whether any positive coefficient is more than accidental. To check this, the computer generates a measure of statistical significance called the "t-statistic" (the coefficient itself divided by the standard error of the variable). If the t-statistic on a coefficient is greater than roughly 1.7, then the odds that a true coefficient of 0 would have generated the estimate we found are less than 10 percent (a 90 percent "confidence level"). If it exceeds 2, we know that the odds are less than 5 percent. Thus, high t-statistics indicate accurate estimates.

We would also like to know how fully the equation explains the dispersion in the data. It could be that we have an accurate estimate of the importance of IQ toward pay, but that what we have found is that IQ matters very little. It could also be that the lawyers all have almost the same IQ, so that not much of the variation in pay among them is explained by it. Toward that end, the computer calculates an "adjusted R^2"—which, roughly, gives the percentage of the variance in the data the equation as a whole explains.[2]

Now return to our example. We first enter the data from table 2.1 and use the computer to generate a standard set of "summary statistics" that give

1. Why minimize the sum of the squared values of the estimated errors rather than just their sum? This is conventional, but there are also good statistical reasons for it that would be too digressive to explain here. It is worth noting, however, that minimizing the square of the error values puts particular importance on not choosing the coefficient values so that some lawyers are described extremely badly. If required to make a choice, OLS chooses coefficient estimates that describe most lawyers slightly badly rather than a few lawyers extremely badly.

2. This is an adjusted R^2 if it is adjusted for the fact that adding extra right-hand-side variables inevitably makes the equation explain the dispersion in the data more fully. In this book, the difference between adjusted and unadjusted R^2 is not important.

Table 2.2 Hypothetical Law Firm—Summary Statistics

Variable	n	Minimum	Mean	Maximum
Pay	26	86,000	100,039	124,000
IQ	26	105	126	145
Hours	26	1,600	2,103	2,700
Seniority	26	1	3.65	6
Pay (male)	19	86,000	99,632	120,000
IQ (male)	19	105	122	135
Hours (male)	19	1,600	2,011	2,400
Seniority (male)	19	1	3.84	6
Pay (female)	7	90,000	101,143	124,000
IQ (female)	7	125	136	145
Hours (female)	7	1,800	2,357	2,700
Seniority (female)	7	2	3.14	6

Table 2.3 Pay Levels in a Hypothetical
Law Firm—Regression Results

	Dependent Variable Pay
Male	4,797 (2.05)
IQ	465 (4.09)
Hours	11.1 (3.39)
Seniority	5,255 (10.8)
Intercept	−4,544 (0.30)
n	26
Adjusted R^2	.87

NOTE: The regression uses OLS. The table gives the coefficients, followed by the absolute value of the t-statistics.

a simple description of each variable separately without trying to relate the variables to each other (table 2.2). This is not strictly speaking necessary to regression analysis, but it is good practice to gain an idea of the sizes of all the variables. We then ask the computer to calculate pay as a function of the other variables in our regression equation. Under the early-twenty-first-century versions of Excel, we can do this by loading "regression analysis" into memory as an "add in." Then, by pulling down "Tools" and going to "Data Analysis," we will find "Regressions." We identify the pay column as the "Y range" and the other columns as the "X range," and generate the coefficients and t-statistics that appear on table 2.3. Other spreadsheets have similarly straightforward methods that would generate the exact same OLS regression estimates from this data.

What does this tell us about an associate's salary at this law firm? The equation in table 2.3 tells us that an associate earns −$4,544 plus his or her IQ times $465, plus billable hours times $11.1, plus his or her seniority times

$5,255—and an extra $4,797 if he is male. Note from table 2.2 that the average associate was a male with an IQ of 126 who worked 2,100 hours and had 3.7 years of experience. Using the coefficients of table 2.3, this means his likely pay would have been about $110,000. Most interesting for the objective of this study, the firm discriminates. Holding constant intelligence, effort, and seniority, the firm pays men about $4,800 more than it pays women.

Note several other things about this example. First, the firm discriminated against women even though the women earned more than the men—$101,143 on average compared to $99,632. We know the bias exists because the computer tests for sex differences holding the other relevant factors constant. Apparently, the firm had hired women who were substantially smarter and harder working than the men.

Second, in the real world we seldom have exactly the important variables that we need. We may know hours billed, for example—though getting that data from the firm will not be easy without a court order—but we will not have IQ unless we can make compulsory IQ testing part of discovery. Even if the judge is compliant, we would not be able to measure other crucial aspects of lawyering such as "judgment" or "temperament," which will therefore fall into our error term. The empirical game will turn on our ability to find adequate proxies for the most important qualities (LSAT score instead of IQ, for example), and on our hope that any important quality without a proxy will not cause confusion by being correlated with our other explanatory variables (that "judgment" will be uncorrelated with IQ or sex, for example).

Third, all t-statistics in the example are extremely high. All coefficients are statistically different from zero at the 95 percent confidence level or higher. Moreover, the adjusted R^2 of 87 percent indicates that these few variables explain most of the variance in the data. The real world is rarely so kind. The high t-statistics and R^2 here result from the fact that we invented these data out of whole cloth. In fact, if such nice results were to show up in a real study, sophisticated readers would properly be skeptical about whether the data are genuine. If someone flips a fair coin ten thousand times, we expect the number of heads to be about half that; but if someone tells us it was exactly five thousand, we start to wonder whether researcher fraud might not be a better explanation than the fairness of the coin for such a stunning result.

C. Complications
1. When the Dependent Variable Is a Dummy Variable

OLS estimates are appropriate when the dependent variable potentially takes any value from negative to positive infinity, including fractions. Lawyers' pay can certainly take fractional values, even if negative pay is as unlikely for associates as pay of $500,000. Yet sometimes we will want to use regressions to predict a "dummy" variable, one that can only take the value 0 or 1. In table 2.7, for example, we will ask which judges begin their careers at the Tokyo District Court (1 if they did, 0 otherwise). In such cases we will need to use "probit" or "logit" regressions rather than OLS. Necessarily, this takes us beyond Excel. For the analysis in this book, we use the program Stata instead.[3]

The problem with OLS is that it is designed to estimate an equation like the one in the example above,

$$\text{Pay}_i = a + b_1 * \text{Sex}_i + b_2 * \text{IQ}_i + b_3 * \text{Hours}_i + b_4 * \text{Seniority}_i + e_i,$$

where the dependent variable, *Pay,* is a linear function of the independent variables. If a lawyer's IQ is ten points above average and OLS tells us that the best estimate is $b_2 = 465$, the regression predicts that his pay will be 4,650 dollars above average, other things equal. But suppose the dependent variable measures whether the lawyer made partner. It thus takes a value of 0 if he fails and 1 if he succeeds:

$$\text{Partner}_i = a + b_1 * \text{Sex}_i + b_2 * \text{IQ}_i + b_3 * \text{Hours}_i + b_4 * \text{Seniority}_i + e_i.$$

If we used OLS, this equation might generate an estimate of $b_2 = .823$, implying that if a lawyer's IQ were ten points higher, his value for *Partner* would increase by 8.23. This, of course, makes no sense. *Partner* has only two potential values, 0 and 1. For the linear equation to fit the data, the unobserved errors e_i would have to take very special values to make the right-hand side of the equation sum to 0 or 1, and we have no reason to assume they would take those values. OLS will faithfully spit back estimates if one tries to use it, but the estimates will not make sense.

Probit and logit regressions take a different approach from OLS. Suppose we have an unobserved variable called *Partnerability* that we can model by

$$\text{Partnerability}_i = a + b_1 * \text{Sex}_i + b_2 * \text{IQ}_i + b_3 * \text{Hours}_i + b_4 * \text{Seniority}_i.$$

Whether someone makes partner depends on a second equation, which is discontinuous instead of linear:

$$\text{Partner}_i = 1 \text{ if Partnerability} + e_i > 0$$
$$= 0 \text{ if Partnerability} + e_i \leq 0$$

3. No such problem arises if any or all of the *independent* variables take 0-1 values, as *Male* did in the example. The problem with dependent variables equaling only 0 or 1 is that this means the error term *e* must take only very peculiar values so as to make the right-hand and left-hand sides equal in the equation being estimated. A right-hand-side variable equaling only 0 or 1 does not constrain the error term that way.

For a given level of *Partnerability,* this pair of equations gives us the probability that a lawyer will make partner. If *Partnerability* = 15.0, for example, it might be that Probability$(15.0 + e_i > 0) = .43$, in which case we could assign a 43 percent chance that he would make partner. If pressed, we would predict that he would be passed over.

Probit and logit both estimate coefficients that bring the predicted values of *Partner* as close to the observed partnership decisions as possible. The two regression techniques differ from each other in whether they assume that the e_i error distribution (which determines the Probability(.) function) takes a normal or logistic distribution. Since the two distributions have similar "bell shapes," ordinarily this distinction will not matter.

Because probit and logit are not linear models, we cannot interpret the coefficients in the straightforward manner we do with OLS. If we estimated $b_2 = .43$, for example, that means that if a lawyer has an IQ ten points above average, he will have a *Partnerability* index 4.3 points higher. We must go a step further, to the *Partner* equation, to figure out how this affects his chances of making partner. Suppose that the average lawyer has *Partnerability* of 15.0, and thus the 43 percent chance of making partner explained above. Our lawyer with an IQ ten points higher and a *Partnerability* of 19.3 might have Probability$(19.3 + e_i > 0) = .52$, for a 52 percent chance of making partner. The effect of the ten IQ points is to add nine percentage points to his probability of making partner.

The coefficient $b_2 = .43$ is much less interesting than the "marginal effect" of how the probability of *Partner* = 1 increases with IQ. When we present probit results, we will therefore present the marginal effects instead of the coefficients. In a linear model, the effect per extra IQ point is the same regardless of the starting IQ or the number of IQ points added. In a nonlinear model, the effect per added IQ point depends on both of those things. We will adopt the conventional measure of reporting the marginal effect to be the rate of change in the dependent variable when the independent variable is increased slightly from an observation with median values for all independent variables (i.e., the values with the same number of observations above and below). Also, instead of the *t*-statistics and R^2s of OLS, the computer will now generate *z*-values and pseudo R^2s, which in general one can treat as close substitutes for the OLS statistics.

2. When the Dependent Variable Is Constrained

Suppose the dependent variable neither ranges over the entire number line from negative to positive infinity, nor is a 0-1 dummy. Instead, it ranges between an upper and a lower bound. For most of chapters 4–6, for instance, we estimate the fraction of a decade that a judge spends in attractive or unattractive jobs. The dependent variable thus ranges from 0 to 1, but includes all fractions in between. For these regressions, the appropriate regression model is "tobit." Tobit regressions generate z-statistics, and analogously to adjusted R^2s they calculate pseudo R^2s.

As with probit, the coefficients calculated by tobit are not as useful as the marginal effects calculated from them. Understanding what we explained in the previous section about probit coefficients and marginal effects is enough to enable readers to be able to interpret the tobit regressions in the following chapters, and the nonstatistically inclined can safely skip the rest of this subsection. For those interested, however, we here explain tobit marginal effects in more detail.

Tobit estimation is bit like a cross between OLS and probit. For extreme observations, the situation is like probit, because y_i cannot change to take values beyond 0 and 1 as the x_i values change. For moderate observations, the situation is like OLS because as x_i values change, the y_i values change smoothly between 0 and 1.

The tobit model begins with the equation

$$s_i = x_i * b,$$

where s_i might be an index of a judge's propensity to be assigned a greater percentage of bad jobs in a decade (not the percentage y_i which we actually observe). In our case, x_i is the set of explanatory variables for the career of judge i, and s_i is the Secretariat's evaluation of judge i. What we observe is not the s_i, but what is called "censored" data.[4] Let u_i be a normally distributed error term. What we observe is y_i the percentage of bad jobs judge i received during the decade, which is determined as follows:

$$y_i = 0 \quad \text{if} \quad s_i + u_i \leq 0$$
$$y_i = 1 \quad \text{if} \quad s_i + u_i > 1$$
$$y_i = s_i + u_i \quad \text{otherwise.}$$

In the present case, s_i is censored because nobody can spend less than 0 or more than 100 percent of a decade in an undesirable job. Thus, we only observe y_i, not s_i. The set of judges for whom $y_i = 1$ included some who just barely avoided getting out of the branch offices, and some who were so annoying that the Secretariat would have put them in branch offices 200 percent of the decade if only it could have.

---

4. This is different from *truncated* data. If the data had been truncated, we would not observe many 0s and 1s—for we would not have those observations in our sample at all.

The probability of observing $y_i = 0$ is $\text{Prob}(x_i b + u_i < 0)$. The probability of observing $y_i = 1$ is $\text{Prob}(x_i b + u_i > 1)$. The probability of observing y_i in between 0 and 1 is just the remaining probability, $[1 - \text{Prob}(x_i b + u_i < 0) - \text{Prob}(x_i b + u_i > 1)]$. The predicted value for y_i given x_i and b is an expected value, based on the probabilities of u_i turning out different ways. For any judge, there is some probability that $y_i = 0$, some probability that $y_i = 1$, and some probability that y_i takes each of the possible values in between. The overall expected value for y_i is

$$\text{Prob}(x_i b + u_i < 0)(0) + \text{Prob}(x_i b + u_i > 1)(1) + [1 - \text{Prob}(x_i b + u_i < 0) - \text{Prob}(x_i b + u_i > 1)]E(x_i b + u_i | 0 < x_i b + u_i < 1),$$

where the last term is the expected value of $x_i b + u_i$ conditional on it being between 0 and 1. For a particular tobit regression, the numbers generated by the computer might give us the following expression for a particular judge's expected percentage of bad jobs during a decade:

$$.23(0) + .48(1) + (1 - .23 - .48)(.76) = .70$$

This equation says that there is probability .23 that a judge with these characteristics would spend no time in a branch office, probability .48 that he would spend 100 percent of the decade there, and probability .29 that he would spend some amount in between, where the average amount in between would be 76 percent of the decade. Our overall prediction, a weighted average of these three possibilities, is that he would spend 70 percent of the decade in bad jobs.

The marginal effects that we report are the rate at which the predicted y_i value changes when x_i changes. Thus, it might be that the coefficients generated by tobit tell us that if a judge made an anti-government decision instead of a pro-government decision, the values in the above equation would change to

$$.03(0) + .67(1) + (1 - .03 - .67)(.85) = .92,$$

which says that now the judge would only have probability .03 of escaping being assigned to a branch office, but would have probability .67 of spending the entire decade there. The marginal effect of an anti-government decision would be an extra 22 percent ($= .92 - .70$) of the decade in a branch office. As with probit, the marginal effect depends on the characteristics of the particular judge, and we will use the median judge as our base.

3. When the Dependent Variable Has Ordinal but Not Cardinal Values

Last, suppose the dependent variable takes ordinal but not cardinal values. For example, in chapter 3 we ask which judges the Secretariat assigns to the best cities. We know most judges would rather be in Tokyo than Osaka, and in Osaka rather than Fukuoka. Yet although we know which cities they consider most attractive, we do not know *how much* more attractive they find one over another. We know the ordinal rankings of the cities, in other words, but those rankings have no cardinal significance. OLS, however, treats the value of the dependent variable as a cardinal number. If we enter a 2 for Tokyo and 1 for Osaka, it treats a Tokyo job as twice as attractive as an Osaka one.

For these tests, the appropriate regression is "ordered probit," which we use in chapter 3. Like plain probit, ordered probit imagines that there is a latent index variable—*Judge_Quality* here—and that as the index variable passes a threshold, the dependent variable of interest jumps from one value to another. In simple probit, the only jump is from 0 to 1. With ordered probit, there can be several thresholds, so the dependent variable can jump from 0 to 1 to 2 to 3. Unfortunately, the coefficients of ordered probit are extraordinarily intricate to interpret. There is no single marginal effect, because an increase in *Judge_Quality* increases a judge's chances of getting both the desirable Osaka job and the even more desirable Tokyo job. We explain the ordered probit coefficients we estimate in appendix C.

II. Judicial Pay and Leftist Judges

A. THE ISSUE

Return now to the leftist Japanese judges. Before asking whether Abe or Fukushima suffered for their opinions, however, consider how one might test whether YJL members suffered more generally. And as an index of career success, consider whether they earned salaries as high as their colleagues who were not League members. We do not have the pay data on individual judges (nor, having written this book, is the Secretariat likely ever to give us that data). Yet we do have a proxy.

During their first ten years on the bench, Japanese judges climb the twelve steps of the assistant judge pay scale, a range from 190,600 to 405,600 yen per month as of 1989, at the end of our period of analysis. During the rest of their career, they move through another nine steps—from 494,000 yen (step 8) to 912,000 (step 3) to 1,115,000 (step 0). Although the Constitution protects judges from explicit pay cuts (Art. 79), the Secretariat need not promote all judges at the same rate. If unhappy with a judge's work, it need not promote him at all.

Although we do not know pay, we do know how many years it takes a judge to reach the moderately prestigious administrative status known as *sokatsu*. Most judges eventually obtain a *sokatsu* post, but some obtain it earlier than others. Because appointment to *sokatsu* comes only at appointment to step 3 on the pay scale (as of the late 1980s), the length of time it takes a judge to obtain *sokatsu* status correlates with how fast he climbed the pay scale.

Hence, to measure pay discrimination we use as our dependent variable the time it takes a judge to reach *sokatsu* status, a variable we call *Time2Sok*. To test for political discrimination, we introduce a variable, *YJL*, that takes the value 1 if a judge was a member of the league and 0 otherwise. As in our hypothetical example of sex discrimination, if the Secretariat did not discriminate against YJL members, the coefficient on *YJL* will equal 0. If it promoted them up the pay scale more slowly, the coefficient will be positive and statistically significantly different from 0.

To this equation, we add several control variables: *Male, Flunks* (the number of times a judge failed the entrance exam to the LRTI—a proxy for IQ and hard work), *Elite_College* (1 if a judge attended either of the two most prestigious universities, the University of Tokyo and the University of Kyoto—again, a proxy for IQ and hard work), *1st_Tokyo* (whether the Secretariat thought the judge a star and assigned him initially to the Tokyo District Court—again a proxy for talent and effort), and *1st_BO* (whether the Secretariat thought the judge a loser and assigned him initially to a branch office).[5] We include more precise definitions of the variables in table 2.4.

We do not try to disentangle the relative importance of intelligence and effort. The issue is important and interesting, but it does not bear on the question of political discrimination. As shown in the correlation matrix in panel B of table 2.5 below, the control variables are themselves correlated with each other. Although this lowers the statistical significance of the coefficients, it does not bias our estimates of the coefficient on *YJL*. Indeed, it is precisely because the variables affecting career success are correlated that we need to use regression analysis in the first place. Note that *YJL* is positively correlated with *Elite_College, 1st_Tokyo,* and *Male,* but negatively

5. To control for unobservable differences among the cohorts, we further include dummy variables indicating the year in which a judge finished his legal education. We omit the coefficients here.

Table 2.4 YJL Pay Discrimination—Variables

Time2Sok	The year a judge first received a *sokatsu* appointment, less the year he graduated from the LRTI. Because judges generally do not receive a *sokatsu* posting until they reach a specific rank in the pay scale, Time2Sok proxies for the rate at which a judge climbs the scale.
YJL	1 if a judge was a member of the Young Jurists League in 1969; 0 otherwise. To the extent that the Secretariat has continued to punish former YJL members, YJL will correlate positively with unattractive job postings and negatively with attractive ones.
Male	1 if a judge is male, 0 if female.
Flunks	The estimated number of years (based on birth year) between college graduation and entrance to the LRTI. Because the LRTI entrance exam passage rate varied between 1 and 4 percent, even the best students usually failed it several times. By approximating the number of times a judge failed this exam, Flunks inversely proxies for a combination of IQ and effort. Because smarter and harder working judges tend to be more successful than others, Flunks will usually correlate positively with attractive job postings and negatively with unattractive ones.
Elite_College	1 if a judge graduated from either the University of Tokyo or the University of Kyoto; 0 otherwise. Because the variable proxies for IQ and effort (and captures any old-school ties), Elite_College will generally correlate positively with attractive job postings and negatively with unattractive ones.
1st_Tokyo	1 if a judge started at the Tokyo District Court; 0 otherwise. When the Secretariat hires a new class of judges it generally assigns the most promising to the Tokyo District Court. Because fast track judges tend to stay on the fast track, 1st_Tokyo will tend to correlate positively with later attractive job postings and negatively with unattractive ones.
1st_BO	1 if a judge started at a branch office; 0 otherwise. When the Secretariat hires a new class of judges, it generally assigns some of the least promising to branch offices from the start. Because slow-track judges tend to stay on the slow track, 1st_BO will tend to correlate positively with unattractive job postings and negatively with attractive ones.

correlated with *Flunks,* and *1st_BO.* This indicates that the leftist lawyers were disproportionately among the most talented male judges—exactly the ones most likely otherwise to succeed. For the same reason that we needed regression analysis to show pay discrimination against women in our hypothetical law firm example, we shall need it to show discrimination against the YJL members.

B. DATA SOURCES

We assemble the data used throughout this book from several sources. As noted in chapter 1, for judicial careers we use the *Zen saibankan keireki soran* (the ZSKS), a book that details all job postings received by judges educated after World War II. The database for our pay regression is based on all judges hired from 1960 to 1969. We make several adjustments for things such as early deaths, detailed in appendix B.

Table 2.5 YJL Pay Discrimination

A. Summary Statistics

Variable	n	Minimum	Mean	Maximum
Time2Sok	501	11	21.711	37
YJL	501	0	.281	1
Elite_College	501	0	.317	1
Flunks	501	0	4.828	18
1st_Tokyo	501	0	.104	1
1st_BO	501	0	.142	1
Male	501	0	.948	1

B. Correlations

	Time2Sok	YJL	Elite_College	Flunks	1st_Tokyo	1st_BO	Male
Time2Sok	1.00						
YJL	.05	1.00					
Elite_College	−.03	.03	1.00				
Flunks	.05	−.12	−.23	1.00			
1st_Tokyo	−.04	.01	.25	−.23	1.00		
1st_BO	.11	−.09	−.15	.30	−.14	1.00	
Male	−.18	.03	.08	−.05	.08	.02	1.00

NOTE: The data reflect all judges hired from 1960 to 1969, subject to the adjustments made in appendix B.

For membership in the leftist YJL as of 1969, we use *Osorubeki saiban* (Shiso, 1969), a book that reproduced the list of members from the league's own newsletter.

Table 2.5 shows the summary statistics for the variables we use in this chapter.

To discover whether family status affected career success, we checked the *Nippon shinshi roku,* the Japanese equivalent of a cross between *Who's Who* and the *Social Register* for 1969. We searched for every judge from the classes of 1961 to 1965. Because not one appeared in the book, we did not construct a variable for family status. This is actually a useful negative finding: the judiciary appears not to be a career for those well-connected by birth, despite the large number of judges who attended prestigious universities.

In chapters 3–6 we use data on judicial opinions. For these cases, we relied on the *Hanrei takei* database (published by Daiichi hoki, formerly known as the LEX/DB database). This source resembles the American Westlaw and Lexis, and includes virtually all postwar published opinions on nine or ten CD-ROMs (depending on whether an annual update is part of the package). Unfortunately the collection is still slightly incomplete. The publisher only began compiling the opinions in the 1980s and had nothing like the West national reporter system from which to work. Nonetheless, we have checked the compilation scheme and have no reason to think the coverage is biased in any way relevant here.

Table 2.6 YJL Pay Discrimination—Regression Results

	Dependent Variable	
	A. Time2Sok	B. Time2Sok
YJL	.919 (1.71)*	.995 (1.87)*
Elite_College	.086 (0.17)	.264 (0.52)
Flunks	.014 (0.19)	−.025 (0.35)
1st_Tokyo	−1.383 (1.72)*	−1.055 (1.32)
1st_BO		1.448 (2.09)**
Male		−3.423 (3.34)**
Intercept	22.905 (29.20)**	25.825 (21.74)**
Adjusted R^2	0.09	0.11

NOTE: $n = 501$. The regression uses OLS. The table gives the coefficients, followed by the absolute values of the t-statistics.

To control for unobservable differences among the cohorts, we further include dummy variables indicating the year in which a judge finished his legal education. We omit the coefficients here.

The data cover all judges hired from 1961 through 1969, adjusted as described in appendix B.

*Statistically significant at the 90 percent confidence level using a two-tailed test.
**Statistically significant at the 95 percent confidence level using a two-tailed test.

Our data and computer programs are available on the Internet at http://pacioli.bus.indiana.edu/erasmuse/jbook/jbook.htm.

C. RESULTS

We report our regression estimates in table 2.6. Most notably, the coefficient on *YJL* is positive and significant (albeit at only the 90 percent confidence level): judges who joined the YJL in the 1960s received their first *sokatsu* assignment later than their peers. The coefficients on *YJL* of .92 in regression A and 1.0 in regression B indicate that they received their posting about a year later. The *t*-statistics of 1.7 in A and 1.8 in B indicate that the coefficients are statistically significantly different from 0 at the 90 percent level. If, as observers claim, a *sokatsu* appointment signals promotion to a defined step on the pay scale, then the Secretariat apparently promoted YJL members up the pay scale more slowly than nonmembers.

As expected, the coefficient on *1st_Tokyo* is negative and significant in at least one specification (regression A). These are the judges the Secretariat initially identified as the most promising. Twenty years later they seem to have risen through the ranks about a year and a half ahead of the rest. The coefficient on *1st_BO* has the opposite effect (regression B). The Secretariat apparently identified these judges as the least talented, and twenty years later they seem to have climbed the ranks a year and a half behind the rest. Because the Secretariat forthrightly assigns the best new recruits to the Tokyo District

Table 2.7 First Postings—Regression Results

	Dependent Variable		
	A. 1st_Tokyo	B. 1st_BO	C. Flunks
Elite_College	.208 (3.76)**	−.017 (0.41)	−1.641 (5.12)**
YJL	−.016 (0.61)	−.023 (0.58)	−.847 (2.55)**
Flunks	−.022 (3.01)**	.022 (3.25)**	
R^2	.15	.11	.06
Regression	Probit	Probit	OLS

NOTE: $n = 501$. The figure for R^2 gives the pseudo R^2 for columns (A) and (B) and the adjusted R^2 for column (C). The table gives the marginal effects at the sample medians, followed by the absolute value of the z-statistics for probit and t-statistics for OLS. The regressions included intercepts, not reported here.

The data cover all judges hired from 1961 through 1969, adjusted as described in appendix B.

**Statistically significant at greater than 95 percent confidence level using a two-tailed test.

Court but says nothing about the apparent policy of starting the worst at branch offices, in the later chapters we focus on *1st_Tokyo*. The coefficient on *Male* is negative (−3.4 in regression B) and statistically significant: men reach *sokatsu* status three and a half years before comparably qualified women. The point is obviously intriguing and important, but as this is a project about politics rather than sex discrimination, we do not pursue it further.

Although the coefficients on *Elite_College* and *Flunk* are not significant, *1st_Tokyo* and *1st_BO* both indirectly incorporate their effects on judicial careers. In table 2.7 (regression A), we ask who the Secretariat sends to the coveted first postings at the Tokyo District Court. Disproportionately they are the graduates of the Universities of Tokyo and Kyoto who failed the LRTI exam the fewest times, and this effect is statistically significant. The marginal effect of .208 for *Elite_College* means that having gone to an elite university increased an otherwise median judge's chances of starting in Tokyo by 20.8 percent, and the marginal effect of −.022 for *Flunks* indicates that having flunked the LRTI exam one extra time reduces the judge's probability of starting in Tokyo by 2.2 percent. In regression B we ask whom the Secretariat sends to the first postings in the branch offices. Disproportionately they are the graduates who flunked the exam the most often, and this is also statistically significant. Quite coincidentally, the marginal effect of *Flunks* is also .022, after rounding.

Note that these first two regressions in table 2.7 are not OLS, but probit, because the variables for first job are binary, taking only the values 0 and 1. The entries in the table are the marginal effects (which are analogous to the coefficients for OLS, but with the differences noted earlier).

According to regressions A and B of table 2.7, the Secretariat seems not to have penalized YJL members in their first job appointments. But there is a simple explanation for this: it did not know who the members were. The YJL roster first became public in 1969. These first postings are for judges hired from 1960 to 1969.

In regression C, we ask who tended to flunk the LRTI exam. Dispropor-tionately (and, again, the effect is statistically significant), they were those who did not graduate from the Universities of Tokyo or Kyoto, and were not mem-bers of the YJL. On average, the judges in this cohort passed the exam after five or six tries. The graduates of the Universities of Tokyo and Kyoto passed it after four tries. Because university and LRTI entrance exams test for similar skills, this phenomenon is hardly surprising.

Thus, the YJL apparently recruited from among the more talented judges. This is crucial to trying to draw conclusions from data about judicial careers. In chapter 1, we explained that if YJL judges were above average in ability, then average careers would not indicate lack of persecution at all—rather, it would be evidence of persecution. Such was the case, it seems, at least regarding time to first *sokatsu*.

III. Our Method

A. INTRODUCTION

You now have seen an example of our basic method, as applied to discovering whether membership in the YJL would hurt a future judge's financial prospects or his first posting. We continue to use that method in the rest of the book. In general terms, we have postulated that both political and control variables such as ability, along with luck, affect a judge's career success. In equation form, we can write this as

$$\text{Success}_i = a + b * \text{Politics}_i + c * \text{Controls}_i + e_i.$$

The *sokatsu* regression took the form

$$\text{Time2Sok}_i = a + b * \text{YJL}_i + c_1 * \text{Elite\_College}_i + c_2 * \text{Flunk}_i$$
$$+ c_3 * \text{1st\_Tokyo}_i + c_4 * \text{1st\_BO} + c_5 * \text{Male} + e_i,$$

and the coefficients estimated by OLS yielded the equation

$$\text{Time2Sok}_i = 25.825 + .995 * \text{YJL}_i + .264 * \text{Elite\_College}_i - .025 * \text{Flunk}_i$$
$$- 1.055 * \text{1st\_Tokyo}_i + 1.448 * \text{1st\_BO} - 3.423 * \text{Male} + e_i.$$

This equation illustrates the importance of using regression analysis. The simple correlation between time to *sokatsu* and membership in the YJL was only .05, very close to zero (table 2.5, panel B), but this was because the independent effect of YJL was almost canceled by the coincidence that YJL members were smarter, as measured by university and exam passage.

The same method is used for the rest of this book. The differences among the various regressions are in how we specify *Success, Politics,* and *Controls.* Of these, *Politics* is the variable we will change most, letting it vary from YJL membership to decisions in tax cases to number of anti-government injunctions, as we map out exactly what it means for politics to affect judicial independence. Changes in how we measure *Success* and in the *Controls* flow from our changes in the *Politics* variable. In some regressions, for example, we look at success in a particular decade for a cohort of judges who all began their careers at the same time, an apt way to measure the influence of their YJL membership. In others, we look at success in the decade after a particular kind of judicial decision, so that the decade will be different depending on the year in which the judge issued his decision.

B. Measuring Success in Judicial Careers

It is worth discussing success generally before we continue with the regressions. Earlier in this chapter, we measured it as the time to a judge's first *sokatsu* appointment, a rough indication of pay increases. Pay certainly matters, even to judges, but money is not the only thing in life. Moreover, all these judges, even the ones who did not go to Tokyo University and who flunked the LRTI exam many times, were extraordinarily talented and hardworking. They all did pass the LRTI exam in the end. Most of them could have made plenty of money in business, and we can deduce that pay is less of a motivation for them than for the average straight-A student.

What, then, motivates judges? Everyone likes more money (you can always give it to charity if you cannot think of anything else to spend it on), but judges must have other motivations for which they are willing to sacrifice cash. This is as true in the United States as Japan, at least for U.S. federal judges, practically all of whom could be earning far more in private practice than as judges.

We propose a "Five P's" theory of judicial motivation, a loose taxonomy that helps us focus on what we might measure.[6] Job characteristics such as pay, location, and plushness of the office are common to all professions, but the pursuit of a career as judge, politician, or central banker has special motivators that we call Policy, Principle, Power, Pride, and Place.

---

6. The name is an allusion to the "Four P's of Marketing": Price, Product, Promotion, and Place. A form of the Five P's taxonomy was introduced in Rasmusen 1997. That article's focus is on central bankers, and the trustee theory applies better to them and to U.S. federal judges than to Japanese judges, but the motivational theory is equally apt here.

Policy refers to the judge's desire to see particular policies in place, usually because of his political or moral preferences.

Principle refers to the judge's desire to take particular actions for their own sakes, rather than for their results. This is distinct from Policy, and can conflict with it. A judge might, for example, dissent publicly (in the United States) or privately (to his fellow judges) in a particular case out of Principle, even when his dissent would have no effect on the outcome and would even reduce his future policy influence.

Power refers to a judge's desire to be able to make important decisions, whether he actually uses that ability or not. The difference between Power and Policy resembles that between wealth and consumption. Usually, for a judge to use his Power to push Policy in a direction it would not otherwise go is to use up his Power at least slightly. But Power, like wealth, can be a good in itself to some people, even when others may wonder what pleasure they could bring unless spent. The judge who values Power will want to be in a position to make as many important decisions as possible. That, in turn, means he will value a high position in the judiciary, and will further value the general power of the judiciary itself.

Pride refers to the value a judge puts on his reputation, whether it is a reputation for competence, honesty, or creativity. Any judge wants to be considered by the legal profession as someone who is wise, articulate, and legally sophisticated.

Place refers to the status of being a judge. Judges are granted deference and perks based solely on their positions, most of which they lose instantly when they leave their positions. Even a judge who is considered a fool by his colleagues and whom they carefully insulate from any power over policy still is a judge, and still must be granted outward respect in his courtroom. Constitutional monarchs such as the Emperor of Japan have the ultimate Place-compensating jobs; they have little Power, and have so few duties besides keeping out of scandals that Pride has little chance to be satisfied, but they have unique and lifetime rewards of Place.

The judiciary in Japan does not offer pay commensurate with the ability of its members, but it does offer ample opportunities to satisfy the other five P's. This, of course, is no accident—the nonmonetary rewards are why the government can staff the judiciary with such talent without paying high salaries. Moreover, by paying less, the government selects for judges who value money less than the five P's and hence are less tempted by either explicit bribery or promises of postretirement benefits.

Whether all five rewards can be enjoyed simultaneously is more dubious. Imagine the situation of a bright young Communist judge in 1965. He is in a good position to influence Policy, which he could do through the Kim Philby strategy of concealing his beliefs, rising eventually to an important position in the Secretariat, and then engineering the promotion of other Communists who would actually change the law.[7] Doing so, however, might well require him to suppress Principle, since he would for years need to lie about his beliefs and decide cases in ways that seem to him unjust. Although the Philby strategy would increase his Power, once he started to interfere in judicial promotions his ability to advance further would decline; power maximization would require never moving out of step with the organization. The Philby strategy would also reduce his opportunity for Pride—he would have prestige within the judiciary for his competence, but not the public profile of a judge who writes brilliantly crafted, if ineffectual, dissents (or articles in Japan, where lower-court opinions lack dissents).

For our study, we need objective, quantitative measures of success. Pay is the standard measure of success in economic studies, and in the regressions above we used the time to a judge's first *sokatsu* appointment to proxy for it. Yet if judges care about the other five P's as well, we need more. Fortunately, other objective measures do have a strong correlation with the five P's. Four of the five are correlated with position in the judiciary. A judge who spends most of his career in a branch office has less power to relish or to use for policy purposes, less opportunity to show his talent, and less prestige attached to his posting. He is spared having to make trade-offs between the career rewards, but only because he has none of them. Being president of a High Court or spending many years in the Secretariat or seconded to the Ministry of Justice, on the other hand, yields him power, which he may use for policymaking, status, and the display of his ability. Trade-offs must be made—the powerbroker in the judicial bureaucracy will not be able to show his abilities in the same way as the High Court president—but clearly he has succeeded in either case.

The exception among these job rewards is Principle. A judge can vote his conscience anywhere, but it will not matter to anyone else if he rules only on traffic tickets. Moreover, if judges cared only about Principle, political intervention in the judiciary would be observed even in equilibrium, yet would have no deterrent effect. Any judge so inclined would rule against the Administration in blind defiance of career effects.

Even then, however, our regressions would be valuable. Deterrence is one of the main goals of punishment, but another is incapacitation. Prison time

7. Kim Philby announced that he had given up his youthful Communist beliefs and rose to become the head of the bureau of the British government in charge of ferreting out Communist spies. He was in line to become head of the entire British secret service until he was detected to be a Soviet spy.

for a criminal takes him off the street even if he steals again the moment he is set free. Time spent in branch offices takes a judge away from administrative power and from the courts where the big issues are decided, even if it leaves his will to issue anti-government opinions unchanged. Below, we ask if anti-government judges are sent to less influential positions. The judge himself may like a branch office position in the hinterland just as much as being secretary-general of the Secretariat, but the Administration would be much happier with him in the hinterland, and the implications for public policy are the same as if he regretted his exile. After the first attempt to influence public policy, he would forfeit future opportunities. Indeed, the administration might even hope for this kind of single-minded judicial motivation—it would make smoking out unreliable judges much easier, at an earlier stage of their careers.

IV. Conclusion

Job assignments in the Japanese judiciary include an element of randomness, to be sure, but they are not entirely random. Smarter judges do better than the duller. Harder working judges do better than the indolent. And—apparently—on some dimensions, conservatives have done better than leftists. They do better in pay, for one. Yet judges also care about various nonmonetary rewards. In the chapters that follow, we ask when politics affects those nonmonetary rewards, and when the opinions judges write affect their careers as well.

3

The Effect of Judicial Decisions:

Anti-Government Opinions and

Electoral Law Disputes

In this chapter, we apply the method described in chapter 2 to what will be the focus of the rest of the book: whether opinions affect the quality of a judge's principal nonmonetary reward—his posting. In section I we construct an exploratory composite measure of "anti-government opinions" and ask whether judges who write such opinions suffer for it in their careers. Tentatively, we find that they may. In chapters 4–6, we then disaggregate this composite index to examine which classes of opinions in the index have what effects.

We actually begin this process of disaggregation at the end of this chapter. Thus, in section II we examine one of the most electorally sensitive set of disputes: cases involving the constitutionality of political campaign restrictions. We explore the dimensions on which the judges who took positions opposed to the Liberal Democratic Party (LDP) suffered. We find that the punishment appears most strongly in the assignment to administrative duties and branch offices rather than in the geographic location of postings. Accordingly, in the later chapters of this book we focus on job characteristics rather than geography.

I. The Impact of Anti-Government Opinions

A. INTRODUCTION

We have shown in chapter 2 that membership in a leftist group can harm a judge's career in Japan. What about the opinions he writes? Will a judge jeopardize his career if he decides cases in ways that reject the government's position? We begin by regressing (through an admittedly complicated procedure) several indices of career success (administrative responsibility and geographical location, both early and late in a career) on a composite measure of a judge's anti-government opinions. Tentatively, we find that such opinions can indeed harm a career. We then turn in section II to the effect of one discrete set of politically very sensitive opinions on judicial careers, and confirm that heterodox opinions can harm a judge's career.

B. DATA AND VARIABLES
1. Data

We start by compiling career data on all judges who entered the courts between 1961 and 1965. In order to compare careers of equal length, we drop judges who left the judiciary before April 1990.[1] Some critics accuse the Secretariat of pressing left-leaning judges into early retirement. To the extent that this happened, our findings understate the true scope of political discrimination.

Because Supreme Court justices have a large group of professional judges at their disposal to work as law clerks, we treat elevation to the Supreme Court as retirement in some other chapters of this book in calculating opinions per year. This does not bias our data for a simple reason: as of 1990, none of the judges in this sample had been named to the Supreme Court.

For judges in the class of 1965 (a subset of the larger group), we investigate every decision that involved the government as litigant in one of four fields: labor, administrative, tax, and criminal law.[2] We include all opinions, whether written alone or by a three-judge panel. We code an opinion as "anti-government" if the party fighting the government won a full or partial victory.

Necessarily, some of these opinions are more strongly anti-government than others. Many do not involve distinctly political issues at all. Nonetheless, we begin with this coding scheme for two basic reasons. First, we intend the test as a deliberately broad and preliminary inquiry. We ask whether there is evidence of biased judicial incentives in this admittedly broad measure, and then disaggregate the measure in the next three chapters. Second, the scheme is simple and objective. In chapter 4 we use more accurately anti-government measures because we pick more obviously political cases, but we recognize that some readers may suspect that we "cooked" the data in the way we selected the cases. To minimize that potential for bias, we here use a less precise but more objective test. Importantly, this objectivity also ensures the close replicability of our results by anyone else choosing to compile this kind of a data set.

1. Of the cohort of 394 judges who finished their legal training in 1961–65, three began their careers in private practice, twelve died in judicial office, four retired at mandatory retirement age, one was fired, ninety-seven resigned, and three were dropped for other reasons. Of the ninety-seven resignations, thirty-one (32 percent) were members of the Young Jurists League (YJL). This is comparable to the judicial population as a whole—according to table 3.2, 35 percent of those who did not resign were YJL members.

2. In disaggregating this index, we explore a subset of administrative cases in chapter 4, tax cases in chapter 5, and criminal cases in chapter 6. Labor cases are explored in Kashimura 1991.

2. Variables

We construct the variables defined in table 3.1. Summary statistics appear in table 3.2. Described more briefly than in table 3.1, the variables are

Flunks: the number of times the judge failed the entrance examination to the Legal Training and Research Institute (LRTI).

Male: a dummy for a judge's sex.

Tokyo_U, Kyoto_U, Chuo_U, No_Univ: graduation from these universities. We disaggregate the *Elite_College* variable used in other chapters to explore any difference between Tokyo and Kyoto Universities. Additionally, because many judges attended Chuo University, we ask whether there is a Chuo "old boy" network.

Opinions/Yr: a judge's published opinions per year.

1st_Post: an ordinal measure of the administrative (i.e., not geographical) prestigiousness of a judge's first assignment. A high ranking indicates high prestige.

1st_Location: an ordinal measure of the geographical attractiveness of the judge's first assignment. A high ranking indicates a desirable city.

1980s_Post: an ordinal measure of the administrative prestigiousness of a judge's assignments during the 1980s.

1980s_Location: an ordinal measure of the geographical attractiveness of the judge's assignments during the 1980s.

YJL: 1 if a judge was a member of the Young Jurists League in 1969, 0 otherwise.

Early_Antigovt: the number of anti-government decisions that a judge issued during the period 1965–74.

Late_Antigovt: the number of anti-government decisions that a judge issued during the period 1975–84.

Any_Early_Antigovt: 1 if a judge issued any anti-government decisions during the period 1965–74, and 0 otherwise.

Any_Late_Antigovt: 1 if a judge issued any anti-government decisions during the period 1975–84, and 0 otherwise.

C. RESULTS

1. First Assignments

Before turning to the effect of anti-government opinions themselves, we begin by replicating in our ordered probit model (we explained the use of this regression model in chapter 2) the gist of the results earlier reported in table 2.7: that the best initial jobs go to the judges showing the highest potential for performance. Thus, in table 3.3 we report the results of an ordered probit

Table 3.1 Anti-Government Opinions—Variables

Flunks	The number of times a judge flunked the entrance examination to the LRTI. We hypothesize that the lower the number of times a person flunked, the higher his cognitive ability and the greater his willingness to work hard. Because the quality of a judge's work depends in part on his intelligence and his drive, these factors should together correlate with judicial performance.
Male	1 if a judge is male, 0 if female.
Tokyo_U	1 if a judge went to Tokyo University; 0 otherwise.
Kyoto_U	1 if a judge went to Kyoto University; 0 otherwise. Traditionally observers have considered the Kyoto University law department second only to Tokyo University.
Chuo_U	1 if a judge went to Chuo University; 0 otherwise. Chuo University operates a large and respectable but not first-tier law department. We include the variable because so many judges attended Chuo, conceivably leading to a clique.
No_University	1 if the ZSKS lists no university for a judge; 0 otherwise. A 1 means either that he attended the LRTI without graduating from a university (possible but unlikely) or that his educational background was unknown (a fact that suggests he graduated from an unprestigious school).
Opinions/Yr	The number of recorded decisions a judge published up to 1990 divided by the number of years he spent on the bench. We exclude those years during which he handled only administrative work.
	Note a potential problem here. The law reporters, both official and unofficial, do not publish all opinions. Instead, they publish an opinion only if the editors find it interesting or important. If a branch office judge hears less important cases, this could mean that he will not publish as much even if he works hard, leading to a simultaneity problem. Suppose opinions/year is positively correlated with career success. That fact could mean either that judges receive inferior assignments because they publish less, or that they publish less because they receive inferior assignments. To check for this problem, we used our Class of 1965 data to create another variable: productivity for all years in courts other than lower-court branch offices or summary courts. Fortunately for our purposes, the correlation between that new variable and Opinions/yr was .98, indicating that adjusting for poor assignments would make little difference.
1st_Post	The prestige of the first assignment a judge receives. The variable is 3 if it involves an administrative assignment, 1 if it is on a District or Family Court, and 0 if it involves a lower-court branch office or Summary Court. For the vast majority of judges, the value was 1.[a]
1980s_Post	The prestige of a judge's assignments during the 1980s. If he spent at least three years in an administrative assignment, it is 3; if he spent at least three years in either an administrative assignment or a *sokatsu* post (but not three years in an administrative assignment only), it is 2; if he does not qualify for the categories above and spent at least three years in a lower-court branch office or Summary Court, it is 0; otherwise, it is 1. For this chapter, but not in later chapters, we count time in the branch office only if the judge was not the official head of the branch office and did not have *sokatsu* status.
1st_Location	The location of a judge's initial assignment. This is 3 if the judge's first assignment was in Tokyo (including Hachioji), 2 if in Osaka, 1 if in another large metropolitan area (Yokohama, Nagoya, Sapporo, Kobe, Kyoto, Fukuoka, Kawasaki, Hiroshima, or Kitakyushu); 0 otherwise.
1980s_Location	A judge's location during the 1980s. It is 3 if he spent at least five years in Tokyo, 2 if at least five years in Osaka or Tokyo (but not five years in Tokyo), 1 if at least five years in a major metropolitan area (but not five years in Tokyo or Osaka); 0 if otherwise.

(*cont.*)

Table 3.1 *(continued)*

YJL	1 if a judge was a member of the Young Jurists League in 1969; 0 otherwise.
Early_Antigovt	The number of anti-government decisions that a judge issued during the period 1965–74.
Late_Antigovt	The number of anti-government decisions that a judge issued during the period 1975–84.
Any_Early_Antigovt	1 if a judge issued any anti-government decisions during the period 1965–74; 0 otherwise.
Any_Late_Antigovt	1 if a judge issued any anti-government decisions during the period 1975–84; 0 otherwise.

[a]We do not let this variable take a value of 2 because we judge there are fewer gradations of quality in the first post than in later posts or locations. Given that the variables are purely ordinal, the cardinal number we assign is unimportant to the econometrics. In the next variable, 1980s_Post, a value of 2 will be used to indicate sokatsu posts, but beginning judges never receive that type of post.

Table 3.2 Anti-Government Opinions—Summary Statistics

	Minimum	Mean	Maximum
Flunks			
Male	0	.96	1
Tokyo_U	0	.16	1
Kyoto_U	0	.19	1
Chuo_U	0	.14	0
No_University	0	.43	0
Opinions/Yr	.04	2.02	10.42
1st_Post	0	.91	3
1980s_Post	0	1.83	3
1st_Location	0	1.00	3
1980s_Location	0	1.06	3
YJL	0	.35	1
Early_AntiGovt	0	1.62	15
Late_AntiGovt	0	.68	4
Any_Early_AntiGovt	0	.57	1
Any_Late_AntiGovt	0	.38	1

NOTE: $n = 276$ ($n = 54$ for the last four variables). Except for the last four variables, data for which is available only for the class of 1965, the data cover all judges hired from 1961 to 1965, with the adjustments described in the text.

regression of two measures of the attractiveness of a judge's first job on his personal characteristics. Consider each regression separately.

Regression A: Recall that *1st_Post* measures whether a judge receives administrative responsibilities, receives a routine District or Family Court assignment, or is stationed to a branch office or Summary Court. Because only a very few judges (three in our sample) begin their careers with administrative responsibilities, the ordered probit results of regression A confirm the probit results of table 2.7: the worst jobs (primarily the branch office assignments) go to the judges who failed the LRTI exam the most often.

Regression B: The regression on *1st_Location* asks who receives the prized Tokyo and Osaka assignments. According to the results, those jobs go to the

Table 3.3 First Assignments—Ordered Probit Regressions

	Dependent Variable	
	A. 1st_Post	B. 1st_Location
Male	−.56 (0.97)	.35 (0.98)
Flunks	−.12 (3.16)**	−.14 (4.87)**
Tokyo_U	−.19 (0.39)	1.36 (4.39)**
Kyoto_U	−.73 (1.60)	.71 (2.43)**
Chuo_U	−.54 (1.17)	.11 (0.32)
No_University	−.49 (1.15)	.18 (0.63)
YJL	−.07 (0.32)	−.01 (0.09)
Pseudo R^2	.08	.12

NOTE: $n = 276$. The data cover all judges hired from 1961 to 1965, with the adjustments described in the text. The table gives the coefficients, followed by the absolute values of the t-statistics.
**Statistically significant at the 95 percent confidence level using a two-tailed test.

judges (i) who failed the LRTI exam the fewest times, and (ii) who attended the most selective universities. They also suggest that Tokyo University graduates do better than Kyoto University ones, and that Chuo graduates do no better than graduates of other universities. Once more, the ordered probit results of table 3.3 confirm the probit results of table 2.7: the best jobs go to the judges most likely to perform well.

Similarly consistent with table 2.7, the coefficient for YJL is insignificant in both regressions. As suggested earlier, because the League's membership rolls did not become public until 1969, the Secretariat probably did not know who was a member in 1961–65, and so membership did not affect the initial job assignments.

2. Opinions and Job Postings
(a) Introduction

Turn now to the connection between the opinions a judge wrote in two periods (1965–74 and 1975–84), and the jobs he held in the 1980s. To study this we start by running the same regressions as in table 3.3, merely changing the dependent variables from *1st_Post* and *1st_Location* to *1980s_Post* and *1980s_Location*, and adding the *Opinions/Yr* variable and dummies for the judge's first posting. In other words, we begin by exploring the impact of the control variables on the jobs held by the entire population of 1961–65 judges during the 1980s. This yields the results in table 3.4.

(b) Late Assignments

In these regressions, several points stand out. First, in the location regression *Flunks* is significant. That *Flunks* continues to be important decades later

Table 3.4 1980s Assignments—Ordered Probit Regressions

	Dependent Variable	
	A. 1980s_Post	B. 1980s_Location
Male	.33 (0.97)	.22 (0.57)
Flunks	−.03 (1.05)	−.07 (2.35)**
Tokyo_U	.03 (0.11)	.02 (0.05)
Kyoto_U	.20 (0.67)	.15 (0.46)
Chuo_U	.19 (0.61)	.48 (1.40)
No_University	−.07 (0.27)	−.04 (0.14)
1st_Location = 1	.33 (1.84)*	.36 (1.85)*
1st_Location = 2	−.14 (0.63)	.30 (1.27)
1st_Location = 3	.79 (3.42)**	1.13 (4.53)**
Opinions/Yr	.19 (4.32)**	.20 (4.27)**
YJL	−.28 (1.94)**	.16 (0.32)
Pseudo R^2	.09	.13

NOTE: $n = 276$. The data cover all judges hired from 1961 to 1965, with the adjustments described in the text. The table gives the coefficients, followed by the absolute values of the t-statistics.

*Statistically significant at the 90 percent confidence level using a two-tailed test.

**Statistically significant at the 95 percent confidence level using a two-tailed test.

suggests that interest in the law, intelligence, and drive matter, and in ways beyond their effect on a judge's first job.

Second, *1st_Location* correlates with a judge's later assignments. Although "*1st_Location* = 2" (Osaka) cannot be significantly distinguished from the other levels, "*1st_Location* = 1" (other metropolitan area) and "*1st_Location* = 3" (Tokyo) are both significantly better than "*1st_Location* = 0" (all other cities), the dummy left out of the regression, and "*1st_Location* = 3" has the bigger coefficient, as one would expect.

Third, *Opinions/Yr* matters: judges who write many publishable opinions do better than those who write few. Although this restates the importance of intelligence and hard work, its significance goes further. From time to time, observers have suggested that Japanese society may reward judges who settle cases rather than decide them.[3] Because of a cultural preference for negotiated settlements, they argue, Japanese judges are encouraged to settle cases when they can. As settlements do not appear in our data, we do not know whether the most successful judges settle the lowest percentage of their disputes. That may well be the case. We do know that the judges who are the most prolific in writing published opinions for the cases that fail to settle are put in better postings by the Secretariat.

Last—consistent with table 2.6—independent of the quality of a judge's work, political affiliation matters. Whether a judge was a YJL member

3. The classic account tying low levels of litigation in Japan to a cultural aversion to clear-cut court outcomes is Kawashima 1963.

inversely correlates with whether he received prestigious administrative responsibilities in the 1980s. Those judges who were part of the YJL in 1969 were still receiving less attractive jobs ten to twenty years later. Curiously, YJL membership seems not to have affected the location where the judge worked. Perhaps the Secretariat was willing to assign leftists to the cities. Crucially, however, it tended not to give them the highest positions within the judicial hierarchy. It is significant that in our definition, these high positions include positions within the Secretariat itself, which would give a judge the opportunity to help determine the success of other judges' careers. Thus, it may be that the Secretariat was quite willing to reward politically undesirable judges for brains and hard work, but not in ways that gave them a hand in running the system.

(c) Method

Our first political variable was YJL membership, which is cleanly defined and relatively easy to collect for the entire cohort of 276 judges. We now turn to the more complex inquiry at the core of this book: whether the way a judge decides a case influences the jobs he obtains. More specifically, we ask whether a tendency to decide cases against the government hurts his career. We find that it may. This inquiry, however, introduces problems in both theory and econometrics.

The theoretical issues arise because of several possible implications of the Priest–Klein (1984) selection effect. Litigated cases are not a random sample of all disputes, and who wins the cases that go to trial may say more about which cases go to trial than about how the judge views the two sides. In order to avoid trial costs, most disputants settle disputes when they agree about the likely litigated outcome. As a result, cases do not go to trial randomly. Instead, they go to trial primarily when the parties involved hold mutually optimistic estimates about the expected litigated outcome. In general, we suspect that this will be more likely to occur when the judge's expected decision is unclear. If so, then the fact that 80 percent of Judge Y's decisions are pro-plaintiff does not necessarily mean he is pro-plaintiff: he may only be pro-plaintiff in the most complicated cases, where the litigants found his decisions hardest to predict. For the purposes of this analysis, settlement could have an even more bizarre effect: at least hypothetically, it could be that the government goes to trial with its most outrageous cases only when it knows the judge is particularly pro-government, and is only moderately displeased when the government's arguments are too weak for even that judge to swallow. Thus the judges who rule against the government might be the most pro-government judges.

Two further complications are that (i) under Japanese public law, the government often finds it hard explicitly to settle cases out of court (as Kaneko [1992: 78] explains), and (ii) some observers claim that many Japanese plaintiffs litigate public law disputes for their publicity effect rather than to win. To the extent that either phenomenon occurs, the selection bias will be less and the percentage of government victories will convey more information about a judge's political preferences.

A potential problem nonetheless remains. Settlement will probably be most common where the parties know a judge's style and biases most precisely. If they know nothing about a judge, he will hear cases that are not selected with an eye to his individual biases. As a result, his verdict rate may indeed disclose his biases. A judge with a shorter track record is one about whom litigants will have less information. Accordingly the selection bias should be strongest among judges at the end of their careers, and weakest at the start.

The econometric issues result from the enormous amount of time necessary to collect this data. Because of this problem, we examined only the opinions of the fifty-four judges in the class of 1965 who stayed in the judiciary through 1985. We now must combine those observations on judicial opinions with our 276 observations on all the other variables relevant to a judicial career. If we were willing to drop 222 observations, the econometrics would be simple: we would repeat the ordered probit regressions in table 3.4, but with opinion variables added to the right-hand side. This not only discards information, but it raises doubts about the validity of the estimates and the standard errors, since ordered probit is a nonlinear, asymptotic technique for which having a large sample is especially important.

Instead we take a different approach. We begin with the regressions of table 3.4, which use all 276 observations to predict career success. These regressions do not explain all the variance in the data, and they generate an unexplained residual for each judge. If we can explain this residual using judicial opinion variables, we will have shown that a judge's opinions matter and ought to have been in the regressions in table 3.4. Moreover, because the residual is a continuous variable, we can use ordinary least squares, which does not rely on asymptotics for its validity.

More specifically, we first turn to our class of 1965 data set and use our table 3.4 regressions to generate a "residual" for each judge: his predicted career quality minus his actual posting of 0, 1, 2, or 3. This residual is a continuous variable that measures Judge X's unexplained career quality. If positive, it indicates that he did better than our regression predicted; if negative, it indicates

Table 3.5 Unexplained Career Success and Anti-Government Decisions

	1. Post Residual	2. Location Residual
A. Number of Anti-Government Opinions		
Early_Antigovt	.03 (.92)	.02 (0.66)
Late_Antigovt	−.11 (1.32)	−.21 (2.60)**
R^2	0.04	0.12
B. Any Anti-Government Decisions		
Any_Early_Antigovt	.18 (0.23)	−.21 (1.34)
Any_Late_Antigovt	−.35 (1.90)*	−.05 (0.28)
R^2	0.07	0.06

NOTE: $n = 54$. Coefficients are followed by the absolute values of t-statistics in parentheses. The test uses OLS on a logistic conversion of the residual from the career regression.
*Statistically significant at the 90 percent confidence level using a two-tailed test.
**Statistically significant at the 95 percent confidence level using a two-tailed test.

he did worse. We then use a logit transformation to map the value of the residual, which lies between −3 and +3, to the entire real line between positive and negative infinity, mapping the raw residual u to $\log[(u + 3)/(3 − u)]$. This allows us to use a formal test of a model in which we test the null hypothesis that this transformed residual is just a normally distributed disturbance against the alternative that it also depends on political variables. If a judge's decisions had no impact on his career, then regressing his residual on a variable summarizing his decisions would yield an insignificant coefficient. If they did have an impact, then, crucial to the analysis here, the coefficient would be significant.

(d) Results

According to table 3.5, judges who decide cases against the government receive less attractive jobs. In panel A, the number of anti-government opinions that a judge wrote in 1975–84 inversely correlates with the odds of receiving a post in an attractive city in the 1980s. In panel B, whether a judge decided any anti-government opinions (a 0 or 1 variable) in 1975–84 inversely correlates (though only at the 90 percent confidence level) with receiving high-status posts in the judicial hierarchy in the 1980s.

The simplest explanation for this phenomenon is that it represents a straightforward punishment strategy: if a judge decides cases against the government, the expected values of his next several jobs fall. The probability of punishment may well be less than 1. Nonetheless, according to table 3.5, anti-government opinions translate directly into less attractive posts in the near future.

II. Electoral Law Decisions

Rather than the composite index of anti-government opinions, consider now some straightforwardly and strongly political disputes. We investigate political cases in more detail in chapter 4, but consider first a preliminary inquiry into the dimensions that the Secretariat's punishments might take. We undertake this inquiry to learn how best to structure the various regressions in chapters 3–5.

Recall (as discussed in chapter 2) the political dimension to these cases. Because incumbents have greater access to the media than challengers and the LDP had more incumbents than any other party, LDP leaders favored the § 138 ban on door-to-door canvassing. For precisely the same reasons, many opposition leaders (particularly among the Communists) opposed it.

The Supreme Court consistently held the ban constitutional.[4] Among the lower-court judges, we located thirty-seven who held the ban constitutional and nine who held it unconstitutional. Using data on these forty-six judges, we test whether a judge's decision on the issue affected his assignments. To this end, we introduce several new variables and give the average values for the two groups of judges in table 3.6:

Prior_Posts: the prestige of a judge's assignment before the § 138 decision. The variable equals 3 if he spent at least three years in an administrative job during the ten years before the decision; 2 if he did not meet that requirement but spent at least three years in an administrative or *sokatsu* capacity; 0 if he did not meet either of those requirements but spent at least three years in a lower-court branch office or Summary Court; and 1 otherwise.

Later_Posts: the equivalent to prior posts for the ten years after the decision. It takes the values 0, 1, 2, or 3.

Prior_Location: the desirability of the judge's location before the § 138 decision. The variable is 3 if the judge spent at least five of the previous ten years in Tokyo; 2 if at least five years in Tokyo or Osaka (but not five in Tokyo); 1 if at least five years in metropolitan areas generally; and 0 otherwise.

Later_Location: the equivalent to prior location for the ten years after the decision. It takes the values 0, 1, 2, or 3.

Prior_Branch: the percentage of years a judge spent in branch offices during the ten years (adjusted appropriately, if fewer years on the bench) before the § 138 decision.

4. See Japan v. Taniguchi, 21 Saihan keishu 1245 (Sup. Ct. Nov. 21, 1967).

Table 3.6 Electoral Law Decisions: Differences between
the Two Groups of Judges

	Constitutional Mean	Unconstitutional Mean
Prior_Posts	1.41	.44
Later_Posts	1.70	1.56
Prior_Location	1.05	.00
Later_Location	1.14	0.44
Prior_Branch	.14	.24
Later_Branch	.10	.50
Prior_Sokatsu	.12	.00
Later_Sokatsu	.28	.03
Prior_Opinions/Yr	1.12	1.28
Male	1.00	1.00
YJL	.14	.56
n	37	9

Later_Branch: the equivalent to *Prior_Branch* for the ten years after the § 138 decision.

Prior_Sokatsu: the percentage of years a judge spent in *sokatsu* assignments for the ten years (adjusted appropriately, if fewer years on the bench) before the § 138 decision.

Later_Sokatsu: the equivalent to *Prior_Sokatsu* for the ten years after the § 138 decision.

Prior_Opinions/Yr: the judge's productivity (published opinions per year on the bench) for the ten years before the § 138 decision.

§ _138_Decision: 0 if the judge held the canvassing ban constitutional and 1 if otherwise.

Table 3.6 suggests that the judges who held the § 138 ban unconstitutional were already in worse jobs before they heard the controversial case. Their average prior post is 0.44 compared to 1.41 for the other thirty-seven judges, prior location is 0.00 compared to 1.05, prior *sokatsu* is 0.00 compared to 0.12, while prior time in branch offices is 0.50 compared to 0.10. The percentage of YJL membership was 0.56 compared to 0.14, so the politics of these judges may have been well known long in advance of their anti-government decisions.

A glance at table 3.6 seems to show that the careers of the unfortunate nine judges actually improved after their § 138 decisions. Ordered probit regressions of later posts and later location on earlier career variables and the § 138 decision failed to show significant relationships, however, and the improvement may just be regression to the mean. When careers are bad enough (e.g., an average location of 0.00), there is nowhere to go but up.

Two other career variables do show a distinct punishment effect, suggesting that these are the elements on which we should focus. Table 3.7 shows the

Table 3.7 Electoral Law Decisions

	Dependent Variable	
	Later_Branch	Later_Sokatsu
Prior_Branch	.236 (1.24)	
Prior_Sokatsu		.476 (2.38)**
Prior_Opinions/Yr	.015 (1.00)	−.117 (1.53)
§_138_Decision	.330 (2.47)**	−.165 (2.45)**
Pseudo R^2	.17	.23
Censoring ($y < 0, y > 1$)	(30, 3)	(23, 2)

NOTE: $n = 46$. The regression uses tobit. The table gives the marginal effects at the median, followed by the absolute value of the t-statistics. The regressions also included intercepts, which were significant and negative for Later_Branch and insignificant for Later_Sokatsu.
**Statistically significant at the 95 percent confidence level using a two-tailed test.

results of two regressions using time in branch offices and time as *sokatsu* as the dependent variables. Tobit, while a nonlinear regression technique, is closer to ordinary least squares than ordered probit. The results support the popular accounts of the § 138 controversy: the position a judge takes on the constitutionality of the § 138 ban significantly affects both the time he spends in branch offices and the time he spends with *sokatsu* duties. Should he hold the § 138 ban unconstitutional, he both increases the amount of time he will likely spend in branch offices over the next ten years (by an average of 3.30 years), and decreases the amount of time he will spend with *sokatsu* responsibilities (by an average of 1.65 years).

III. Conclusion

The anecdotes in chapter 1 suggest that the Secretariat uses its control over personnel matters to create a distinctly political set of incentives. Using comprehensive data sources and a multivariate approach, in chapters 2 and 3 we have begun to explore those anecdotes more systematically. We find that the Secretariat may indeed maintain a politically skewed incentive structure. First, judges who joined a left-leaning organization in the 1960s had less successful careers thereafter. Second, judges who decided cases contrary to government positions seem to have suffered in their careers as well.

The Secretariat manipulated a wide variety of incentives: pay, geographical location, and internal prestige. We lack the data to study pay discrimination following distinct opinions. Geography is amenable only to the relatively difficult to interpret technique of ordered probit. And the Secretariat seems to manipulate internal prestige rankings more directly than geography anyway. Accordingly, in the rest of this book we focus on measures of internal prestige. In the next three chapters, we ask *which* anti-government opinions hurt a judge's career. Toward that end, we use a simpler dependent variable (the fraction of a decade with administrative duties or branch office time) and a simpler regression model (tobit). We will, however, be able to apply the tests on a disaggregated basis to a much broader range of opinions.

4

Political Disputes: Military, Malapportionment, Injunctions, and Constitutional Law

Judges in Japan who oppose the government can suffer for it, chapter 3 suggested. But are all disputes equal? We doubt it, and in the course of chapters 4–6 we disaggregate the composite index we used in chapter 3 to ask which type of disputes generate the largest career impact. In section II of chapter 3 we suggested that it might be the politically most highly charged cases. In this chapter, we pursue that suggestion. Following our findings in chapter 3, we focus on incentives tied to internal prestige in the courts: access to administrative power and time in branch offices.

In this chapter, we analyze a broad range of politically charged cases. We use several proxies (as discussed in chapter 2) for a judge's seniority, intelligence, effort, and ideology. We hold constant those proxies and examine the careers of judges who held either the Self-Defense Force (the SDF) or U.S. bases unconstitutional; judges who rejected national electoral apportionment schemes advantageous to the Liberal Democratic Party (LDP); and judges who enjoined the national government in administrative-law suits. Systematically, we find that they suffered in their careers. We conclude by comparing the incentives presented by these disputes with the incentives in important but less politically charged cases in constitutional and commercial law.

We begin by briefly discussing the context of public-law litigation in Japan at the Supreme Court level (section I). We then explore the connection between lower-court opinions in such cases and judicial careers (section II). Finally, we compare those results with the career effects of two sets of less political but still important cases (section III).

I. Public-Law Litigation

The Japanese Supreme Court is deferential in the extreme. To be sure, even the U.S. Supreme Court does not void legislation as a matter of course. Yet as of 1993 the Supreme Court in Japan had denied the validity of legislation on constitutional grounds only half a dozen or so times in its entire history.[1] The reason is straightforward: almost all the justices have been recent LDP appointees, and the party passing the legislation has also been the LDP.[2]

Compare this with the United States. Given the frequent political turnover between Republicans and Democrats, U.S. presidents regularly try to stack the Supreme Court with relatively young justices. This produces the motley ideological Supreme Court composition that Americans take for granted. The Court includes both Democrat and Republican justices. Because they often serve twenty years or more on the Court, it also includes justices who have shifted ideological positions since they were appointed.

LDP leaders faced a different political scene. During the period of our study, they tightly controlled the party; the party controlled the national legislature, the Diet; and no other party had a serious chance of taking power in the near future. Given that LDP leaders could rationally expect to stay in power and to continue appointing justices indefinitely, they could afford to appoint justices late enough in life (generally in their early sixties) that the justices would be unlikely to change their views before mandatory retirement at age seventy (Ramseyer and Rosenbluth 1997: ch. 8).

The real puzzle is not the Supreme Court's conservatism but that of the lower courts—the over two thousand judges in the District Courts, High Courts, and Family Courts. While not as uniformly deferential as the Supreme Court, these judges, too, have tended to side with the LDP in cases that were politically sensitive. In this chapter, we explore the link between this deference and the career structures they face.

1. See Okudaira 1993: 20; Haley 1998: 179–80; Tomatsu 1993: 194. Compare this with the some 124 statutes declared unconstitutional in the United States (Witt 1990: 1001–9). Note too, however, that voiding statutes was also extremely rare in the United States in the first fifty years after its constitution was written.

2. See, e.g., Okudaira 1993: 24. Also note that courts in a parliamentary system will generally tend to be more conservative than in a presidential system. The reason for this is that the head of the executive in a parliamentary system is necessarily the head of the legislature. As a result, leaders of the majority party can more readily reverse judicial decisions by statute. See Ferejohn 1995: 208–9.

II. Political Opinions and Judicial Careers

A. INTRODUCTION

To study systematically the effect of public-law opinions on judicial careers, we need disputes that involve large numbers of judges. Unfortunately, this limits our inquiry to a handful of disputes. Although we base our conclusions on results that are statistically significant at the 90 percent level or better, readers should take our results with caution. Very few judges flout the LDP. In our chapter 3, section II sample, we find that of the thirty-seven judges who reviewed the canvassing ban, only nine held it unconstitutional. In this chapter, we find forty-seven judges ruled on Article 9 of the Constitution (concerning the status of the Self-Defense Force), but only five of them held the military unconstitutional. We find eighty-nine judges who addressed electoral districting rules, but only seven who struck down the rules before the 1984 opinion that, as we will discuss below, marked a crucial turning point.

Because of these small numbers, we potentially could have omitted some variable that was the real cause of the damaged careers. At least hypothetically, those judges who flouted LDP policies could also have shared some characteristic correlated with unsuccessful careers but not captured by our control variables. The judges who held the military unconstitutional might, for example, have happened to be bald, overweight, and divorced, and the Secretariat could have maintained a bias against bald, fat, divorced judges. Given our lack of explicit control variables for such characteristics, some such combination of factors might explain the punishment we observe.[3]

Precisely because of the small number of heterodox judges in some of our samples, however, we repeat the tests on several independent data sets— different issues, and different judges. We look at three types of cases: Article 9 cases involving the military, malapportionment cases, and injunctions against local and national governments. Note that the last of these sets of disputes does include a larger number of judges who took positions against the national government.

B. ARTICLE 9—THE SELF-DEFENSE FORCE

1. Cases

Start with what is the best-known constitutional dispute in Japan: the argument over Article 9 of the Constitution. As explained in chapter 1, Article 9

---

3. Note, however, that our *Prior_Good_Jobs* and *Prior_Bad_Jobs* variables will capture much of the effect of even those factors: we will be looking not just for bad careers, but for careers that *become* worse. It would only be judges who became fat, bald, and divorced in about the same year as their decision striking down the military who would cause trouble for our technique.

proclaims that "land, sea, and air forces, as well as other war potential, will never be maintained" (see appendix A for the complete text). By any but the most tortured interpretation, this would ban the Self-Defense Force (SDF). The LDP always has claimed it did not. By no stretch of the imagination could Douglas MacArthur, godfather of the clause, have thought it banned U.S. military bases. Occasionally, the opposition parties said it did.

Periodically since the 1950s, the Supreme Court has faced challenges to the SDF and the presence of American bases. Each time, it has refused to hold either unconstitutional (Beer and Itoh 1996; Auer 1993). From time to time, however, lower-court judges have done just that. We found twenty-five District Court opinions addressing Article 9, three of which held either the SDF or the bases unconstitutional. Excluding unsigned opinions, judges who do not appear in the ZSKS (generally judges educated before the war), and judges with less than one and a half years of experience before or two and a half years of experience after the opinion, we obtain a sample of forty-seven judges who wrote opinions on Article 9, three of whom wrote two opinions each. To avoid improperly weighting judge-specific effects, we include dummy independent variables for each of those three judges.

2. Variables

For each judge we first construct a decision variable that gives the judge's decision in the Article 9 opinion itself:

Unconstitutional: 1 if a judge held either the SDF or U.S. bases unconstitutional; 0 otherwise.

We then construct (i) two alternative dependent variables that measure the quality of jobs the judge held over the decade after the crucial opinion, and (ii) a series of control variables that proxy for intelligence, effort, seniority, and ideology. Because the Supreme Court consistently held the SDF and bases constitutional, we do not include a variable specifying whether the Supreme Court reversed the opinion.

Most of the control variables track those we introduced in chapter 2. At the risk of redundancy, we describe those variables again and note the predicted effects. Table 4.1 gives the definitions; table 4.2 the summary statistics.

3. Results

Table 4.3 shows the regression results. Note first that the *Unconstitutional* coefficient in the *Post_Good_Jobs* regression is negative and statistically significant. Compared to otherwise similar judges who held the SDF or U.S. bases

Table 4.1 Politically Charged Disputes—Variables

A. Dependent Variables

Post_Good_Jobs	The percentage of time during the decade after the crucial opinion in which a judge held prestigious appointments—either as chief judge, with *sokatsu* (largely personnel) responsibilities, or in another administrative post.
Post_Bad_Jobs	The percentage of time during the decade after the opinion in which a judge was in a branch office (other than the relatively desirable Hachioji office).

Because these dependent variables are censored, only taking values between 0 and 100, we use tobit rather than OLS in our regressions. Note that Post_Good_Jobs and Post_Bad_Jobs will not sum to 100 for an individual judge, because not all jobs are good or bad—most are mediocre. Our interest is in carrots and sticks, not in the boring middle.

B. Control Variables

Prior_Good_Jobs	Equivalent to Post_Good_Jobs for the decade before the opinion. We use it on the right-hand side to capture otherwise unobserved information about the judge's position within the judicial hierarchy (and thereby to mitigate potential omitted variable issues). Because fast-track judges will generally stay on the fast track (and slow-track judges on the slow), Prior_Good_Jobs correlates positively with Post_Good_Jobs.
Prior_Bad_Jobs	Equivalent to Post_Bad_Jobs for the decade before the opinion. Generally, Prior_Bad_Jobs correlates positively with Post_Bad_Jobs.
Seniority	The number of years between the opinion and the year a judge graduated from the LRTI. In general, the more senior the judge the better the job he will have. As a result, Seniority correlates positively with Post_Good_Jobs and negatively with Post_Bad_Jobs.
Flunks	The estimated number of years (based on birth year) between college graduation and entrance to the LRTI. Because the LRTI entrance exam passage rate varied between 1 and 4 percent, even the best students usually failed it several times. By approximating the number of times a judge failed this exam, Flunks inversely proxies for IQ and effort. Because smarter and harder working judges tend to be more successful than others, Flunks correlates positively with Post_Bad_Jobs and negatively with Post_Good_Jobs.
Elite_College	1 if a judge graduated from either the University of Tokyo or the University of Kyoto; 0 otherwise. Because the variable proxies for IQ and effort (and captures any old-school ties), Elite_College will correlate positively with Post_Good_Jobs and negatively with Post_Bad_Jobs.
Opinions/Yr	A judge's average productivity (measured in published opinions per year on the bench) for the decade before the opinion. Given that observed productivity will correlate with intelligence and effort, Opinions/Yr will positively correlate with Post_Good_Jobs and negatively with Post_Bad_Jobs.
1st_Tokyo	1 if a judge started at the Tokyo District Court; 0 otherwise. When the Secretariat hires a new class of judges it generally assigns the most promising to the Tokyo District Court. Because fast-track judges tend to stay on the fast track, 1st_Tokyo tends to correlate positively with Post_Good_Jobs and negatively with Post_Bad_Jobs.
YJL	1 if a judge was a member of the Young Jurists League in 1969; 0 otherwise. To the extent that the Secretariat has continued to punish former YJL members, YJL will correlate positively with Post_Bad_Jobs and negatively with Post_Good_Jobs.

Table 4.2 Article 9 (Military)—Summary Statistics

	Minimum	Median	Mean	Maximum
Post_Good_Jobs	0	0.39	0.44	1
Post_Bad_Jobs	0	0	0.17	0.92
Unconstitutional	0	0	0.12	1
Prior_Good_Jobs	0	0	0.22	0.93
Prior_Bad_Jobs	0	0	0.09	0.8
Seniority	2	11	13.12	29
Flunks	0	3	3.84	12
Elite_College	0	1	0.56	1
1st_Tokyo	0	0	0.24	1
Opinions/Yr	0	2.23	3.36	29.75
YJL	0	0	0.12	1

NOTE: $n = 50$. The times spent in good and in bad jobs do not sum to 1 because mediocre jobs are an omitted category.

Table 4.3 Article 9 (Military)—The Effect of Opinions on Careers

	Dependent Variable	
	A. Post_Bad_Jobs	B. Post_Good_Jobs
Unconstitutional	−.009 (0.14)	−.274 (2.56)**
Prior_Good_Jobs		.629 (2.20)**
Prior_Bad_Jobs	−.026 (0.24)	
Seniority	.003 (1.18)	.016 (1.79)*
Flunks	.009 (1.43)	−.015 (0.94)
Elite_College	−.134 (2.03)**	.159 (1.78)*
1st_Tokyo	.028 (0.43)	.204 (1.65)
Opinions/Yr	−.035 (1.73)**	−.019 (1.59)
YJL	.063 (0.48)	−.087 (0.34)
Pseudo R^2	.45	.54
Censoring ($y < 0$, unc., $y > 1$)	(26, 24, 0)	(11, 34, 5)

NOTE: $n = 50$. These are tobit regressions. The marginal effects for a judge at the median values of the independent variables are followed by the absolute values of z-statistics in parentheses. The regressions included intercepts and dummies for the three judges with multiple opinions, but the coefficients are not reported here.
* Significant at the 90 percent confidence level using a two-tailed test.
** Significant at the 95 percent confidence level using a two-tailed test.

constitutional (or who otherwise ducked the issue), those who held either unconstitutional received fewer prestigious administrative duties in the decade after the opinion, by an average of 2.74 years.

The *Unconstitutional* coefficient on *Post_Bad_Jobs* is not statistically significant. When the Secretariat punishes judges, it could use either longer assignments to branch offices or shorter administrative appointments. Here, it apparently cares more about avoiding putting the erring judges in administrative appointments.

Where statistically significant, the control variables all have the predicted signs. Thus, *Prior_Good_Jobs* has a significant and positive effect on

Post_Good_Jobs: the more administrative responsibilities a judge had before deciding the Article 9 case, the more he had afterwards. *Seniority* and *Elite_College* are also significant: administrative responsibilities tended to go to the more senior judges and to those from the Universities of Tokyo and Kyoto, even beyond the effect these things might have had on the judge's career prior to the Article 9 decision. *Post_Bad_Jobs* depends on *Opinions/Yr* and *Elite_College:* judges with Kyoto and Tokyo degrees and those who published more opinions spent less time in branch offices.

C. MALAPPORTIONMENT

1. Disputes

Electoral apportionment is a perennial issue in Japanese courts. Through the 1960s and into the 1970s, the LDP relied heavily on the rural vote. During that time, however, Japanese families were steadily migrating to the leftist-dominated metropolitan centers. As a result, the LDP gained by stalling reapportionment. By keeping the old apportionment rules, it maximized the number of representatives from the heavily LDP rural districts.

Increasingly, LDP leaders recognized that delaying reapportionment was a bad long-term strategy. Sooner or later, they would have to reposition their party away from the farm vote and create a new identity as a party for urban consumers. Naturally, many in the LDP rank and file, particularly Diet members from the rural districts, fought this change. For the LDP, the 1970s and 1980s were a time of internal turmoil—a time of tension between the leaders who would eventually lose their jobs if the party did not reposition itself and the rank-and-file members who would immediately lose their jobs if it did (Ramseyer and Rosenbluth 1997, ch. 3).

Faced with challenges to the existing apportionment schemes, the Supreme Court wrote opinions that generally tracked the positions of the LDP leaders. During the first period, the Court rejected challenges to the overrepresentation of rural voters. In the 1979 case of *Kurokawa v. Chiba,*[4] however, it switched sides. By this point, the LDP leaders were pushing the party to jettison the agricultural vote. Faced with plaintiffs who claimed that some votes counted five times as heavily as others, the Court held the apportionment unconstitutional. In the process it aided LDP leaders who would have found it more difficult to force LDP Diet members to redistrict themselves out of jobs without judicial pressure. In 1985, in *Kanao v. Hiroshima,* the Court reiterated the point: rural

---

4. Kurokawa v. Chiba ken senkyo kanri iinkai, 808 Hanrei jiho 24 (Sup. Ct. Apr. 14, 1979) (en banc), *rev'g* 30 Saihan minshu 288 (Tokyo High Ct. Apr. 30, 1974); see Haley 1998: 179–80.

Table 4.4 Malapportionment—Summary Statistics

	Minimum	Median	Mean	Maximum
Post_Good_Jobs	0	0.64	0.60	1
Post_Bad_Jobs	0	0	0.10	1
Invalid ≤ 73	0	0	0.02	1
Invalid ≥ 74	0	0	0.31	1
Invalid ≤ 83	0	0	0.07	1
Invalid ≥ 84	0	0	0.26	1
Invalid.Rev	0	0	0.04	1
Valid.Rev	0	0	0.01	1
Prior_Good_Jobs	0	0.31	0.39	1
Prior_Bad_Jobs	0	0	0.12	0.73
Seniority	5	24	23.01	39
Flunks	0	2	3.00	9
Elite_College	0	0	0.46	1
1st_Tokyo	0	0	0.20	1
Opinions/Yr	0	4.85	5.88	22.22
YJL	0	0	0.12	1

NOTE: $n = 97$.

overrepresentation was unconstitutional.[5] The Court needed more than one opinion to make the point forcefully because of the fact-specific nature of the problem. After all, it did not require that every vote have *exactly* the same effect. Instead, it needed several opinions to clarify just how much variation in electoral power it would allow. By 1985, however, LDP leaders were solidifying the party's position as an urban party and abandoning the farmers to the Socialists and Communists. The Supreme Court dutifully followed, and held the rural overrepresentation unconstitutional.

Given this shift in the position of the LDP leadership and the Supreme Court, one would not expect the Secretariat to have always punished judges for holding apportionment rules unconstitutional.[6] Instead, one would expect it to punish a judge only if either (i) the judge held an apportionment scheme unconstitutional prior to the 1974 and 1984 lower-court opinions in *Kurokawa* and *Kanao,* or (ii) the judge held an apportionment scheme unconstitutional and found that opinion reversed on appeal. To test these hypotheses, we assemble a new data set and define several additional variables. Summary statistics appear in table 4.4.

5. Kanao v. Hiroshima ken senkyo kanri iinkai, 1163 Hanrei jiho 3 (Sup. Ct. July 17, 1985 (en banc), *aff'g* 1134 Hanrei jiho 27 (Hiroshima High Ct. Sept. 28, 1984).

6. And it did not. When we create a general variable equaling 1 if a judge held any apportionment scheme improper and run a regression with the same control variables as in table 4.5, we obtain coefficients and *t*-statistics of −.040 (0.24) (for the *Post_Bad_Jobs* regression) and .018 (0.21) (for the *Post_Good_Jobs* regression); the effect on careers of striking down rural overrepresentation *averaged over the entire period* is nil. But that is like saying that if one averages together the Gulf War and the Kosovo War, the U.S. Democratic Party did not take any position on foreign intervention.

2. Data and Variables

The data set begins with the sixty-nine lower court opinions that raised the propriety of electoral apportionment schemes, whether on constitutional or statutory grounds. By law, most electoral challenges begin at the High Court level (so for these cases the trial court will actually be a High Court). Consequently, the judges in this sample will already be in somewhat prestigious positions at the time of their decisions. Excluding unsigned opinions and judges whose career data did not appear in the ZSKS or who had less than one and a half years of experience before or two and a half years of experience after the opinion, we are left with a set of eighty-nine judges (eight of whom wrote two opinions, for whom we again use judge-specific dummy variables). Of the cases, fifty-four involved challenges to national elections and fifteen to local elections. We then define the following new variables:

Invalid≤73: 1 if a judge held a national apportionment scheme[7] illegal prior to the 1974 trial court opinion in *Kurokawa;* 0 otherwise.

Invalid≥74: 1 if a judge held a national apportionment scheme illegal in or after the 1974 trial court opinion in *Kurokawa;* 0 otherwise.

Invalid≤83: 1 if a judge held a national apportionment scheme illegal prior to the 1984 trial court opinion in *Kanao;* 0 otherwise.

Invalid≥84: 1 if a judge held a national apportionment scheme illegal in or after the 1984 trial court opinion in *Kanao;* 0 otherwise.

Invalid.Rev: 1 if the Supreme Court reversed a judge's opinion holding a national apportionment scheme illegal; 0 otherwise.[8]

Valid.Rev: 1 if the Supreme Court reversed a judge's opinion holding a national apportionment scheme legal; 0 otherwise.

3. Results

The results, shown in table 4.5, confirm both sets of hypotheses. First, judges who held a national apportionment scheme improper during the years when the LDP depended on the rural vote found themselves punished. The variable

---

7. We also ran the first four regressions in table 4.5 using a variable that combined judges involved in all apportionment challenges, whether local or national. Because (for reasons detailed below in the context of preliminary injunctions) many local electoral schemes benefited parties other than the LDP, one would expect the effect to be less pronounced. The coefficients and *t*-statistics on a variable equal to 1 if the judge held improper any (national or local) pre-*Kurokawa* apportionment scheme were 1.32 (2.81) (*Prior_Bad_Jobs*) and −.689 (2.07) (*Prior_Good_Jobs*); for pre-*Kanao* apportionment schemes, they were .453 (1.86) (*Prior_Bad_Jobs*) and −.046 (.30) (*Prior_Good_Jobs*).

8. Here and elsewhere in this study, some appeals were hard to classify as affirmances or reversals. In such cases, we looked to the substance of the opinion and tried to capture the gist of the appellate decision.

Table 4.5 Malapportionment—The Effect of Opinions on Careers

	Dependent Variable					
	A. Post_Bad_Job	B. Post_Good_Job	C. Post_Bad_Job	D. Post_Good_Job	E. Post_Bad_Job	F. Post_Good_Job
Invalid≤73	.792** (5.23)	-.487** (3.57)				
Invalid≥74	-.006 (0.11)	.014 (0.19)				
Invalid≤83			.327* (1.87)	-.197 (1.43)		
Invalid≥84			-.047 (0.93)	.028 (0.34)		
Invalid_Rev					.590** (2.58)	-.302* (1.85)
Valid_Rev					.222 (0.71)	-.162 (0.51)
Prior_Good_Jobs		-.042 (0.25)		-.013 (0.08)		-.020 (0.12)
Prior_Bad_Jobs	-.046 (0.34)		-.061 (0.44)		-.084 (0.61)	
Seniority	.003 (0.96)	.016** (2.01)	.004 (1.19)	.016** (2.00)	.004 (1.11)	.015** (2.01)
Flunks	.0001 (0.02)	-.013 (0.89)	-.003 (0.29)	-.012 (0.79)	-.004 (0.40)	-.012 (0.79)
Elite_College	-.087** (1.99)	.104 (1.36)	-.066 (1.51)	.085 (1.10)	-.073* (1.70)	.092 (1.19)
1st_Tokyo	.083 (0.84)	-.087 (0.83)	.090 (0.89)	-.089 (0.86)	.101 (1.01)	-.087 (0.86)
Opinions/Yr	-.030** (2.26)	.024** (2.26)	-.032** (2.18)	.021** (1.97)	-.032** (2.36)	.023** (2.11)
YIL	-.051 (0.75)	.024 (0.21)	-.033 (0.43)	.023 (0.20)	-.036 (0.52)	.024 (0.22)
n	97	97	97	97	97	97
Pseudo R^2	0.33	0.30	0.31	0.29	0.33	0.29
Censoring ($y < 0$, unc., $y > 1$)	(71, 24, 1)	(13, 64, 19)	(71, 24, 1)	(13, 64, 19)	(71, 24, 1)	(13, 64, 19)

NOTE: These are tobit regressions. The marginal effects for a judge at the median values of the independent variables are followed by the absolute value of z-statistics in parentheses.
Coefficients for dummies for the eight judges with multiple opinions and an intercept were estimated but are not reported.
* Significant at the 90 percent confidence level using a two-tailed test.
** Significant at the 95 percent confidence level using a two-tailed test.

Invalid≤73 in regressions A and B is significant in the predicted directions, and with sizable marginal effects; a judge who struck down reapportionment then both increased his time in branch offices and reduced it in prestigious postings. The variable *Invalid≤83* in regression C is significant and similarly has a positive effect on *Post_Bad_Jobs*. If a judge held the apportionment scheme improper before 1983, he spent more than three extra years in branch offices after the opinion.[9]

We find no evidence of any punishment against judges who held the schemes improper after that time, however; *Invalid≥84* is insignificant in regressions C and D. Note also that the punishment seems to have been imposed mainly through more branch office time rather than less time in prestigious postings; the coefficient for the effect of *Invalid≤83* on *Post_Good_Jobs* in regression D is insignificant, though with the predicted sign.

Second, if the Supreme Court reversed a judge's opinion invalidating an apportionment scheme, the Secretariat punished the judge. The variable *Invalid.Rev* in regressions E and F has a significant positive effect on *Post_Bad_Jobs* and a significant negative effect on *Post_Good_Jobs*. If a judge found his opinion invalidating an apportionment scheme reversed, he spent more time in branch offices (5.90 years) and less time with administrative responsibilities (3.02 years).

Where significant, the control variables again have the predicted effect. *Seniority* has positive effect on *Post_Good_Jobs:* the more senior the judge, the more time he spent with administrative responsibilities. *Elite_College* has a negative effect on *Post_Bad_Jobs:* judges from the Universities of Tokyo and Kyoto spent less time in branch offices. *Opinions/Yr* is positive for *Post_Good_Jobs* and negative for *Post_Bad_Jobs:* the most productive judges spent the most time with administrative responsibilities and the least time in branch offices.

This set of regressions helps resolve an issue that the Article 9 regressions could not address. One explanation for the Article 9 regressions could be that the Secretariat was run by judges who, although completely independent from LDP pressure, were generally conservative politically and in judicial temperament, and hence were reluctant to use Article 9 to weaken national defense. Conservative politics and temperament, however, would not explain a Secretariat that was not bothered by rural overrepresentation until 1984, but that favored striking it down after that. Our results suggest instead that judges were following the preferences of the LDP leadership, whether because they

---

9. The effect is strongest for the very earliest opinions (*Invalid≤73*), but we do not base our analysis on that because of the small number of observations.

independently held the same beliefs or because they had an eye to their future careers.

D. PRELIMINARY INJUNCTIONS

1. Introduction

In administrative litigation, if a plaintiff can show the potential for irreparable harm, he can demand a preliminary injunction against the government.[10] Does a judge risk his career in granting it?

For reasons we outline in chapter 5, we would not expect a judge to find his career jeopardized if he decides a routine administrative case against the government. Injunctions against the government, however, can be decidedly nonroutine. It is one thing to hold that a taxpayer owes only X in back taxes rather than the $2X$ claimed by a dishonest bureaucrat. It is quite another to block government policy. Given that national bureaucrats answer to the Cabinet, if LDP leaders want a national agency to stop taking action Y they can simply tell it to stop, and fire the agency head if he refuses. Suppose a dispute raises significant enough issues that elected officials would have found it worthwhile to intervene themselves if they had wished to do so. For a court in such a dispute to order the agency to desist from doing Y would now directly jeopardize LDP-mandated policy. Given all this, one might plausibly suspect that a judge who readily enjoins the national government jeopardizes his career.

By the same logic, a judge would not always face this threat for enjoining local governments. During the 1960s, the LDP increasingly lost control over these governments. By 1975, only 12.5 percent of mayors had run on an exclusively LDP ticket.[11] As a result, even if the Secretariat punished judges for enjoining LDP policy, we should not observe the punishment among judges who enjoined local governments. From the LDP's point of view, to enjoin the national government was to jeopardize policies important for national prosperity; to enjoin a local government was to protect the rule of law against creeping socialism.

2. Variables

To test these hypotheses, we first code all published administrative cases from 1961 to 1970 in which a petitioner demanded a preliminary injunction. We restrict ourselves to one decade to limit the potential length of time between

10. Gyosei jiken sosho ho, Law No. 139 of 1962, § 25.

11. Ramseyer and Rosenbluth 1997: 48 tab. 3.3. This was the kind of concern that led to the LDP leadership's wishing to reposition the party away from the overrepresented rural districts.

Table 4.6 Preliminary Injunctions—Summary Statistics

	Minimum	Median	Mean	Maximum
Post_Good_Jobs	0	0.07	0.26	1
Post_Bad_Jobs	0	0.09	0.21	0.9
#National_Inj_Granted	0	0	0.37	3
#National_Inj_Denied	0	0	0.5	7
#Local_Inj_Granted	0	0	0.4	4
#Local_Inj_Denied	0	0	0.40	2
Prior_Good_Jobs	0	0	0.06	0.75
Prior_Bad_Jobs	0	0	0.11	0.81
Seniority	2	8	9.42	22
Flunks	0	4	4.32	16
Elite_College	0	0	0.46	1
1st_Tokyo	0	0	0.09	1
Opinions/Yr	0	1.49	2.07	10.67
YJL	0	0	0.12	1

NOTE: $n = 130$.

multiple injunctions issued by any one judge and because injunctions are common enough that we can obtain a good-sized sample even over one decade. Judges seem to have issued fewer preliminary injunctions in recent years, for reasons that may be understandable once we report our findings.[12]

We drop unsigned opinions, judges not in the ZSKS, and judges without one and a half years of experience before or two and a half years of experience after the opinion. This leaves us with a sample of 130 judges. Where a judge has handled injunctive petitions over several years, we code his career by the most recent year in which he granted an injunction. Summary statistics appear in table 4.6. Because we were able to locate only five opinions in which a higher court reversed the grant of an injunction, we do not include a variable dealing with reversals.

We define the following new variables:

#National_Inj_Granted: the number of petitions for preliminary injunctions against the national government granted by a judge. We use the number of times he enjoins the government (rather than a dummy variable) to capture how readily he uses the remedy.

#National_Inj_Denied: the number of petitions for preliminary injunctions against the national government that a judge denied.

#Local_Inj_Granted: the number of petitions for preliminary injunctions against a local (municipal or prefectural) government that a judge granted.

12. From 1971 through 1980, there were twenty reported District Court opinions granting preliminary injunctions; from 1981 through 1997, there were seventeen.

Table 4.7 Preliminary Injunctions—Effect of Opinions on Careers

	Dependent Variable	
	A. Post_Bad_Jobs	B. Post_Good_Jobs
#National_Inj_Granted	−.024 (0.51)	−.050 (1.55)
#National_Inj_Denied	−.085 (1.92)**	.032 (1.92)*
#Local_Inj_Granted	.033 (0.92)	−.001 (0.06)
#Local_Inj_Denied	.049 (1.09)	.019 (0.72)
Prior_Good_Jobs		.460 (3.97)**
Prior_Bad_Jobs	.134 (0.98)	
Seniority	−.023 (3.83)**	.019 (4.34)**
Flunks	.006 (0.71)	−.017 (2.64)**
Elite_College	−.091 (2.01)**	.063 (1.70)*
1st_Tokyo	−.068 (0.86)	.025 (0.42)
Opinions/Yr	.013 (0.75)	−.011 (1.10)
YJL	.020 (0.28)	−.041 (1.02)
Pseudo R^2	.21	.43
Censoring ($y < 0$, unc., $y > 1$)	(64, 66, 0)	(61, 65, 4)

NOTE: $n = 130$. These are tobit regressions. The marginal effects for a judge at the median values of the independent variables are followed by the absolute value of z-statistics in parentheses. The regressions included intercepts, not reported here.
* Significant at the 90 percent confidence level using a two-tailed test.
** Significant at the 95 percent confidence level using a two-tailed test.

#Local_Inj_Denied: the number of petitions for preliminary injunctions against a local government that a judge denied.

3. Results

The results confirm that enjoining the national government does indeed affect a judge's career. To be sure, the marginal effect on *Post_Good_Jobs* for the median judge of granting such injunctions, shown in table 4.7, just misses significance at the 90 percent level, but the tobit regression coefficient itself (not shown in the table) is significant, with a z-statistic of 1.70 and a significance level of 91.8 percent. Some judges who enjoin the national government do indeed jeopardize their careers, though the effect is nonlinear, and smaller for the median judge than for less typical ones. This contrasts sharply with the fate of judges who deny injunctions. The effect of *#National_Inj_Denied* is positive and significant in regression B (again, at the 90 percent level), and negative and significant in regression A (at the 95 percent level): judges who refuse to grant injunctions against the national government receive additional administrative assignments (.32 years per injunction) and spend less time in branch offices (.85 years less per injunction). The results also confirm the predicted distinction between national and local bureaucrats. In both regressions A and B, the granting or denial of injunctions against local governments has no significant effect on the judge's career.

Where significant, the coefficients on the control variables once more have the predicted signs. *Prior_Good_Jobs* positively affects *Post_Good_Jobs:* fast-track judges continue to receive fast-track administrative assignments. *Seniority* positively affects *Post_Good_Jobs* and negatively affects *Post_Bad_Jobs:* the more senior the judge, the more time he spends with administrative responsibilities and the less time in branch offices. *Flunks* negatively affects *Post_Good_Jobs:* the judges who failed the LRTI exam most often were least likely to be trusted with administrative responsibilities. *Elite_College* affects *Post_Bad_Jobs* negatively and *Post_Good_Jobs* positively: judges from the Universities of Tokyo and Kyoto spent the least time in branch offices and the most time with administrative duties.

Crucially, this set of regressions helps distinguish among the different explanations for judicial behavior. It is not that the Secretariat is judicially conservative, unwilling to thwart the actions of elected officials or to intervene in political issues. Rather, it seems to be conservative with respect to the national government and neutral with respect to the local government—exactly as the LDP would wish it to be.

III. Litigation over Prominent but Less Sensitive Issues
A. THE ISSUE

So judges who go against the government in some sensitive cases suffer. Does this phenomenon reflect politicization, or just bureaucratization?[13] After all, Japanese courts are nothing if not bureaucratic. Were judges punished because they favored the political opposition, or just because they refused to conform to the dictates of a large, routinized organization? Judges who held the SDF unconstitutional could calculate the odds that the Supreme Court would reverse them, as could those who held the ban on door-to-door canvassing unconstitutional or those who held the early electoral districts unconstitutional. They knew they were flouting implicit orders from on high. They were mavericks, and nobody would expect a bureaucratic personnel office to treat mavericks well, politics or no politics. (Let us table the distinction between national and

13. In confidential conversations with judges, we have heard that the performance variable many courts care most about is the classic bureaucratic one of a judge's docket clearance rate—how fast paper passes through his courtroom. Some courts, at least, circulate monthly reports to every judge of every other judge's docket clearance rate as a spur toward better performance.

local government injunctions, for which it is hard to see any but a political logic.)

B. Data and Variables

To test whether the Secretariat maintained an apolitical bureaucratic bias against nonconformists, we compare the results above with the careers of judges reversed on appeal in two sets of important but politically less charged disputes: cases involving important but less salient constitutional issues, and cases construing the even less political Commercial Code. We deliberately sought cases that all would agree were important to Japanese law. These cases simply are not important politically. On the one hand, if the judges reversed in these cases incur a career penalty analogous to those incurred by the judges above, that would suggest that the dynamic is heavily bureaucratic—or, if you like, emphatically hostile to judges who get the law wrong. On the other, if the reversed judges suffer no significant penalty, that would suggest that the dynamic is primarily political.

To construct these data sets, we identify the trial court judges involved in all Supreme Court opinions that appear in both an annotated version of the Constitution (Mohan 1997) and a standard casebook on constitutional law (Abe and Ikeda 1989). We drop cases without a published, signed trial court opinion, judges not in the ZSKS, and judges without one and a half years of experience before the opinion or two and a half years of experience after it. This leaves us with a sample of seventy-five judges from forty-six cases.[14]

Second, we produce a corresponding sample of trial judges in cases construing the Commercial Code that were appealed to the Supreme Court.[15] To match them with the constitutional cases, we use commercial cases decided by the Supreme Court in the same years as the Court's opinions in our constitutional sample. Since there were more commercial cases than constitutional cases that need matching, within the years of our constitutional sample we randomly choose a matching number of commercial cases. After dropping unsigned opinions and judges not in the ZSKS or lacking the requisite years of experience before and after the opinion as above, we have a commercial sample of sixty-one judges from forty cases.

14. There is some overlap with the judges analyzed earlier in the chapter, since we do not exclude SDF or malapportionment cases from this sample.

15. Note that such a comparison would be more difficult for a study of the United States, because under our federal system, the federal Supreme Court decides most constitutional cases while state supreme courts decide most questions concerning commercial law.

Table 4.8 Prominent Opinions by Trial Judges—Summary Statistics

	Minimum	Median	Mean	Maximum
Post_Good_Jobs	0	0.30	0.34	1
Post_Bad_Jobs	0	0.16	0.20	1
Constitutional	0	1	0.54	1
Con.Aff-Aff	0	0	0.15	1
Con.Rev-Rev	0	0	0.10	1
Con.Aff-rev	0	0	0.12	1
Con.Rev-Aff	0	0	0.17	1
Commercial	0	0	0.46	1
Comm.Aff-Aff	0	0	0.21	1
Comm.Rev-Rev	0	0	0.04	1
Comm.Aff-Rev	0	0	0.07	1
Comm.Rev-Aff	0	0	0.13	1
Prior_Good_Jobs	0	0	0.12	1
Prior_Bad_Jobs	0	0	0.15	1
Seniority	2	8.50	10.99	33
Flunks	0	3	3.70	13
Elite_College	0	1	0.51	1
1st_Tokyo	0	0	0.27	1
Opinions/Yr	0	1.75	3.02	17.45
YJL	0	0	0.11	1

NOTE: $n = 136$.

We construct the following new variables, summary statistics for which appear in table 4.8:

Con.Aff-Aff: 1 if a judge's opinion in the constitutional sample was affirmed by the High Court and then affirmed again by the Supreme Court; 0 otherwise.

Con.Rev-Rev: 1 if a judge's opinion in the constitutional sample was reversed by the High Court and then reversed again by the Supreme Court (i.e., the High Court reversal was in turn reversed); 0 otherwise.

Con.Aff-Rev: 1 if a judge's opinion in the constitutional sample was affirmed by the High Court and then reversed by the Supreme Court (i.e., the High Court affirmance was reversed); 0 otherwise.

Con.Rev-Aff: 1 if a judge's opinion in the constitutional sample was reversed by the High Court and then affirmed by the Supreme Court (i.e., the High Court reversal was affirmed); 0 otherwise.

Comm.Aff-Aff: 1 if a judge's opinion in the commercial sample was affirmed by the High Court and then affirmed again by the Supreme Court; 0 otherwise. This will be the omitted variable in the table 4.9 regressions.

Comm.Rev-Rev: 1 if a judge's opinion in the commercial sample was reversed by the High Court and then reversed again by the Supreme Court; 0 otherwise.

Table 4.9 Prominent Opinions by Trial Judges—Effect of Opinions
on Careers

	Dependent Variable	
	A. Post_Bad_Jobs	B. Post_Good_Jobs
Con.Aff-Aff	−.099 (1.73)*	.082 (1.31)
Con.Rev-Rev	−.078 (1.37)	.144 (1.84)*
Con.Aff-Rev	−.006 (0.09)	.111 (1.65)*
Con.Rev-Aff	−.054 (0.93)	.090 (1.46)
Comm.Rev-Rev	.027 (0.22)	.126 (0.94)
Comm.Aff-Rev	−.100 (1.48)	.151 (1.66)*
Comm.Rev-Aff	−.065 (1.04)	.078 (1.16)
Prior_Good_Jobs		.161 (2.10)**
Prior_Bad_Jobs	.235 (2.39)**	
Seniority	−.016 (3.86)**	.020 (3.98)**
Flunks	.008 (1.14)	−.009 (1.42)
Elite_College	−.104 (2.22)**	.061 (1.86)*
1st_Tokyo	−.061 (1.27)	.144 (2.68)**
Opinions/Yr	.0004 (0.06)	−.008 (1.57)
YJL	.004 (0.06)	.056 (0.90)
Pseudo R^2	.31	.48
Censoring ($y < 0$, unc., $y > 1$)	(60, 74, 2)	(47, 85, 4)

NOTE: $n = 136$. These are tobit regressions. The marginal effects for a judge at the median values of
the independent variables are followed by the absolute value of z-statistics in parentheses. The
regressions included intercepts, not reported here.
* Significant at the 90 percent confidence level using a two-tailed test.
** Significant at the 95 percent confidence level using a two-tailed test.

Comm.Aff-Rev: 1 if a judge's opinion in the commercial sample was affirmed
by the High Court and then reversed by the Supreme Court; 0 otherwise.
Comm.Rev-Aff: 1 if a judge's opinion in the constitutional sample was reversed
by the High Court and then affirmed by the Supreme Court; 0 otherwise.

C. RESULTS

Consistent with the notion that judges suffer more for political than for bureaucratic sins, the judges reversed in these cases suffered only modestly if at
all. First, as the negative coefficient on *Con.Aff-Aff* in regression A of table 4.9
shows, a judge who is affirmed by both courts in a constitutional law case will
tend to avoid branch office time (the confidence level is 90 percent). Perhaps
more to the point, he will be more likely to do so than a judge who is affirmed by both courts in a commercial law case—the omitted variable in this
regression—which is generally less politically sensitive.

Second, as the positive coefficient on *Con.Rev-Rev* in regression B shows
(with a 90 percent confidence level), a judge who is reversed by both courts in
a constitutional case will also spend *more* time in prestigious assignments. This

is less bizarre than it might seem. After all, a judge who is reversed by the High Court but whose High Court reversal is then in turn reversed by the Supreme Court may well have effectively received the Supreme Court's blessing.

Less explicably, as the positive coefficients on *Con.Aff-Rev* and *Com.Aff-Rev* in regression B show, a judge who is affirmed by the High Court but then reversed by the Supreme Court also spends more time in prestigious assignments. It is hard to know what to make of this, except to conclude that the clear incentives present in politically charged disputes largely disappear in these less sensitive cases.

Note that despite the absence of clear incentives tied to the decision variables in these politically less sensitive cases, the coefficients on the control variables continue to track the patterns above. *Prior_Good_Jobs* has a positive effect on *Post_Good_Jobs,* as does *Prior_Bad_Jobs* on *Post_Bad_Jobs.* Both *Seniority* and *Elite_College* have negative effects on *Post_Bad_Jobs* and positive effects on *Post_Good_Jobs. 1st_Tokyo* affects *Post_Good_Jobs* positively. Where the coefficients on opinion variables in these politically nonsensitive cases are significant at the 90 percent level if they are significant at all, the coefficients on the control variables are almost all significant at the 95 percent level. This helps confirm the power of the regressions—that the insignificance of the other opinion variables is not due to too small a sample size, but to their truly not mattering much.

Comparison of the summary statistics in this chapter's tables shows that these various samples are similar in some dimensions and different in others. The preliminary injunctions judges are the closest to the average judges in Japan, with lower means for *Prior_Good_Jobs, 1st_Tokyo,* and *Opinions/Yr* and a higher mean for Flunks compared to the other three samples. The malapportionment sample contains older and more distinguished judges, with a much higher mean for *Seniority* (23.01, compared with 13.12, 10.99, and 9.42), higher means for *Prior_Good_Jobs* and *Opinions/Yr,* and a lower mean for *Flunks.* This is what one might expect, since this type of lawsuit is decided in a High Court, which tend to be staffed by older and better judges. The Article 9 and prominent opinions samples are intermediate in their summary statistics, but each has its own special features. We hope that by looking at several different groups of judges, our results are more robust than if we had simply aggregated all of our data.

IV. Conclusion

Do judges who flout the ruling party in politically charged cases have worse careers? They do indeed. Apparently, lower-court judges defer to the LDP in politically charged disputes for a simple reason: those who do receive better posts. For example, take the constitutionality of the SDF: judges who sided with the LDP on Article 9 received better assignments than those who did not. Take the apportionment debate: those who held apportionment schemes valid during the time when the LDP relied on overrepresented rural districts did better than those who did not. Or suppose a judge faced demands for injunctions against a national agency: if he granted them, he was likely to do worse than if he denied them.

Note several points. First, in all the politically sensitive sets of cases, we obtain results that are significant at at least the 90 percent confidence level, and often at the 95 percent level. Second, not all our tests involve the punishment of a small number of judges. Among the 130 judges who ruled on petitions for preliminary injunctions, forty-two enjoined the national government. And recall that in chapter 2 we found evidence of pay discrimination against the 140 leftists among all five hundred judges hired between 1959 and 1968. Politics does seem to matter. As always with statistical work, one should not take the results as final. Consistently, however, the multivariate regressions suggest that judicial independence in Japan has real limits. In politically sensitive cases, judges seem to indulge their true political preferences at their peril. Should they flout the preferences of the LDP, they potentially pay with their careers.

5

Administrative Disputes: Taxpayers against the Government

When sued, the Japanese government always wins. At least, almost always. Year in and year out, well over three-quarters of the time, it wins. The question is why. By the occasional word on the street in Japan, it wins because it cheats. By a cynicism cultivated by reading too many of the regressions in this book, our readers, too, might think it wins because it cheats.

Does the government cheat? In chapter 3 we found evidence that judges who write anti-government opinions can suffer in their careers. In chapter 4 we found even clearer evidence that judges who flouted the government in politically charged cases paid with their careers. Is it the same if they decide even ordinary administrative cases against the government?

Several considerations suggest the government's high win rate has nothing to do with judicial career incentives. First, our own work in section III of chapter 4 suggests that the incentives mainly appear in politically sensitive disputes. Second, the basic dynamics of litigation and settlement (the Priest–Klein theory discussed in chapter 3) suggest that parties to a dispute will generally anticipate judicial bias and incorporate it into the terms of the settlement, leaving win rates unaffected. Finally, politicians in modern democracies try to offer their constituents a portfolio of government policies and services that includes reasonably honest and responsive bureaucrats. Toward that end, they will often find the courts a convenient monitoring and constraining mechanism. Judges, however, can constrain bureaucrats effectively only if they do not suffer career penalties for doing so.

We begin by detailing verdict rates in Japan and explaining why one might not expect this to result from skewed judicial incentives (section I). We then use data from reported opinions and judicial careers to test whether the

Secretariat does in fact use its control over judicial appointments to reward pro-government opinions in one class of routine administrative cases—tax cases (section II).

I. The Problem

A. VERDICT RATES

In 1994 (to take a recent year at random), Japanese District Courts decided 154 civil disputes between taxpayers and the government. Of these, the government won 94 percent. The government also litigated another 622 non-tax-related administrative cases. Of those, it won 93 percent (Saiko 1994: tab. 80). This is not unusual. Year after year, the government wins by similar odds (Ramseyer 1989, 1990: ch. 3).

Although we as researchers have access only to published opinions, through internal personnel reports the Secretariat would have access to all opinions. Nonetheless, because the Japanese government publishes a relatively high proportion of the tax opinions, the verdict rate among published opinions tends to track the total. Given that the case reporters had apparently not yet finished publishing 1994 opinions at the time of our initial research, consider a year sufficiently far back that the opinions were safely out. In 1989, the government litigated 182 tax cases and won 87 percent. It litigated another 355 non-tax-related administrative cases and won 90 percent (Saiko 1994: tab. 80). Of the tax cases, 92 were published (51 percent, including both civil and criminal tax cases). Of those published cases, the government won 92 percent. Thus, the win rates on published and unpublished tax cases are almost identical.

B. EXPLANATIONS
1. Introduction

Chapter 2 suggests a straightforward explanation for high government verdict rates in administrative cases: the government rewards pro-government judges. But for several reasons one should wonder about that. First, as already described in chapter 4, the incentive effects appear mainly in political cases and disappear in ordinary commercial cases. Granted, the composite measure of anti-government opinions in chapter 3 included routine administrative cases. Yet the analysis of chapter 4 suggests that the career effect of the composite might just have been caused by the more politically charged cases within the composite index. In addition, two theoretical considerations that we consider next also suggest that government win rates in administrative cases have nothing to do with any bias in judicial incentives.

2. The Effect of Settlement

Even if the courts relentlessly favored the government, rational taxpayers and bureaucrats would take that bias into account when they bargained. If they did, the bias would shape the terms of their out-of-court settlements. It would not, however, necessarily result in a high government win rate in the few cases that proceeded to trial. We explained why in chapter 2, but a review here may be helpful.

The effect works like this. Suppose the courts were heavily biased in favor of the government. Lawyers would soon discover this and advise their clients accordingly. Government lawyers would similarly take it into account. Hypothetically, they might even feel emboldened by the biased judges, and bring outrageous cases that they know would lose before unbiased judges. The combination of private-party caution in settlement and government boldness in pressing suit would not necessarily result in the government's winning most of the cases that went to trial. Indeed, if—hypothetically again— private parties surrender in all but the most outrageous cases and the gov- ernment brings sufficiently weak ones, the outcome could even be govern- ment losses in most cases that make it to trial, despite a clear government advantage.

According to the original Priest–Klein (1984) study, legal bias or no, ob- served verdict rates should hover around 50 percent. Researchers since have failed to confirm this 50 percent hypothesis (Kessler, Meites, and Miller 1996; Waldfogel 1995). They have, however, left intact the intuition that legal bias will not correlate with verdict rates.[1] Thus, the Japanese tax office may win consistently, but that is no evidence of biased judicial incentives. Instead, ver- dict rates depend on how the government and taxpayers decide which cases to press on to trial.

A straightforward reason for high government win rates is a simple repeat- player strategy (Ramseyer 1989, 1990). Suppose one party faces repeated dis- putes over similar issues. Suppose further that judges generally follow prece- dent, breaking it only reluctantly. Repeat players will then disproportionately select for litigation those cases where they see a good chance of shifting the law in their favor. As Priest and Klein observed, a "systematic difference in

---

1. We have already noted one reason why win rates might not be 50 percent under the selection effect: the government might bring so many outrageous cases that its win rate falls even when judges are biased in its favor. Another reason that cases fail to settle out of court might be that both sides think that the plaintiff will win but they disagree as to how much damages would be. The idea that cases that go to trial are not a random sample of all cases filed is still valid, but we cannot then predict that the win rate will be near 50 percent.

stakes to the parties" will cause the observed verdict to differ from 50 percent (1984: 40). The Japanese tax office is exactly such a repeat player. If it sees a chance officially to set a precedent for future courts—something the particular taxpayer in the case cares nothing about—the tax office will refuse even the most generous settlement offer, preferring to get their point on the record. The tax office will litigate and send to trial cases that both sides expect it to win, refusing settlement, while any taxpayer who could win most of what he wants without going to trial would gladly forgo having his name appear in the court reporter.

3. Political Economy

Basic considerations of electoral politics suggest that rational politicians will not want to punish judges routinely for second-guessing bureaucrats. In Japan, as in other modern democracies, voters elect legislators to obtain a broad portfolio of policies and services. In turn, politicians hire bureaucrats to deliver that portfolio. Like other employees, however, bureaucrats can both shirk their job and deliberately sabotage the policy preferences that legislators want to implement but the bureaucrats dislike. That bureaucrats shirk reflects the basic human proclivity to minimize effort. That they misbehave reflects that individual bureaucrats will not always share the policy preferences of the politicians who hired them.

Given the divergence in objectives, politicians face the task of monitoring and constraining their bureaucratic agents. When the issue is major, the politician can of course simply telephone the misbehaving bureaucrat and tell him to change course. This is particularly true in parliamentary regimes like Japan, in which Congress and the presidency are not controlled by different parties. If the bureaucrat adopts regulations the leaders of the majority party do not like, they can not only fire him, but repeal the regulation by statute. Again, this is particularly easy in a parliamentary regime, where there is no threat of executive veto of the repealing statute and the bureaucrat cannot play the legislature off against the executive. Thus, there is no reason why politicians need judges to monitor bureaucrats as far as major policies go. For just that reason, in chapter 4 we found judges punished for *injoining* the government—cases that disproportionately flout LDP preferences. And indeed, in a variety of ways Japanese administrative law places major political decisions beyond the scope of judicial review (Ramseyer and Nakazato 1999: ch. 8).

Although politicians can readily monitor major policies, they cannot efficiently monitor the routine decisions that mid-level and low-level bureaucrats make. They can perhaps review the siting of a new nuclear power plant, but they cannot spend the time to review every taxi license revocation without exorbitant opportunity cost in terms of foregone legislation.[2] For such routine disputes, courts offer politicians a way to monitor (McCubbins and Schwartz 1984). By giving disaffected constituents the right to bring mundane complaints before an impartial judge, they improve the quality of policies and services they provide their constituents. In the process, they improve their own odds of reelection.[3]

II. The Test

A. INTRODUCTION

Consider two contrasting hypotheses concerning whether judges who publish opinions favoring taxpayers at the expense of the government will find that their careers suffer. If the word on the street in Japan is right, a judge who writes pro-taxpayer opinions incurs a nontrivial risk of damaging his career. This may not show up in every career, but disproportionately such judges should receive worse assignments than those who favor the government.

By contrast, if the LDP hopes to encourage judges to monitor lower-level bureaucrats in mundane cases, then the Secretariat will simply try to reward judicial accuracy. If a judge writes an opinion that is wrong, in the sense of being reversed by a higher court, he will receive a worse assignment, but that should be true whether he favors the government or the taxpayer. Given the results in commercial litigation (chapter 4), we would also expect such an effect to be relatively weak. Wrong decisions hurt a judge's career slightly, but they are not the most important thing for his success.

---

2. The point is not that they never review such decisions. In fact, Japanese majority politicians do offer constituents a wide range of bureaucratic intervention services. The point is rather that even a party like the Liberal Democratic Party (LDP) that specializes in such bureaucratic intervention services may find it cost effective to delegate some disputes to the courts. A special twist on this for Japan is that Diet members have relatively small government-paid staffs. Given that LDP members can hope for more cooperation from the LDP-managed executive branch, this is perhaps because larger staffs would help non-LDP members more than LDP members. If this is true, delegating intervention services to judges would be part of the general delegation that Diet members do.

3. Crucially, the theory here applies only to the most mundane disputes, and to disputes involving government sectors (such as low-level divisions of the bureaucracy) that the LDP does not directly control. If a dispute is sufficiently major that a legislator could cost-effectively intervene, the LDP has an incentive positively to disable the courts, so as to increase the value of legislative services. On why injunctive cases are not mundane, see chapter 4.

If the dispute involves a government unit run by the opposition (such as big city governments in the 1970s), the LDP similarly has an incentive to encourage judicial review.

B. DATA

We use tax disputes as an example of mundane administrative litigation to test between these two hypotheses. Accordingly, we examined all published cases (whether civil or criminal) that construe either the Income Tax Act (for individual taxpayers) or the Corporate Tax Act (for firms).[4] We then coded a tax case according to whether the taxpayer or the government won, whether the case was appealed, and whether it was reversed on appeal.[5]

We use this material to assemble two samples. These can be used in combination for some purposes but must be used separately for others.

In the "Tax Trials" data set, we examined *all* District Court tax cases published in either 1976 or 1979. We located 113 tax opinions for 1976 and 116 for 1979. Because some judges wrote several tax opinions, this produced a set of 179 judges who wrote at least one tax opinion in either of the two years. We chose years in the late 1970s because at the time we began collecting the material our data on judicial careers (ZSKS 1990) expired in 1990 and our regressions require ten years of postopinion career data. Choosing sample years that were three years apart yielded two cohorts with little overlap, since most judges are reassigned every three years. Some judges specialize by subject matter—including tax—during a three-year assignment. Rarely, however, does a judge write many tax opinions for more than three years in a row.

In the "Tax Appeals" sample, we collected data on those trial court decisions that were appealed. We used a longer time horizon for this, since appealed decisions are less common and we need a large enough sample of each type of decision for regressions to give meaningful results. We included all the appealed cases in 1976 and 1979, since we already had them from the Tax Trials sample. We added to that all cases reported for the other years between 1975 and 1984 in which either the trial judge was reversed on appeal or a pro-taxpayer opinion was affirmed (a total of seventy-eight cases). Finally, we collected a random sample of seventy-eight pro-government opinions written during those years and affirmed on appeal. Affirmed, pro-government decisions are by far the most common kind of appeals case, so we did not need

4. We include criminal tax cases (there were thirty-three cases, two with acquittals) because we believe the case selection dynamic in tax fraud cases is often close to that of civil tax cases. We dropped judges not in the data source (primarily judges educated before World War II and prosecutors seconded to the courts) and judges who joined the bench less than a year before the year of the decision or who quit less than two years after the year of the decision. Where a judge had opinions in both 1976 and 1979, we coded the career data based on the year in which he decided a pro-taxpayer decision. If he wrote a pro-taxpayer decision in both or neither of the two years, we based the career data on 1979.

5. We treat a case as a taxpayer victory if the court adopted any or all of the taxpayer's position.

Table 5.1 Taxes—Summary Statistics

	Minimum	Median	Mean	Maximum
A. Tax Trial Sample ($n = 179$)				
AnyProTP	0	0	.34	1
AnyRev	0	0	.09	1
Prior_Good_Jobs	0	0	.20	1
Post_Good_Jobs	0	.27	.34	1
Prior_Bad_Jobs	0	0	.16	.73
Post_Bad_Jobs	0	.20	.22	.85
Seniority	2	13	13.52	29
Flunks	0	3	4.03	17
Elite_College	0	0	.39	1
1st_Tokyo	0	0	.10	1
Opinions/Yr	0	1.85	2.88	20.6
YJL	0	0	.07	1
B. Tax Appeal Sample ($n = 284$)				
TP_Aff	0	0	.11 (.19)	1
TP_Rev	0	0	.15 (.26)	1
J_Aff	0	1	.70 (.45)	1
J_Rev	0	0	.12 (.20)	1
Prior_Good_Jobs	0	0	.17 (.17)	1
Post_Good_Jobs	0	.19	.33 (.33)	1
Prior_Bad_Jobs	0	0	.18 (.11)	.81
Post_Bad_Jobs	0	.20	.24 (.24)	.97
Seniority	2	12	12.93 (12.93)	31
Flunks	0	3	4.01 (4.01)	17
Elite_College	0	0	.36 (.36)	1
1st_Tokyo	0	0	.12 (.12)	1
Opinions/Yr	0	1.90	2.91 (2.91)	29.02
YJL	0	0	.06 (.06)	1

NOTE: This is a stratified sample. The values as weighted to estimate the population values are followed in parentheses by the unweighted sample values. For the median, weighting happens not to alter the values. For the minimum and maximum, weighting can never make a difference, and population values are not estimated.

to analyze all of them to determine their effect on judicial careers. Thus, by using this simple form of stratified sampling, we were able to concentrate on the most interesting decisions.[6]

C. VARIABLES

Using this data, we construct the following new variables. Summary statistics appear in table 5.1.

6. We used the following sampling procedure. We first determined how many cases in a given year had *TP_Aff, TP_Rev,* or *J_Rev* equal to 1, and all of those went into the sample—nine cases for 1975, for example. We then numbered the cases that year with *J_Aff* equal to 1—thirty-seven of them for 1975. Using STATA, we generated nine different random numbers from 1 to 37, and used those *J_Aff* cases for our sample. Thus, we end up sampling the same numbers of *J_Aff* cases as all other cases for each year except for 1976 and 1979, for which our sample was the entire population of tax cases.

Table 5.2 Dependent and Control Variables—Summary

A. Dependent Variables

Post_Good_Jobs	The percentage of time during the decade after the crucial opinion in which a judge held prestigious appointments.
Post_Bad_Jobs	The percentage of time during the decade after the opinion in which a judge was in a branch office.

B. Control Variables

Prior_Good_Jobs	Equivalent to Post_Good_Jobs for the decade before the opinion.
Prior_Bad_Jobs	Equivalent to Post_Bad_Jobs for the decade before the opinion.
Seniority	The number of years between the opinion and the year a judge graduated from the LRTI.
Flunks	The estimated number of years (based on birth year) between college graduation and entrance to the LRTI.
Elite_College	1 if a judge graduated from either the University of Tokyo or the University of Kyoto; 0 otherwise.
Opinions/Yr	A judge's average productivity (measured in published opinions per year on the bench) for the decade before the opinion.
1st_Tokyo	1 if a judge started at the Tokyo District Court; 0 otherwise.
YJL	1 if a judge was a member of the Young Jurists League in 1969; 0 otherwise.

AnyProTP: 1 if a judge published a tax opinion (in 1976 or 1979, depending on the judicial cohort) in which the government lost on any count; 0 otherwise.

AnyRev: 1 if a judge published a tax opinion in a reference year (1976 or 1979) that was reversed on any issue; 0 otherwise.

We then add the variables used in chapter 4 and described in table 4.1. For ease of reference, we include table 5.2 as a summary.

D. RESULTS

1. Preliminary Considerations

We perform three sets of regressions:

1. preliminary regressions illustrating the determinants of early or intermediate judicial careers (on the combined samples),
2. regressions examining the effects on the trial judge of pro-taxpayer opinions and of reversals generally (on the Tax Trials sample), and
3. regressions testing for different effects on trial judges whose decisions were appealed of pro-government and pro-taxpayer reversals (on the Tax Appeals sample).[7]

In the first regressions, we examine the determinants of a judge's early or intermediate career. Unaware of any relevant bias that would result from merging the two data sets, we combine them here. By using as the dependent

7. Note that the Tax Trial sample has 179 observations, the Tax Appeals sample has 329 observations, and the combined sample has 335 observations. The number of observations in the first two samples adds up to more than 335 because there is some overlap between the Trials and Appeals samples.

Table 5.3 Early and Intermediate Judicial Careers in the Combined Samples

	Dependent Variable		
	A. 1st_Tokyo	B. Prior_Bad_Jobs	C. Prior_Good_Jobs
Flunks	−.012 (1.86)*	.006 (2.12)**	−.001 (0.84)
Elite_College	.110 (2.56)**	−.028 (1.44)	.022 (1.51)
YJL	−.041 (0.83)	.101 (1.91)*	−.022 (1.50)
1st_Tokyo		.004 (0.13)	.081 (2.36)**
Seniority		.007 (5.36)**	.011 (6.90)**
Opinions/Yr		−.029 (5.10)**	.004 (2.33)**
Pseudo R^2	.05	.20	.58
Censoring ($y < 0, y > 1$)		(211, 0)	(202, 4)
	probit	tobit	tobit

NOTE: $n = 335$. The marginal effects for a judge at the median values of the independent variables are followed by the absolute value of z-statistics in parentheses. The regressions also included intercepts, not reported here.
* Significant at the 90 percent confidence level using a two-tailed test.
** Significant at the 95 percent confidence level using a two-tailed test.

variables *1st_Tokyo, Prior_Bad_Jobs,* and *Prior_Good_Jobs,* we first explore the determinants of early and intermediate judicial careers (see regressions A, B, and C of table 5.3).[8] Consistently, the results confirm our findings in chapter 3 about Japanese judicial career structure: they show that the Secretariat identifies the most promising new recruits and assigns them to the Tokyo District Court for their first job. Having gone to an elite university and having graduated from the Legal Research and Training Institute (LRTI) at a young age both confer significant advantage. Having been a member of the Young Jurists League (YJL) is not statistically significant.

Regressions B and C of table 5.3 go further, and show some of the factors that determine the quality of jobs a judge receives relatively early in his career.[9] Again consistent with regressions on other data sets, writing few opinions (low *Opinions/Yr*), having flunked the LRTI exam more often (high *Flunks*), and having joined the YJL all lead to longer stints in branch offices.

Interestingly, the coefficient on *Seniority* is significant and *positive* in regression B: in the *Prior_Bad_Jobs* regression, more senior judges spent more time in branch offices during the decade before the tax opinions, contradicting the more general result that length of time in branch office declines with seniority. What regression B captures, however, is the nonlinearity in this relationship:

8. The regressions in table 5.3 are not weighted by sampling probability.
9. Obviously, some judges are more senior than others during this period. We say "relatively early" only for the simple reason that for each judge, it is a decade earlier than in our next set of regressions. Note that *Opinions/Yr* cannot technically be a determinant of either *Prior_Good_Jobs* or *Prior_Bad_Jobs,* since it is calculated over the same period. We use it here on the theory that it proxies for the judge's general rate of published productivity.

branch office time is generally a *mid*career phenomenon. The very youngest judges generally avoid branch office stints. Only after judges have worked several years (often a decade) in a supervised setting are they sent to branch offices. It is primarily at that point that branch office time starts to function as a potential punishment. Because regression B uses *Prior_Bad_Jobs* as the dependent variable, the coefficient on *Seniority* reflects the early-to-mid-career transition—a point at which branch office time increases. To capture the different effect that *Seniority* has on junior and senior judges, we transformed *Seniority* into exponential form. Estimating that the break occurs shortly after a judge finishes his first ten-year term, we constructed a variable equal to (*Seniority* − 13) squared, and reran regression B (on *Prior_Bad_Jobs*). The coefficient on the transformed variable was now negative and statistically significant.

Regression C of table 5.3 illustrates the determinants of the most prestigious midcareer jobs. Again, we see that writing many opinions (*Opinions/Yr*), starting in the Tokyo District Court (*1st_Tokyo*), and having considerable experience (*Seniority*) help a judge.

2. Tax Cases

(a) Introduction

Turn now to the question central to this chapter: whether a judge's tax decisions affect his career. Table 5.4 shows the regression results for the Tax Trials sample. It includes both *AnyProTP* and *AnyRev*.

Note first that where significant the control variables have the predicted effects. *Seniority* is negatively and significantly correlated with *Post_Bad_Jobs,* and positively and significantly correlated with *Post_Good_Jobs*. *1st_Tokyo* is negatively and significantly correlated with *Post_Bad_Jobs* and positively and significantly correlated with *Post_Good_Jobs*. *Flunks* is positively and significantly correlated with *Post_Bad_Jobs* and negatively and significantly correlated with *Post_Good_Jobs*. *Elite_College* is positively and significantly correlated with *Post_Good_Jobs*.

(b) AnyProTP

Finally, we come to the opinion variables. *AnyProTP* has no significant effect in the regressions, while *AnyRev* does. Whether a judge writes a protaxpayer opinion has no significant effect on the jobs he obtains in the succeeding years but being reversed by a higher court does have an effect. Even the signs on the insignificant variables are not consistently in the directions predicted. And the results remain the same whether the two variables are put in separately (the first four columns of table 5.4) or together (the last two

Table 5.4 The Effect of Tax Opinions on Judicial Careers in the Tax Trials Sample

	Dependent Variable					
	A. Post_Bad_Jobs	B. Post_Good_Jobs	C. Post_Bad_Jobs	D. Post_Good_Jobs	E. Post_Bad_Jobs	F. Post_Good_Jobs
AnyProTP	.024 (0.63)	−.006 (0.13)			−.001 (0.05)	.026 (0.47)
AnyRev			.151** (2.04)	−.137** (2.40)	.152* (1.92)	−.143** (2.57)
Prior_Good_Jobs		−.046 (0.42)		−.042 (0.38)		−.046 (0.42)
Prior_Bad_Jobs	.033 (0.37)		.012 (0.14)		.012 (0.13)	
Seniority	−.009** (4.40)	.027** (6.26)	−.010** (4.83)	.029** (6.46)	−.010** (4.63)	.029** (6.46)
Flunks	.010* (1.69)	−.015 (1.63)	.010* (1.76)	−.014 (1.55)	.010* (1.71)	−.014 (1.59)
Elite_College	−.030 (0.91)	.079 (1.52)	−.036 (1.11)	.092* (1.76)	−.036 (1.10)	.089* (1.72)
1st_Tokyo	−.126** (3.21)	.148 (1.62)	−.131** (3.53)	.159* (1.72)	−.132** (3.49)	.160* (1.73)
Opinions/Yr	−.009 (1.24)	.011 (1.33)	−.006 (0.96)	.008 (1.07)	−.006 (0.93)	.007 (0.86)
YJL	.091 (1.15)	−.069 (0.90)	.093 (1.18)	−.073 (0.94)	.093 (1.18)	−.072 (0.95)
Pseudo R^2	.21	.33	.23	.34	.23	.34
Censoring ($y < 0$, $y > 1$)	(76, 0)	(76, 18)	(76, 0)	(76, 18)	(76, 0)	(76, 18)

NOTE: $n = 179$. These are tobit regressions. The marginal effects for a judge at the median values of the independent variables are followed by the absolute value of z-statistics in parentheses. The regressions also included intercepts, not reported here.

* Significant at the 90 percent confidence level using a two-tailed test.

** Significant at the 95 percent confidence level using a two-tailed test.

columns). Given the possibility that judges who write pro-taxpayer opinions write them regularly, and that *Prior_Good_Jobs* and *Prior_Bad_Jobs* would then incorporate the punishment imposed for past pro-taxpayer opinions, we reran the regressions with *Prior_Bad_Jobs* and *Prior_Good_Jobs* omitted. Notwithstanding the change, *AnyProTP* remained insignificant.

In contrast, whether a higher court reverses a judge's opinion does affect his career. The coefficient on *AnyRev* is negative and significant in the *Post_Good_Jobs* regressions; and positive and significant in the *Post_Bad_Jobs* regressions.[10] Compared to judges who are not reversed, judges who are reversed spend less time in the best jobs and significantly more in the worst jobs. Thus, it does not matter whether a judge decides for the taxpayer or for the government. It does matter whether he decides correctly.[11]

(c) Appeals

Might it be that what matters for a judge is not being reversed, but being reversed when he favors the taxpayer? Maybe a judge is not penalized when his mistakes favor the government. Maybe he suffers only when he mistakenly favors taxpayers. Because our Tax Trials database has too few cases appealed to test this proposition, we turn to our augmented Tax Appeals sample.

The Tax Appeals data set includes only judges whose cases were appealed to a higher court. Of those, the great majority were pro-government opinions that were upheld by the higher court, so we will use that as our base situation and omit the variable *J_Aff* from our regressions. The question is whether the other variables—*J_Rev, TP_Aff,* and *TP_Rev*—have a significant effect compared to the base situation. Table 5.5 shows the results.

The findings surprised us. The second column is the less surprising of the two: judges who rule in favor of the government and are reversed on appeal get fewer good jobs than those who are affirmed. It is odd, however, that ruling in favor of the taxpayer and being reversed has no such effect. The first column's results are different from either the government-bias hypothesis or the reversals-are-bad hypothesis. Two of our new variables are significantly different from the *J_Aff* baseline: *TP_Aff* and *TP_Rev*. It seems that a judge who rules in favor of the taxpayer and has his decision appealed—even if he is reversed on appeal—has less chance of going to a branch office than

10. The correlation between *AnyRev* and *AnyProTP* is .34.

11. By the logic behind Priest–Klein (1984), if both parties agree that a decision issued by a trial court is wrong, they will not appeal. Instead, they will settle out of court on the basis of the expected reversal on appeal. As a result, the lack of an appeal is not evidence that a trial judge decided correctly. An actual reversal on appeal, however, is relatively clear-cut evidence that other judges believe that the trial court was wrong.

Table 5.5 The Effect of Tax Opinions on Judicial Careers
in the Tax Appeals Sample

	Dependent Variable	
	A. Post_Bad_Jobs	B. Post_Good_Jobs
TP_Aff	−.128 (3.32)**	.012 (0.21)
TP_Rev	−.096 (2.63)**	.056 (1.07)
J_Rev	.028 (0.62)	−.078 (1.90)*
Prior_Good_Jobs		.010 (0.11)
Prior_Bad_Jobs	.258 (2.98)**	
Seniority	−.010 (5.15)**	.023 (6.56)**
Flunks	.004 (0.84)	−.011 (1.72)*
Elite_College	−.000 (0.00)	.048 (1.25)
1st_Tokyo	−.169 (5.67)**	.141 (2.24)**
Opinions/Yr	−.003 (0.47)	.014 (2.30)*
YJL	−.105 (2.01)*	.028 (0.40)
Pseudo R^2	.20	.34
Standard error	.33	.45
Censoring ($y < 0, y > 1$)	(126, 0)	(110, 32)

NOTE: $n = 284$. These are tobit regressions that weight observations by the inverse of the sampling probability. The marginal effects for a judge at the median values of the independent variables are followed by the absolute value of z-statistics in parentheses below. The regressions also included intercepts, not reported here.
* Significant at the 90 percent confidence level using a two-tailed test.
** Significant at the 95 percent confidence level using a two-tailed test.

one who has a pro-government opinion affirmed on appeal. In the Tax Trials sample, ruling in favor of the taxpayer had no effect either way, but here it seems to help a judge. We speculate that perhaps the Secretariat noted the talent it took for a judge to spot the unusual case in which the merits arguably favored the taxpayer. Indeed, not only were the cases unusual, but given the government's decision to appeal them, they probably involved complex and difficult legal or factual questions as well.[12] For purposes of testing between our two hypotheses, however, it suffices that the regressions more than confirm the absence of pro-government bias in mundane administrative cases.

III. Conclusion

Consistently, the Japanese government wins in court. Crucially, it does not win by manipulating the career judiciary to produce biased courts. Japanese judges do not enjoy better careers if they favor the government in mundane cases. Instead, it most likely wins because as a rational repeat player it dispropor-tionately selects for litigation those cases that will shift precedent in an ad-vantageous direction. In mundane administrative litigation involving disputes

12. In other words, perhaps the ability to spot the taxpayer-favored case is correlated with the ability to decide other cases correctly, and the Secretariat is rewarding this general talent.

between the government and taxpayers, the system favors accurate judges rather than biased judges. Those judges who find their opinions reversed on appeal do incur a penalty. Those judges who occasionally favor taxpayers incur none.

These results illustrate the potential benefits to bureaucratic judiciaries, in contrast to the less savory aspects we discuss in most of chapters 3 and 4. The Secretariat's ability to reassign and manipulate the promotion of judges does facilitate exerting political pressure. In simple routine cases, however, it also facilitates pressure toward enhancing quality: judges who are talented and hard working and who decide difficult cases correctly receive better jobs and greater responsibilities. Such would not be the case in a system in which judges are independent of rewards and punishments based on their performance.

6

Criminal Cases: Suspects against the Government

The regressions in chapter 3 included criminal cases in the composite index used to ask whether judges in Japan with anti-government opinions incurred a career penalty. Did the criminal cases help drive those results? Or did we obtain our findings despite the criminal cases?

The answer relates to the infamously high Japanese conviction rates. Depending on how one defines the rate, Japanese courts convict somewhere between 98 and 99.8 percent of all criminal defendants. Why? Might it be that a judge who acquits jeopardizes his career? After all, that the government chose to prosecute a defendant indicates that prosecutors concluded he was probably guilty. Might a judge who second-guesses that conclusion incur a career hit? If so, Japanese defendants might still be guilty. But, then again, they might not.

Alternatively, maybe Japanese judges convict because Japanese prosecutors only prosecute true criminals. Most ingenuously, perhaps they prosecute only the guilty out of deep-seated principle, or out of a fear that a false conviction might later come to light and embarrass them. More plausibly, perhaps they prosecute only the guilty because of their budget constraint. Chronically understaffed, Japanese prosecutors lack the time to prosecute any but a small fraction of the suspects forwarded by the police. Rather than waste their time with dubious cases (other than perhaps the occasional politically driven corruption or leftist activism case), if rational they would tend to prosecute only the most obviously and gruesomely guilty. Because they would prosecute only the guilty, judges would convict everyone tried.

Using data on the careers of all 321 judges who published an opinion in a criminal case in 1976 or 1979, we explore the effect of criminal opinions on a judge's career. On the one hand, we find that judges who convicted did indeed receive better posts than those who acquitted. Apparently, a judge sitting alone who acquits will spend an extra year and a half in branch offices over the next decade. A judge who finds a conviction reversed on appeal will suffer no significant penalty, but one who finds an acquittal reversed will spend an extra three years in branch offices.

On the other hand, judges incur this punishment only if the acquittal involves politically sensitive crimes or issues of statutory interpretation. As a result, judicial fear of second-guessing prosecutors cannot explain the high conviction rates, for the Secretariat simply does not punish judges for deciding that a prosecutor charged the wrong man. The punishment that acquitting judges receive is not punishment for acquitting per se. Instead, it is either punishment for flouting majority party policy on sensitive political issues (consistent with the results of chapter 4), or punishment for making major legal mistakes (consistent with the results of chapter 5).

We begin by comparing conviction rates in Japan and the United States (section I). We then discuss why the severe budget constraints in Japanese prosecutorial offices could result in a high ratio of guilty to innocent prosecutions (section II). Finally, we ask whether Japanese judges face incentives to convict (section III).

I. Comparative Conviction Rates
A. INTRODUCTION

Conviction rates are high in Japan. They are high in most countries, of course, but they are particularly high in Japan. In U.S. federal courts, prosecutors win 85 percent of all criminal cases (46,773 out of 54,980 in 1995) and convict 83 percent of murder defendants (265 out of 313). In U.S. state courts, they win roughly 87 percent of their felony cases and 88 percent of their misdemeanors. Japanese District Court judges convict 99.9 percent of all defendants (49,598 out of 49,643 in 1994). Of the defendants up on murder charges, they convict 99.7 percent (587 out of 589).[1]

---

1. In a majority of Japanese murder cases, the charges against the suspect are dropped, as we discuss in section II.B.2. For Japanese figures, see Homusho 1996: 122; Saiko 1994 gives slightly different figures. For U.S. federal courts, see Administrative Office 1995: tab. D-4 (murder includes first and second degree; figures for Oct. 1994–Sept. 1995); for state courts, see U.S. Dept. of Justice (1996).

International comparisons of criminal statistics are famously problematic. One might have thought at least murder statistics were reliable. Yet even here, there are problems, for the Japanese police agency pools attempts with actual murders, a point missed in the criminal law discussion in Ramseyer and Nakazato 1999.

Conviction rates like 83.3 or 99.7 percent are not the odds a defendant who contests his guilt actually faces, either in the United States or Japan. The data for both countries include cases where defendants decided not to contest the charges. In Japan, to be sure, the law does not allow plea bargains. Instead, all defendants prosecuted face trial, and courts convict them only if prosecutors prove their guilt beyond a reasonable doubt. Or so goes the theory.

Yet the lack of formal plea bargains in Japan does not mean the parties ignore analogous calculations. Defendants need not contest their guilt. Instead, they can freely confess. In exchange, prosecutors can freely suggest a sentence lower than the sentence the defendant would receive at a contested trial. The suggestion matters, because courts routinely accept prosecutors' recommended sentences.[2] Although such an implicit bargain would not be enforceable formally, both sides will generally find it worthwhile to stick to the deal. If only to encourage defendants to confess, the prosecutor's office will want to maintain its reputation for playing by customary norms. Having already confessed, the defendant would find it hard to renege even if he wanted.[3]

B. Confessions in Japan

For both the prosecutor and the defendant, uncontested proceedings create gains from trade (Easterbrook 1983). By agreeing not to contest his guilt, the defendant saves the prosecutor resources he can use to prosecute others. So long as the deterrent effect of these additional convictions outweighs the lessened punishment of the settling defendant, the arrangement increases the deterrent value of the law. Perhaps more important, it increases the prosecutor's observable work product: the convictions he can show his present bureaucratic supervisors or potential private-sector employers. The gains to the defendant are equally obvious: he gains if the plea-bargained sentence is less costly to

2. Foote 1992: 352. The parallel between Japanese confessions and U.S. plea bargains is made explicitly in Johnson 1996: ch. 7. For an analogous debate in the German context, see Langbein 1979: 214–15.

3. Where lack of enforceability matters is in plea bargains in which the defendant wishes to promise cooperation as a witness in other cases. In such bargains, the cooperation sometimes comes after the prosecutor has recommended a sentence, and U.S. prosecutors, keenly aware of the potential for defendant breach, use all the formal legal tools at their disposal to prevent it. See, e.g., Rasmusen 1998. Lack of enforceable plea agreements, like low budgets, is an obstacle in the path of the Japanese prosecutor, because it is harder to punish criminal witnesses for breaking deals to testify at other defendants' trials. This is perhaps one reason for the well-known fact that Japanese trials are usually based on documentary evidence and confessions rather than on live testimony (on which see, e.g., Ishimatsu 1989).

him than the sum of the expected risk-adjusted value of the sentence from a contested trial and his expected litigation costs.[4]

Procedural protections for defendants in Japan loosely track those in America. Although courts hesitate to mandate a blanket exclusionary rule, they do exclude coerced confessions on reliability grounds, they impose a presumption of innocence, and they demand proof at levels close to the reasonable doubt standard in U.S. trials. They enforce a right to counsel at trial (with state-appointed counsel for the poor), a right to remain silent, and a right to interrogate witnesses, and they require warrants for searches and seizures (Ramseyer and Nakazato 1999: 168–75). Moreover, if defendants do happen to be acquitted at trial, they receive an indemnity from the state as compensation for their trouble, unlike in the United States (Nomura 1981: 7).

Absent an explicit or implicit bargain, a rational defendant gains little by confessing. In Japan as in the United States, some defendants do confess or plead guilty without a promise of a lower penalty. Exceptions do not prove rules, however, and we have little reason to think defendants anywhere systematically act against their self-interest. If Japanese defendants routinely file confessions, that very fact suggests that they routinely receive lower sentences.

Japanese defendants certainly do confess. Of the 49,856 criminal cases in Japanese District Courts in 1994, defendants contested prosecution in only 7.3 percent. If a confession performs the same function as a plea bargain (obviously, they are not exact equivalents), then Japanese defendants cut a bargain all but about 7 percent of the time. By contrast, of the 54,980 criminal cases in U.S. federal District Courts in 1995, defendants pleaded innocent in 22 percent, and in state courts, they pleaded innocent in 11 percent. Notwithstanding the formal absence of plea bargains, Japanese defendants seem no more likely to contest prosecution than Americans (Saiko 1994: vol. 2, tab. 31-4; Administrative Office 1995: tab. D-4; U.S. Dept. of Justice 1997).

C. Logic of the Comparative Rates

One reason for the low frequency of contested prosecutions in Japan despite the absence of formal plea bargains is the greater predictability of trials there. The logic follows from the well-known model of litigation and settlement (Landes 1971; Posner 1973). A prosecutor faces lower costs if he can simply meet with the defendant's lawyer and bargain than if he must prove his case in a contested trial. A defendant similarly saves time and expense by avoiding

---

4. The Japanese Constitution guarantees counsel to indigent defendants, but about half the defendants use privately retained lawyers. See Ramseyer and Nakazato 1999: 172.

trial. In bargaining, moreover, both sides reduce risk by exchanging a gamble between conviction with a high sentence and acquittal with no sentence for a sentence that is definite. If both sides similarly estimate the odds of the various trial outcomes, then unless one of them enjoys risk they will plea bargain. Even if they do not agree completely on the odds, so long as their opinions are close enough and the cost and risk of trial are high enough, they will cut a deal.

In Japan, several factors dramatically increase the predictability of criminal litigation compared to the United States (Ramseyer and Nakazato 1989). First, trials are discontinuous. The prosecutor and defendant begin the trial by assembling before a judge. They discuss the issues at stake and then recess to gather evidence. Having collected evidence on the first issue, they reconvene, litigate that issue, and recess again to gather evidence on the next. During this process, the judge has considerable opportunity to disclose how he leans. As he discloses his inclinations, the parties obtain increasingly accurate estimates of the outcome.

Second, as noted in chapter 2 all trials are bench trials—Japanese courts do not use juries. Unlike juries, judges have "seen it all before," and the lawyers have seen them seeing it. Judges have histories that lawyers can investigate to find out how they approach cases. Whether because they take professional pride in uniformity, or because (like most mortals) they economize on effort, judges tend to decide similar cases similarly.

Yet third, that uniformity is not just a function of professional pride or economizing on effort. It is also a matter of professional incentives. Precisely because they face the supervision and discipline of the Secretariat, Japanese judges will manage cases more uniformly than their U.S. counterparts. Trial judges in the United States face reversal if they make important mistakes, but no professional penalty: for them, reversal is at most an embarassment. As we saw in chapter 5 (and as we explore below in the criminal context), trial judges in Japan face career consequences if they err. In general, this will make it easier for litigants to predict how a judge will rule.[5]

This predictability reduces the variance in the prosecutor's and defendant's estimates of success. Plea bargains fail and litigation ensues when both parties are optimistic—where the difference in their estimates of the contested outcome is so great that they cannot agree to meet in the middle

---

5. In addition, in Japan but not the United States, if a judge in a criminal trial mistakenly acquits, the prosecution can appeal the decision and ultimately obtain a conviction (Ramseyer and Nakazato 1999: 175). This reduces the effect of pro-defendant judicial error.

and save their trial costs. To the extent that the predictability of the judicial system reduces variance, it reduces the frequency with which prosecutors and defendants will arrive at dramatically different estimates. If their estimates are more accurate, they are more likely to be close to each other; if the estimates are closer to each other, the parties are more likely to cut a deal.

Evidence from civil suits corroborates this explanation (Ramseyer and Nakazato 1989). As observers often note, disputants in Japan settle a larger fraction of civil disputes than in the United States. They settle them, however, in the shadow of the law. Out of court, defendants pay and plaintiffs collect amounts that track the amounts a court would award. They settle because the trial outcome is usually clear, and so neither side has reason to bother litigating. Rather than sue, they settle along the lines a judge would rule.

D. RESIDUAL CONVICTION RATES

Given the high rate of uncontested proceedings in Japan, what is the residual conviction rate in contested cases? The contrast with the United States is stark. In 1994 Japanese defendants refused to confess in 3,648 cases. Courts acquitted them in forty-five, yielding a contested conviction rate of 98.8 percent. In 1995, U.S. federal defendants pleaded innocent in 11,877 cases. Courts acquitted them (or dismissed the charges) in 8,207, yielding a contested conviction rate of 30.9 percent.[6] In state courts, the contested conviction rate apparently stands even lower.[7]

II. Prosecutorial Incentives

A. INTRODUCTION

For a scholar, the high conviction rates in Japan are a bedeviling puzzle. They might be high because prosecutors only prosecute the guilty, and judges then duly convict. Or they might be high because judges dutifully convict everyone prosecuted, guilty or no. To determine the truth, we would seem to need independent evidence of the guilt of the accused. That, of course, is information

---

6. Saiko 1994: tabs. 31-4, 36-3; Administrative Office 1995: tab. D-4. If we ignore dismissals—which might be part of negotiating ploys by prosecutors—defendants were acquitted in 1,095 of the 4,765 trials in the United States, a conviction rate of 77 percent. Somewhat analogous calculations appear in Johnson 1996: ch. 7.

7. A point implied by federal surveys placing both the aggregate conviction rate and the plea bargaining rate in the high 80 percent range. See U.S. Dept. of Justice 1996.

Table 6.1 Prosecutorial Screening and Judicial Review

	Prosecutorial Screening	Judicial Review	Conviction Rates	Innocents Convicted
a.	High	Fair	Higher	Fewer
b.	High	Unfair	Higher	Fewer
c.	Low	Fair	Lower	Fewer
d.	Low	Unfair	Higher	More

we rarely have. If we had it, so would the courts, and surely they would use it for their decisions.

As a simple heuristic, consider table 6.1. In this summary, prosecutors can screen suspects carefully or cursorily. The courts, in turn, can decide the cases fairly (carefully and without a pro-conviction bias) or unfairly (either cursorily or with bias).[8]

If a prosecutor screens suspects carefully, then whether a court reviews cases fairly (row a) or unfairly (row b), conviction rates will be high and few innocent defendants will be convicted. If a prosecutor screens only cursorily, then if a court reviews cases fairly it will periodically acquit (row c). Conviction rates will be lower, but here too few innocent defendants will stand convicted. If a court merely rubber-stamps prosecutions, then conviction rates will remain high and innocent defendants may indeed comprise a substantial fraction of those convicted (row d).

The puzzle is which case best describes Japan. Given the high conviction rates, it cannot be row c. Given that prosecutors will not have much incentive to be careful if judges rubber-stamp all prosecutions, row b would be hard to maintain as a subgame-perfect equilibrium.[9] But which of the other two might it be? Is it the intuitively troubling row d, or the apparently less problematic row a? Lacking independent evidence of the guilt of the suspects, we cannot test the issue directly. To explore it indirectly, we proceed in two steps. We first explore the likely effect of the resource constraints on prosecutorial screening. As a way to ask whether we are in row a (with unbiased adjudication) or row d (biased adjudication), we then test empirically whether judges in Japan face unbiased incentives (section III).

8. Hypothetically, of course, courts could also have a pro-acquittal bias. Given that no one has suggested such a phenomenon in Japan, we ignore the possibility here.

9. Though one can overstate the point. Prosecutors ultimately answer to politicians, and politicians who do not keep their prosecutors in line will—all else equal—do worse at the ballot box. A major function of judicial review of prosecutors, however, is to aid politicians (and ultimately voters) in monitoring prosecutors to make sure they only bring strong cases. Without that review, politicians would have to use more direct monitoring or rely on complaints from the people prosecuted, which is not an unbiased source of information.

B. Prosecution Budgets
1. The Argument

One need not posit differences in prosecutorial clairvoyance or scruples to suggest that Japanese and American courts might differ in their ratios of innocent to guilty defendants. Instead, one need only show a difference in budgets. Suppose, as seems likely, a prosecutor promotes his career by convicting defendants. A win helps. A loss is at best neutral, but even then has the opportunity cost of time wasted that might have been used to obtain more convictions.

How does a prosecutor win cases? Obviously, he could try to be brilliant, experienced, and prepared. He could also, however, just prosecute easy cases. By only filing cases with overwhelming evidence, he could avoid ever losing. If averse to even a small chance of losing, he could offer such generous plea bargains that no rational defendant would ever plead innocent.

Things are not so simple, of course. Given the usual bureaucratic structures, a prosecutor cannot maximize his current conviction rate by prosecuting one easy larceny case each year and dropping everything else brought to his desk. He must at least keep busy, and busy with more than one case a year, because he also faces pressure from police and public to convict as many criminals as possible.[10]

Even given these pressures, a prosecutor will have strong incentives to prosecute mostly strong cases. Any prosecutor in any system has more cases than he has time to handle.[11] Indeed, if that were not the case, the government would proceed to save money by reducing the number of prosecutors until it

10. In Japan, this pressure is formalized in prosecution review commissions, each of which is made up of eleven randomly chosen citizens who hold hearings on nonindictments and issue nonbinding recommendations to prosecutors. There are 207 such commissions, serving for six-month terms. Between 1949 and 1989 they held 77,000 hearings for 22 million nonindictments, a rate of .3 percent (West 1992: 697–98). The commissions recommended indictment in only about 7 percent of cases they heard, and only about 20 percent of these resulted in changed decisions by prosecutors (ibid., 702). The commissions are similar to German "motions for judicial decisions" (Jescheck 1970). The United States has only a weak equivalent, the statutes that in a few states allow private persons to challenge prosecutorial inaction (Green 1988). Perhaps Japan, with its lower prosecution rates, has more need of a formal check on prosecutorial discretion. See also Goodman 1986 and Ishimatsu 1989.

11. This is not accidental. Any justice system in which prosecutors have the resources to prosecute every possible case is grossly overfunded. It is more efficient to prosecute only a fraction of cases, and usually only the strongest. If a criminal cannot determine in advance whether he will be one of those prosecuted, such a system preserves deterrence and reduces costs. This is one corollary of the large-punishment-with-low-probability theory of Becker (1968).

did become the case. Rationally, a prosecutor will turn to his strongest cases first. In exceptional circumstances, he will try evidentially weak cases involving politically visible or particularly heinous crimes. Yet even then he will start with the most straightforward political or heinous cases and move to the more problematic ones only as time permits.[12]

Japanese prosecutors face particularly stark incentives to win cases. Like the judges, prosecutors are part of a national bureaucracy. Within it, some posts are prestigious and some are not. Every two years, prosecutors find themselves moved from post to post on the basis of their performance. Whether they move to a better post or worse depends on that performance, and according to many observers, losing a case is a sure path to demotion. As one Tokyo prosecutor put it, "[p]rosecutors regard acquittal as a very serious problem. . . . Each prosecutor examines each case very, very carefully, and if he doubts that it's a strong case or if there are extenuating circumstances he doesn't indict" (Mayer 1984: 119). The sociologist David Ted Johnson (1996: 499) made the connection between career failure and acquittals more explicitly: "[p]rosecutors found to be 'negligently' responsible for acquittals pay heavy fines in this currency of status" within the Ministry of Justice.

A prosecutor's career does not depend on his standing with people who look only at a few summary statistics. That may well be the case with state prosecutors in the United States, whose careers often depend on voters for whom the prosecutor's race is not the most important on a ballot. Those prosecutors do worry heavily about conviction rates and high-profile cases at election time, because voters do not devote time to a careful study of their careers. In Japan, however, the Ministry of Justice evaluates a prosecutor both on the abilities he demonstrates in particular cases and on the number of people he convicts. As a result, a Japanese prosecutor has less reason to care about his success rate per se than an elected prosecutor in the United States. Instead, his position more closely resembles that of an assistant U.S. district attorney, an appointed official whose career depends on evaluation by professionals in his field.

Given this dynamic, if prosecutorial offices try to maximize the number of convictions, then one with a lower budget (Japan, as we suggest below) may have a higher conviction rate than one with a greater budget (the United

12. There is, of course, a trade-off between ease of prosecution and seriousness of the offense, as explored more fully in Posner 1998: sec. 22.3. The prosecutor who just wants to win will not prosecute murders (which elicit heavy spending on defense) or fraud (which has complicated elements of proof). Even prosecutors who focus on the most serious classes of crimes, however, will tend to start with the easiest cases in each class and move to harder ones as budget and time permit.

States). Because of the severe resource constraints, the leaner office will have time to prosecute only the most egregious cases. In the extreme, a resource-starved office would only be able to prosecute one case a year, but have a conviction rate of 100 percent. Given more generous resources, a fatter office would move to prosecute riskier cases too, and its conviction rate would drop.[13] This is not because the prosecutor is trying to maximize his conviction rate—the fatter office would always have the higher conviction rate if that were true. It is because trying to put more criminals behind bars will result in more acquittals as well as more convictions.

2. Comparative Statistics

Consider a few back-of-the-envelope comparisons between Japan and the United States.[14] Japan employs about twelve hundred prosecutors.[15] The United States, with about twice the population, employs about thirty-two thousand prosecutors—almost twenty-five times as many.[16]

Japan does have much less crime than the United States. Does this explain why it employs so many fewer prosecutors? Each year, police in the United States clear about 14 million crimes by arrest, excluding traffic

13. See generally Posner 1998: sec. 22.3, 1990: 216. Take the independent special prosecutors in the United States such as Lawrence Walsh and Kenneth Starr. With enormous budgets, they can afford to indict people who may be guilty but are far less obviously guilty than the typical defendant tried on burglary or auto theft charges. Their low conviction rates reflect this.

14. The calculations that follow rely on the following sources. On the United States, see U.S. Dept. of Commerce 1996: 323, 333; U.S. Dept. of Justice 1996. On Japan, see Watanabe et al. 1997: 110; Homusho 1996: 402–3, 411–13, 430–31. The resource shortage in Japan is rightly noted in Haley 1991: ch. 6. Johnson (1996: 84) claims that Japanese prosecutors are not overworked, but primarily because he calculates indictments per prosecutor rather than arrests per prosecutor.

15. Watanabe et al. (1997: 110) report that as of 1996, there was one chief general prosecutor, one vice chief general prosecutor, eight chief prosecutors, 1,198 prosecutors, and 919 assistant prosecutors. Prosecutors must generally be graduates of the Legal Research and Training Institute (LRTI), but assistant prosecutors, who serve only in the Summary Courts, can be former bureaucrats. Kensatsu cho ho (Prosecutorial Office Act), Law No. 61 of 1947, §§ 16, 18. For the argument that one should add assistant prosecutors to these figures, see Saxonhouse 2002.

16. Carol Defrances and Greg Steadman (1998) of the U.S. Bureau of Justice Statistics report that there were 26,170 local prosecutors in 1996. Federal U.S. Attorney offices employed 4,892 attorneys in 1999 (Department of Justice, http://www.usdoj.gov/jmd/2001summary/BSpage5.pdf [August 14, 2001]). That sums to 31,062. In addition, state governments employ prosecutors in the offices of the attorneys general to handle appeals of cases initially brought by local prosecutors, for example. Guessing that there are about a thousand of these yields the total of thirty-two thousand in the text.

To gauge how overworked prosecutors are, it would also be useful to know the size and quality of their support staffs. Paralegals in the United States, assistant prosecutors in Japan, and police personnel in both countries potentially reduce prosecutor workloads considerably. Given the difficulty of measuring this, and the fact that in this context (unlike, say, in corporate legal practice) litigation (which requires attorneys) is central, we simply use the number of attorneys for our calculations.

offenses.[17] Given that there are thirty-two thousand prosecutors, that comes to 438 crimes per prosecutor. In contrast, Japanese police clear about 1.4 million Criminal Code violations per year.[18] This comes to 1,166 crimes per prosecutor. Crime is low in Japan, but the number of prosecutors is even lower.

What data we have seems to show that differences in prosecution rates reflect these differences in workload.[19] In 1994, state courts in the United States convicted 870,000 people of a felony, and the federal courts another 44,000. Given the conviction rates cited earlier, prosecutors must have brought felony charges against slightly more than 1 million defendants. If we use the FBI's definition of 2.4 million "index crime" arrests as a rough indicator of the number of felony arrests, we obtain a 42 percent prosecution/arrest ratio for felonies.[20] In Japan, by contrast, of the 919,000 people arrested for Criminal Code violations in 1995, prosecutors filed charges against a scant 17.5 percent.[21] Not much weight can be put on the U.S. figures because of data problems—index crimes both include some misdemeanors and exclude some felonies, and

17. In 1999 in the United States there were 14,031,070 nontraffic crimes cleared by arrest. *Sourcebook of Criminal Justice Statistics Online,* http://www.albany.edu/sourcebook/1995/pdf/t41.pdf (August 14, 2001). This figure is mostly taken from reports of local police departments, with estimates made for jurisdictions that failed to report. Although it excludes most traffic offenses, it includes 1,511,300 arrests for drunk driving.

18. In 1995 there were 2,435,000 Criminal Code crimes known to police, 1,406,000 cases cleared, and 970,000 people arrested. Homusho 1996: 406. The last two figures differ because some people are arrested for committing more than one crime. The figure for cases cleared seems most similar to the American standard published statistic "cleared by arrest." Despite its name, the U.S. figure does include cases cleared without arrest, if the police "identified the offender, possess enough evidence to support arrest, and identify the offender's location." See U.S. Federal Bureau of Investigation, *Crime in the United States—1999,* "SECTION III: Crime Index Offenses Cleared," http://www.fbi.gov/ucr/Cius_99/99crime/99cius3.pdf (September 5, 2001).

There are certainly many offenses that police refer to prosecutors for possible prosecution for which no arrest is made. In 1978, for example, there were 1,136,698 thefts known to police in Japan. Of these, 599,309 were "cleared," meaning the police had identified the likely offender or decided no crime had in fact been committed. For those, there were 231,403 offenders. Of these offenders, 62,540 were dropped by the police, 132,073 were referred to prosecutors without arrests, and 36,790 resulted in arrests by bench warrant or otherwise. George 1984: 52.

19. The figures in this paragraph are from Homusho 1996: 432; U.S. Dept. of Commerce 1996: tabs. 316, 323; U.S. Dept. of Justice 1996, 1997.

20. Similar calculations yield prosecution/arrest ratios in the United States of 60 percent for drug trafficking; 45 percent for robbery; 44 percent for burglary; and 16 percent for aggravated assault.

21. Note that the lower prosecution budget in Japan is not an indication that either the United States or Japan is behaving suboptimally. Lower prosecution rates have the cost of less crime deterrence, but the benefits of lower cost and fewer innocent people prosecuted. We discuss this issue more fully in section III.E. Japanese prosecutors can choose to suspend prosecution in selected cases, by which they hope to signal to the public (how credibly is another question) that they believe the suspect is guilty even though they decided to forgo prosecution. Foote 1986.

felony arrests are often plea bargained down to misdemeanor convictions—and the Japanese figures include both serious and nonserious crimes.[22] This is some indication, however, that Japanese prosecutors are more willing to let arrested offenders off the hook if the evidence is not overwhelming.

C. PROSECUTORIAL BUDGETS AND INCENTIVES

1. Clarification

Our argument that an increased budget will reduce conviction rates does not apply under all circumstances. In appendix D we use a formal model to unravel the connection between budgets and conviction rates.[23] For two reasons, we believe that a prosecutor in Japan who is given a greater budget would tend to spend it on prosecuting more cases rather than on prosecuting his existing cases more intensely. The result would be that an increase in budgets would decrease the conviction rate.

First, as just discussed, Japanese prosecutors try only a very small fraction of the cases forwarded to them from the police. The rest they simply drop unprosecuted. Hence, they face a large pool of cases they can add to their docket. Second, in bench trial jurisdictions like Japan, the investments a prosecutor makes in a case should earn high returns initially, quickly raising the expected conviction rate from near zero to a comfortable probability. Yet they will run into sharply diminishing marginal returns thereafter. After investing enough effort in a case to make the basic showing, the U.S. prosecutor devotes much of the rest of his time to such tasks as *voir dire* in jury selection, showmanship before the jury, or simply explaining to the jury the basics of crime and criminal life. By contrast, a Japanese prosecutor argues before professional judges. He must present the facts and the law, but how he presents them (a factor with otherwise enormous potential for polishing and artistry) matters less.

Let us put this argument slightly differently. Japanese prosecutors currently take only a small fraction of their cases, and leave a large number of crimes unprosecuted. This suggests they leave unpursued many cases that they could try if only they had more resources. If given a larger budget, they would need to choose between prosecuting more aggressively the cases they already try, or taking additional cases. Given the high conviction rates they currently

22. The data problem is that the FBI collects U.S. arrest data by offense, not seriousness of the offense, so a larceny could be either a misdemeanor or a felony, and the Department of Justice statistics exclude misdemeanor convictions.

23. Surprisingly little work has been done on the economic analysis of prosecutor behavior. One exception is the recent working paper by Glaeser, Kessler, and Piehl (2000), which focuses on the interaction between choices of federal and state prosecutors.

obtain, we doubt they would opt to spend the extra resources on the existing cases. Instead, we suspect they would turn to the cases they currently drop. Given that they will tend to try their best cases first, those additional cases will disproportionately be weaker than the cases they now prosecute.

2. Qualifications

What of the Priest–Klein (1984) hypothesis outlined in chapter 5: that because of settlement and plea bargaining, litigated verdict rates do not reflect the distribution of liability or guilt in the underlying population of cases? The point is simply irrelevant to our discussion. The effect of prosecutorial poverty in Japan is to remove the credibility from the prosecutor's threats to try hard cases. If the threat is not credible, then only the obviously guilty will plead guilty. Accordingly, if a prosecutor has only a small budget, *both* the plea-bargained and the contested cases will be disproportionately selected from defendants who are clearly guilty. The rest of the cases will be neither settled nor tried, but simply dropped.

Nor does it matter whether the average success *rate* at trial enters directly into the prosecutor's utility function as a separate argument from the expected *number* of convictions. This is plausible. Particularly when running for office, American prosecutors do like to boast about the percentage of their cases that result in convictions. In a typical press release for a local prosecutor's race, for example, we read: "Attorney Thomas Broderick Jr. will formally announce Tuesday that he is a candidate for the Democratic nomination for Madison County prosecutor. . . . He was chief deputy for Prosecutor William F. Lawler Jr. for more than seven years, claiming a 98 percent personal conviction rate on cases ranging from drugs to murder."[24]

That the conviction rate enters directly in a prosecutor's utility function, however, still would not eliminate the effects of budget increases that we have described. In allocating a budget of any size, a prosecutor would slant his allocation toward improving his percentage won, but if he were given an extra yen, he would split it between his two objectives of improving his percentage and increasing his number of cases won. Increasing the number of cases would be a better use of the money under the circumstances we have described above, even if it lowered his conviction rate.

An interesting implication is that criminal conviction rates should be much higher than civil plaintiff victory rates, particularly in U.S. state courts. The reason has nothing to do with jury unanimity or burden of proof. Such requirements will not affect the percentage of trials that end in convictions,

24. "Attorney Says He'll Be Candidate for Prosecutor," *Indianapolis Star,* 17 January 1998, at N02.

since prosecutors will take them into account in deciding whether to pursue a case. Rather, criminal conviction rates are higher than civil plaintiff win rates because elected prosecutors who care about conviction rates have more reason than plaintiffs to avoid losing at trial.

III. Empirics

A. INTRODUCTION

If prosecutors in Japan prosecute a higher percentage of guilty defendants than in the United States, higher conviction rates will result under unbiased adjudication. In this section, we ask whether the Japanese judicial bureaucracy does reward unbiased accuracy, or instead rewards convictions. We first explain our data and variables (section B), then turn to our regression results (section C). We conclude by reexamining the details of our data (section D).

B. DATA AND VARIABLES
1. The Test

To explore whether Japanese judges face biased incentives to convict, we use a simple test. We take all 455 District Court criminal case opinions published in 1976 or 1979 (our reference years), and identify the deciding judges. These are the same years we used in chapter 5 for our study of tax cases.[25] We divide our judges into two groups according to whether they acquitted a defendant in one of the reference years. We further divide those who acquitted a defendant into those who did so as part of a three-judge panel and those who did so as a single judge. Concurrently, we also divide all judges who had a case appealed according to whether the appeal resulted in a reversal or an affirmance.

For each of our judges, we measure the attractiveness of the jobs he held during the ten years after the relevant reference year. Holding constant the usual control variables, we then test whether an acquittal led to a worse job posting.

---

25. We dropped those cases that did not give the name of the deciding judge (fourteen convictions, six acquittals), those cases whose outcome was hard to code (eleven cases), and those judges who did not appear in our career records (they were probably prosecutors seconded to the courts—an occasional practice). In addition, we dropped those judges who had been appointed less than a year before the reference year, and those who quit less than two years after the reference year (about twenty judges). For the two judges for whom we lacked the information on *Flunks,* we used the sample-wide mean.

We also examined the High Court opinions in 1976 and 1979 and traced back the judges who wrote the District Court opinions. Perhaps because of the wider variation in years written, however, the results are more haphazard and inconclusive. We thus limit ourselves to the more uniform sample of District Court opinions written in 1976 or 1979.

Table 6.2 Dependent and Control Variables—Summary

A. Dependent Variables

Post_Good_Jobs	The percentage of time during the decade after the crucial opinion in which a judge held prestigious appointments.
Post_Bad_Jobs	The percentage of time during the decade after the opinion in which a judge was in a branch office.

B. Control Variables

Prior_Good_Jobs	Equivalent to Post_Good_Jobs for the decade before the opinion.
Prior_Bad_Jobs	Equivalent to Post_Bad_Jobs for the decade before the opinion.
Seniority	The number of years between the opinion and the year a judge graduated from the LRTI.
Flunks	The estimated number of years (based on birth year) between college graduation and entrance to the LRTI.
Elite_College	1 if a judge graduated from either the University of Tokyo or the University of Kyoto; 0 otherwise.
Opinions/Yr	A judge's average productivity (measured in published opinions per year on the bench) for the decade before the opinion.
1st_Tokyo	1 if a judge started at the Tokyo District Court; 0 otherwise.
YJL	1 if a judge was a member of the Young Jurists League in 1969; 0 otherwise.

Table 6.3 Criminal Decisions—Summary Statistics

	Minimum	Median	Mean	Maximum
Prior_Good_Jobs	0	0	.078	.970
Post_Good_Jobs	0	.27	.341	1
Prior_Bad_Jobs	0	.20	.204	1
Post_Bad_Jobs	0	.20	.234	1
Seniority	2	13	13.5	29
Flunks	0	3	4.22	17
Elite_College	0	0	.321	1
1st_Tokyo	0	0	.112	1
Opinions/Yr	0	.85	1.34	14.11
YJL	0	0	.109	1
Any_Acq	0	0	.271	1
Solo_Acq	0	0	.053	1
Acq_Rev	0	0	.034	1
Acq_Aff	0	0	.040	1
Con_Rev	0	0	.050	1
Con_Aff	0	0	.150	1

NOTE: $n = 321$.

2. Variables

We define several new variables relating to whether a judge acquits defendants, and then construct the usual job-quality and control variables as well. The new variables are described below, along with a quick summary of our standard job quality and control variables in table 6.2. We include summary statistics in table 6.3.

Any_Acq: 1 if a judge participated in an opinion acquitting a defendant (or accepting part of a defendant's argument), 0 otherwise.

Solo_Acq: The same as *Any_Acq,* but excluding acquittals by three-judge panels.

Acq_Rev: 1 if a judge participated in an opinion acquitting a defendant (as defined above) that was reversed by a High Court (or where the High Court increased the penalty on appeal), 0 otherwise.[26]

Acq_Aff: 1 if a judge participated in an opinion acquitting a defendant that was affirmed by a High Court, 0 otherwise.

Con_Rev: 1 if a judge participated in an opinion convicting a defendant (or rejecting all of the defendant's claims) that was reversed by a High Court (or where the High Court reduced the penalty on appeal), 0 otherwise.

Con_Aff: 1 if a judge participated in an opinion convicting a defendant that was affirmed by a High Court and has values of zero for *Acq_Rev, Acq_Aff,* and *Con_Rev,* 0 otherwise.

C. RESULTS
1. Introduction

In table 6.4, we report the results of two sets of regressions. Regressions A and B use *Any_Acq* as the key explanatory variable; regressions C and D use *Solo_Acq.* Within each set, the first column shows the regressions with *Post_Good_Jobs* as the dependent variable, and the second with *Post_Bad_Jobs.*

2. Job Quality and Control Variables

The job quality and control variables generate results consistent with that shown in previous chapters. *Prior_Good_Jobs* is positively correlated with *Post_Good_Jobs,* though it does not quite reach statistical significance, and *Prior_Bad_Jobs* is significantly correlated with *Post_Bad_Jobs.* Those judges who spent more time with prestigious administrative responsibilities in the 1970s spent more time with such responsibilities in the 1980s. Those who spent more time in branch offices in the 1970s spent still more time there in the 1980s.

Seniority is positively and significantly correlated with *Post_Good_Jobs,* and negatively and significantly correlated with *Post_Bad_Jobs:* the more senior the judge, the more time he spent with administrative responsibilities and the less time in branch offices. *Flunks* is negatively and significantly correlated with *Post_Good_Jobs:* the fewer the times a judge failed the LRTI entrance exam, the more time he spent with administrative responsibilities. *1st_Tokyo* is

26. Japanese courts do not consider this double jeopardy (Ramseyer and Nakazato 1999: 175).

Table 6.4 The Effect of Acquittals on Judicial Careers

	Dependent Variables			
	A. Post_Good_Jobs	B. Post_Bad_Jobs	C. Post_Good_Jobs	D. Post_Bad_Jobs
Prior_Good_Jobs	.137		.130	
	(1.51)		(1.41)	
Prior_Bad_Jobs		.201**		.188**
		(2.87)		(2.66)
Seniority	.032**	−.014**	.032**	−.014**
	(10.90)	(6.62)	(10.97)	(6.82)
Flunks	−.010*	.002	−.010*	.002
	(1.86)	(0.63)	(1.75)	(0.62)
Elite_College	−.001	−.036	.007	−.030
	(0.04)	(1.21)	(0.20)	(1.00)
1st_Tokyo	.088	−.081*	.105	−.088**
	(1.42)	(2.16)	(1.62)	(2.39)
Opinions/Yr	.004	−.003	.003	−.002
	(0.38)	(0.39)	(0.32)	(0.23)
YJL	.006	.097*	.006	.097*
	(0.12)	(1.87)	(0.12)	(1.87)
Any_Acq	.025	.052		
	(0.65)	(1.50)		
Solo_Acq			−.104	.140*
			(1.72)	(1.88)
Pseudo R^2	.31	.16	.31	.17
# Censored	(132, 28)	(134, 5)	(132, 28)	(134, 5)
$(y < 0, y > 1)$				

NOTE: $n = 321$. These are tobit regressions. The marginal effects for a judge at the median values of the independent variables are followed by the absolute value of z-statistics in parentheses. The regressions also included intercepts, not reported here.

* Significant at the 90 percent confidence level using a two-tailed test.

** Significant at the 95 percent confidence level using a two-tailed test.

negatively and significantly correlated with *Post_Bad_Jobs:* judges who began their careers at the Tokyo District Court spent less time in branch offices in the 1980s. Last, *YJL* is positively and significantly correlated with *Post_Bad_Jobs:* those judges affiliated with the left-wing Young Jurists League in 1969 were still spending more time in branch offices in the 1980s.

3. Opinions

(a) Acquittals in General

To test whether judges face biased career incentives in criminal cases, consider first regressions A and B. These test whether a judge involved in any published opinion acquitting a defendant incurred a career penalty over the next decade. The results are inconclusive. The coefficient on *Any_Acq* is positive in the *Post_Bad_Jobs* regression, but is not significant at the 10 percent level. In the *Post_Good_Jobs* regressions, the coefficient is not even in the predicted direction.

(b) Solo Acquittals

The data include convictions and acquittals authored both by three-judge panels (107 cases) and single-judge panels (317). This loosely mirrors the way courts decide criminal cases more generally. Of all cases (published and unpublished) decided in 1994, three-judge panels decided 7.6 percent (3,751 cases), and single judges decided 92.4 percent (45,529) (Saiko 1994: tab. 29).

By law, three-judge panels must decide the most serious criminal cases.[27] Single judges generally decide the rest. Although the assigning mechanism depends on the local court, commonly a minor incoming criminal case will go directly to a single judge, who will then decide it himself. If it is unusually hard, he will route it to a three-judge panel.

In general, if prosecutors seldom prosecuted obviously innocent defendants (as suggested in section II), if judges were fair and unbiased, and if single judges handled the most straightforward cases themselves, then cases decided by single judges would show lower acquittal rates than those handled by three-judge panels. The data are consistent with this hypothesis. Among the published opinions, 33 percent of the panel opinions were acquittals, but only 7 percent of the single-judge opinions. Of all 1994 cases published and unpublished, 1.2 percent of all panel opinions were acquittals, but only 0.09 percent of all single-judge opinions.[28]

Yet, one should not be so sanguine. Consider regressions C and D, in which we test whether a single judge who acquits a defendant incurs a career penalty. According to regression D, a judge who acquits alone does indeed suffer—a result that is significant at better than the 5 percent level. And consider the size of the punishment. The marginal effect of .140 on *Solo-Acq* in regression D of table 6.4 suggests that a judge who acquits a defendant will spend an extra 1.4 years in branch offices. It can be calculated using the tobit coefficients that a median judge (with $Solo\_Acq = 0$) can expect to spend .23 of the next decade in branch offices; an otherwise median judge with $Solo\_Acq = 1$ can expect therefore to spend .37 of the next decade there.

The puzzle is what to make of this. On the one hand, the difference between the not-quite-significant results for *Any_Acq* and the strongly significant ones for *Solo_Acq* could reflect the fog involved in collegial panels. Many of the acquitting panels might have been split. Because Japanese lower courts never

27. Saibansho ho (Courts Act), Law no. 59 of 1947, § 26.
28. Saiko 1994: tab. 29. The published acquittal rates are higher both because acquittals are generally more newsworthy to commercial case reporters, and because the unpublished convictions mostly involve uncontested proceedings.

publish dissents (though the Supreme Court does), we would not know which of the judges favored acquittal and which opposed it. Because the judges themselves knew, however, the internal personnel reports may reflect that information. If so, then the Secretariat might well punish only the two judges who favored acquittal. Accordingly, perhaps the contrast between the two sets of regressions simply results from the fog in the *Any_Acq* variable.

Alternatively, the difference between regressions B and D might reflect a policy mandating that judges forward hard cases to a multijudge panel.[29] If so, then perhaps the Secretariat had no intent to punish judges who acquit after group deliberation. Instead, it wanted to punish those who flouted court policy and refused to forward ambiguous cases to three-judge panels. Perhaps, in short, the Secretariat did not punish judges for acquitting; it punished them for ignoring case-routing policy.

(c) Reversals

The *Solo_Acq* results thus leave a puzzle: whether the career penalties paid by judges who acquit on single-judge panels reflect penalties for acquitting or penalties for not forwarding hard cases to collegial panels. Because even a Secretariat with a pro-conviction bias might see some acquittals as proper and not want to reward all convictions, we explore the careers of judges who find their cases reversed. If the Secretariat punishes only for case-routing violations rather than acquittals, then judges who find acquittals reversed should do no worse than those who find convictions reversed—*holding constant* the effect of *Solo_Acq*.

To explore these issues, we divide all appealed cases into four groups: acquittals reversed, acquittals affirmed, convictions reversed, and convictions affirmed. We then rerun the regressions with *Post_Good_Jobs* and *Post_Bad_Jobs* as the dependent variables. As the coefficients on the opinion variables were insignificant in the *Post_Good_Jobs* regressions in table 6.4, we focus on the *Post_Bad_Jobs* regressions. We report the results in table 6.5.

In regression A we show the result a judge faces if he finds an acquittal overturned: over the next ten years, he will spend substantially more time in branch offices (2.26 years). The result is more than significant at the 5 percent level. By itself, regression A does not necessarily show a pro-conviction bias. Instead, it could reflect a general Secretariat policy of punishing judges who make mistakes, with a reversal indicating that the trial judge was wrong.

29. Note that the Secretariat will, quite rationally, always hold strong priors that a prosecuted suspect is guilty. This follows from the prosecutor's incentive to economize on his resources by only prosecuting guilty suspects. This idea is explored in Rasmusen 1995.

Table 6.5 The Effect of Appeals on Judicial Careers

| | Dependent Variables | | |
	A. Post_Bad_Jobs	B. Post_Bad_Jobs	C. Post_Bad_Jobs
Prior_Bad_Jobs	.208 (2.95)**	.204 (2.96)**	.187 (2.75)**
Seniority	−.014 (7.00)**	−.014 (6.93)**	−.014 (6.87)**
Flunks	.003 (0.75)	.003 (0.71)	.002 (0.62)
Elite_College	−.038 (1.25)	−.041 (1.38)	−.041 (1.43)
1st_Tokyo	−.086 (2.30)**	−.084 (2.34)**	−.090 (2.64)**
Opinions/Yr	−.002 (0.28)	−.001 (0.16)	−.0005 (0.06)
YJL	.105 (2.00)**	.106 (2.04)**	.105 (2.04)**
Acq_Rev	.226 (2.29)**	.241 (2.43)**	.211 (2.14)**
Acq_Aff		.071 (0.90)	.071 (0.91)
Con_Rev		.001 (0.02)	.007 (0.11)
Con_Aff		.057 (1.35)	.064 (1.52)
Solo_Acq			.122 (1.67)*
Pseudo R^2	.17	.17	.19

NOTE: $n = 321$. These are tobit regressions. The marginal effects for a judge at the median values of the independent variables are followed by the absolute value of z-statistics in parentheses. The regressions also included intercepts, not reported here. In each regression, 134 observations are censored because of the bound of 0 and 5 because of the bound of 1 on the left-hand-side variable.
* Significant at the 90 percent confidence level using a two-tailed test.
** Significant at the 95 percent confidence level using a two-tailed test.

Accordingly, in regression B we use all four appeal-related variables. Here the results do show a bias: the Secretariat only punishes judges who find their acquittals reversed. Only the coefficient on *Acq_Rev* is either large or significant. In terms of judicial bias, the relevant question is whether the coefficient on *Acq_Rev* is greater than that on *Con_Rev*. And indeed it is.

It remains possible that the penalty paid by judges who find their acquittals reversed merely reflects the penalty paid by single-panel judges who (to continue the earlier argument) failed to follow the policy of forwarding hard cases to three-judge panels. Given that the correlation between *Acq_Rev* and *Solo_Acq* is only .11, we were skeptical. Yet to test for that phenomenon directly, in regression C we include both the four appeal-related variables and *Solo_Acq*.

The results in regression C confirm the independent bias against those who write reversed acquittals. Both *Acq_Rev* and *Solo_Acq* are independently significant. Holding constant the effect of *Solo_Acq,* judges who find their acquittals reversed still suffer larger penalties over the next decade. The median judge had no acquittals reversed or solo acquittals. The coefficients from regression C imply (after calculations omitted here) that such a median judge could expect to spend .22 of the next decade in branch offices. For a judge with a three-judge panel acquittal reversed, the prediction rises to .42, an extra two years in branch offices over the decade. For a judge with a solo acquittal that was later appealed and affirmed, the prediction is .44. This is surprising. A judge is punished heavily for a solo acquittal even if his judgment is later confirmed by an appellate court. Rather less surprising, a judge who both acquits in a solo trial and is later reversed has a predicted percentage of time in branch offices of .59—over three and a half years more than the median judge.

D. ACQUITTALS IN DETAIL

If, as tables 6.4 and 6.5 imply, Japanese judges face skewed incentives to convict, then we have no assurance that the high conviction rate reflects a high percentage of guilty defendants (row a in table 6.1). Instead, since judges would be rubber-stamping prosecutorial choices, prosecutors would have less incentive to screen cases, and Japanese judges may well be convicting innocent defendants regularly (row d in table 6.1).

Unfortunately, we have very few acquittals, and the cases ending in acquittals could well raise other characteristics that the Secretariat sought to punish. To explore this potential omitted variable problem, we examine the $Solo\_Acq$ and Acq_Rev cases in more detail. More specifically, we take all judges with $Solo\_Acq = 1$ or $Acq\_Rev = 1$ and compare the time they actually spent in branch offices in the decade after the opinion (observed $Post\_Bad\_Jobs$) with the time they would have spent (given their other personal characteristics) had they not acquitted (predicted $Post\_Bad\_Jobs$). If the latter (predicted $Post\_Bad\_Jobs$) exceeds the former (observed $Post\_Bad\_Jobs$), then by definition the judge suffered no punishment.

Tables 6.6 and 6.7 summarize our results, and confirm our concerns. The Secretariat, they imply, punishes acquitting judges primarily when they acquit in politically sensitive cases or misconstrue statutes in ways that raise questions of judicial ability. Of the judges punished in table 6.6, Hirayu and Ogawa acquitted defendants for violating the statutory ban on door-to-door canvassing. As noted in chapter 2, these were highly visible politically charged cases that regularly resulted in judicial punishments. Fujita acquitted leftists for beating a police officer during a riot on the grounds that the police were making illegal arrests. Torai let off a violent mobster by interpreting broadly the scope of an earlier summary proceeding that generated a trivial fine. Most of the other punished judges acquitted defendants on grounds of statutory interpretation: what constitutes mental capacity, whether consensual sex can be statutory rape, whether the statute of limitations has run, or when negligence rises to manslaughter. In none of the cases where judges' careers seemed to suffer did a judge rule "The defendant didn't do it."

Table 6.7 suggests much the same phenomenon. Again, one judge (Hirayu) held the door-to-door canvassing ban unconstitutional. Koike, Yamazaki, and

Table 6.6 Judges with Solo Acquittals

Judge Name	A. Observed Post_Bad_Jobs	B. Predicted Post_Bad_Jobs If No Solo Acquittal
Kunio Ogawa	1.00	.33
Politician acquitted of violating campaign limits, on grounds that limits are unconstitutional.		
Kazumichi Hirai	.90	.30
Defendant acquitted, on grounds of mental capacity.		
Yoshito Morita	.87	.40
Defendant construction supervisor acquitted of manslaughter charge for negligently leaving construction site, where negligence not shown.		
Masato Hirayu	.83	.27
Politician acquitted of violating campaign limits, on grounds that limits are unconstitutional.		
Yasuhiro Igaki	.80	.39
Prosecution dismissed, on basis of interpretation of statute of limitations.		
Narishige Futakami	.70	.26
Allegedly largely rehabilitated juvenile ordered released.		
Kenji Fujita	.60	.27
Rioters acquitted of battery of riot police, on grounds that police were acting illegally in making arrests.		
Shigeo Yamamori	.60	.28
Defendant acquitted of injuring a minor, where defendant had consensual sex with sixteen-year-old.		
Osamu Okushi	.43	.33
Juvenile released from correctional facility, where reliable guardian petitioned for custody.		
Yasuo Torai	.40	.26
Indictment of violent *yakuza* member dismissed, where series of violent batteries (perhaps mob discipline) were covered by summary proceeding on related charge leading to 100,000 yen ($330) fine.		
Satoshi Kataoka	.04	.02
Partial acquittal on grounds that crime B is lesser included offense to crime A.		
Kenichi Hiruma	.03	.17
Administrative traffic fine of juvenile vacated.		
Niro Shimada	.00	.04
Prosecution for fraud in commercial loan application dismissed, on grounds of inadequately specific indictment.		
Kazunobu Araya	.00	.06
Real estate broker acquitted of corporate tax fraud on factual grounds.		
Tetsuo Hirai	.00	.28
Construction firm acquitted of tax fraud on factual grounds.		
Ryujiro Sugiura	.00	.13
Upon petition of suspect, freer access to attorney ordered.		

(*cont.*)

Table 6.6 *(continued)*

Judge Name	A. Observed Post_Bad_Jobs	B. Predicted Post_Bad_Jobs If No Solo Acquittal
Yasushi Sato	.00	.27
Juvenile who confessed to burglary sent to juvenile detention instead of criminal system.		
Masaru Miyamoto	.00	.28
Prosecution dismissed in tax case (facts not clear).		

NOTE: Column A shows the proportion of bad jobs the judge received in the decade after his decision. Column B shows the prediction by OLS regression if the judge had no solo acquittals.

Table 6.7 Judges with Reversed Acquittals

Judge Name	A. Observed Post_Bad_Jobs	B. Predicted Post_Bad_Jobs If No Solo Acquittal
Masato Hirayu	.83	.00
Politician acquitted of violating campaign limits, on grounds that limits are unconstitutional. (See also table 6.6.)		
Yasuhiro Igaki	.80	.07
Prosecution dismissed, on basis of interpretation of statute of limitations. (See also table 6.6.)		
Yokichi Koike	.57	.13
Labor union activists acquitted of destroying property by posting signs on company building; held, property not damaged.		
Katsuyuki Ikeda	.48	.10
a. Defendant acquitted partially, based on exclusion of evidence obtained through unreliable confession. b. Defendant convicted of customs duty violations on primary counts; supplementary trial on additional counts held unconstitutional as cruel punishment.		
Ushio Yamazaki	.40	.00
See Koike case, above.		
Kizo Noguchi	.37	.00
See Koike case, above.		.
Seichi Omasa	.35	.00
See Ikeda cases a and b, above.		
Yasuhiro Morioka	.30	.02
Fraud prosecution dismissed on statutes of limitations grounds.		
Reiji Noma	.00	.00
See Morioka case, above.		
Kiyoshi Inoue	.00	.00
See Ikeda cases a and b, above.		
Tetsuo Hirai	.00	.00
Defendant acquitted, on grounds of mental capacity. (See also table 6.6.)		

NOTE: Column A shows the proportion of bad jobs the judge received in the decade after his decision. Column B shows the prediction by OLS regression if the judge had no acquittals that were solo or reversed. Negative numbers (possible because OLS is used instead of tobit) are replaced by 0.

Noguchi acquitted defendants of crimes involving labor unrest. Given the role that Socialists and Communists played in Japanese labor unions (especially public-sector unions), union cases can be very political and sometimes did result in punishments imposed on pro-labor judges.[30] Ikeda and Omasa invoked the exclusionary rule, which the Japanese Supreme Court has long viewed skeptically (Ramseyer and Nakazato 1999: 168–72). Only two other punished judges remain, and both acquitted on grounds that turned on the interpretation of the statute of limitations. Here too, none of the judges acquitted on the grounds that the government prosecuted the wrong man.[31]

More simply, the point is this: despite the economically and statistically significant coefficients in tables 6.4 and 6.5, the regressions provide no evidence that judges who second-guess whether the police and prosecutor found the right defendant suffer. Instead, the only evidence of punishment appears in nonroutine cases—cases where the judges arguably interpreted statutes wrongly or favored the leftist opposition.

E. THE POLITICAL ECONOMY OF CONVICTIONS

One remaining puzzle is why Japan and the United States differ so strikingly in their decisions of how much to spend on criminal prosecution. In both countries, politicians face competitive elections. Yet Japanese politicians hire so few prosecutors that they leave a majority of the people arrested for serious crimes unprosecuted. Politicians in the United States, on the other hand, hire so many that they prosecute even many cases they cannot win.

The Japanese system is the easier to explain. Assume, as seems plausible, that citizens in both countries want politicians to minimize crime subject to a budget constraint.[32] By this metric, Japanese politicians have done extraordinarily well. On the one hand, they have kept violent crime low. Murders run 1.6 per 100,000 population, compared to 10.1 in the United States. The Japanese rate is lower than the U.S. rate even correcting for the fraction of

30. For an empirical study finding evidence that Japanese judges were punished for taking positions opposed to that of the ruling Liberal Democratic Party in labor cases, see Kashimura (1991).

31. That most of the few acquittals are due to procedure rather than factual innocence is not special to our sample. Based on a government white paper, Kitamura (1993: 265) reported that in 1985, out of 2,493,721 accused persons brought to trial, the conviction rate was 99.88 percent, leaving 117 substantive acquittals and 2,788 acquittals on procedural grounds. He reported a similar pattern for 1989: a 99.91 percent conviction rate, 131 defendants declared not guilty, and 1,063 defendants acquitted on procedural grounds.

32. Citizens also want minimal error, of course. We have no reason to think the Japanese system has greater error than the United States, though that is of course partly the subject of this chapter. For a summary of the literature suggesting a high accuracy rate in the Japanese judiciary, see Johnson 1996: ch. 1.

young males in the population and the murders in the urban ghettos.[33] On the other hand, Japanese politicians have kept down the costs of law enforcement too. Not only do they use fewer prosecutors, they use fewer police. In the mid-1990s, Japan had 18 police officers per 10,000 population, while the U.S. rate was 24 per 10,000.[34] So the low budgets of Japanese prosecutors seem quite appropriate; the system is doing a good job of satisfying the voters' demand for crime control.

The U.S. system presents the harder puzzle. Why do American politicians win elections even though crime rates stay high and prosecutors waste resources bringing losing cases? In part, perhaps the answer lies in a constraint politicians cannot correct: the constitutional right to trial by jury. This right has two consequences. First, it raises the cost of deterrence. As novices, juries tend not to realize what all legal professionals know: that nearly all defendants prosecuted in modern democracies are guilty.[35] Probably, they are guilty of the crime charged but, if not, then at least of some similar crime. Indeed, for just that reason U.S. criminal defense lawyers routinely demand jury trials. And precisely because convictions are harder to obtain from juries, deterrence in the United States will always come at a higher price. High U.S. prosecution budgets cannot keep crime low, but reducing the budgets would let crime increase even further.

Second, the right to trial by jury gives prosecutors a private incentive to try more cases than is socially optimal. As explained in section I.C, the jury system increases the variance in the parties' estimates of the expected litigated verdict. In the process, it increases the fraction of civil disputes that go to trial, and that increased probability of trial raises the returns to trial expertise. Those increased returns, in turn, present prosecutors with an incentive to use their job to obtain the trial experience they cannot find in the large modern law firms dominated by massive cases. The jury trial right creates, in other words, the agency slack that induces U.S. prosecutors to litigate more cases than U.S. citizens would like.[36] The agency slack is costly, but it is a constitutionalized cost that politicians can do little to reduce.

33. Ramseyer and Nakazato 1999: 176–78 (1993 data). It is also noteworthy that murder rates in Japan have actually declined since the 1950s (ibid., 176). Japanese murder statistics include attempts, a point not noted in Ramseyer and Nakazato 1999.

34. For speculation about why the violent crime rate in Japan is so low, see ibid., ch. 7.

35. Not all, obviously. After all, *how* likely the defendants are to be guilty is exactly the issue we try to explore indirectly in this chapter. The implication here is that, holding constant the level of guilt within a given pool of defendants and the level of resources devoted to prosecution, the conviction rate for the pool will be higher in Japan than in the United States. Restated, part—though not all—of the reason for the high Japanese conviction rate is simply the absence of jury trials in Japan.

36. On why the returns to private practice are low in Japan despite the small number of lawyers (essentially, the ease with which one can circumvent the bar's monopoly on legal practice), see Ramseyer and Nakazato 1999: ch. 1.

The large increase in crime in the United States from 1960 to 2000 is clearly relevant to the politics of all this (though too large a topic to explore here). If we take it as given that the United States has a higher propensity toward crime (for whatever reason), then vote-maximizing politicians might reasonably decide to spend more on prosecution. Because crime rates are high enough to create severe social disruption, they may even reasonably decide to spend more on prosecutions *per crime*. By contrast, because crime reduction is subject to diminishing returns and increasing cost, Japanese politicians may conclude that further reducing crime from the already very low level is not worth the expense.

IV. Conclusion

Japanese courts convict. Courts convict in America too, of course, but in Japan they convict with a vengeance: over 99 percent of the time. Even in cases where the defendant contests his guilt, they convict over 98 percent of the time. Are courts convicting the guilty and innocent alike, or are prosecutors merely choosing the guiltiest defendants to try? Absent independent evidence of the guilt of the accused, we cannot directly tell.

In this chapter, we pursue indirect evidence on point. First, Japanese prosecutors are woefully understaffed. Tied as they are to a severe budget constraint, one might expect them to try only the most obviously guilty. Unbiased courts would then convict. The conviction rate would approach 100 percent, but only because most of the defendants were guilty. To return to our heuristic in table 6.1, Japan would fit best the case as described in row a.

Are Japanese courts unbiased? Initially, Japanese judges seem to face significantly skewed incentives: judges who acquit seem more likely to suffer a career penalty than those who convict. Yet a closer look at the judges punished for their acquittals suggests a classic omitted-variable problem, and returns us to our hypothesis about prosecutorial resources. The acquittals that generate apparent punishment are sometimes cases in which judges sided with opposition parties in politically charged cases, and otherwise cases in which the judges simply misinterpreted the law. Never is it a case in which the judge decided that the prosecutors had brought charges against the wrong man. Instead, we know from chapters 4 and 5 that the Japanese courts generally reward political reliability and legal accuracy—and the observed punishment simply reflects that broader phenomenon.

7

Toward a Party-Alternation Theory of Comparative Judicial Independence

In this book, we have focused on promotions as incentives. For promotions matter: carrots are as much incentives as sticks, and the withholding of a reward can be as effective as the infliction of a punishment. Even where members of an organization cannot be expelled or have their salaries reduced, if they care about future promotions they will work under the potential influence of whoever decides personnel policy. Thus, despite the rhetoric of independence, nations in whose courts judges start young and rise through the ranks depending on their talent and achievement leave an opening for political influence. We find that in one of those nations, Japan, this structure has indeed produced politically skewed incentives.

On the one hand, Japanese politicians offer parties to private quarrels fiercely independent judges. They do so because the independent judicial resolution of such disputes is a service voters value highly. On the other hand, when parties are locked in a dispute with the government, the calculus changes. Independent judges for private disputes are part—but only a part—of the portfolio of policies and services for which voters elected the politicians. Suppose the majority party were to keep judges rigorously independent of itself not just in private quarrels, but also in public-law disputes. If judges bore personal preferences that diverged from those of the majority electorate, they could use their independence to stymie the delivery of the policies the majority wanted. As a result, the majority party will be strongly tempted to use its power to control the judiciary: where a dispute involves politically charged issues, judges may need to worry about more than just what they think the law says or what they personally would like to see happen.

To be sure, in some public-law disputes even Japanese politicians keep judges independent. As we found in our analysis of tax disputes, in mundane administrative disputes they can and do use independent judges to help moni-tor their bureaucratic agents. These disputes seldom raise major issues of policy but often involve misbehaving bureaucrats. By helping to keep bureaucrats in line, independent judges help politicians deliver what they promised to the voters (McCubbins and Schwartz 1984). In ordinary criminal disputes too, majority politicians apparently subject their judges to unbiased incentives. And we do not contradict the conventional wisdom that Japanese politicians refrain from using such crude methods as telling judges how to write particular opinions or firing judges who disagree with them. The political influence is more subtle.

In finding that Japanese politicians give judges some independence but retain indirect political influence, we raise two comparative puzzles. First, why do Japanese politicians choose a different degree of judicial independence than many of their counterparts elsewhere? More specifically, why do they impose on judges a politically biased incentive structure where U.S. federal politicians do not? Second, does the same logic apply to bureaucrats? Perhaps not, but why not? Why do politicians often keep judges more independent than they keep other bureaucrats? We will address those questions in this chapter.

In predicting the use of independent judges, the usual bromides about ju-dicial independence protecting "discrete and insular minorities" will take us nowhere. Even in the United States, the most prominent examples of judicial protection of minorities turn out to involve groups that are part of the coalition behind one of the principal political parties: U.S. politicians protect minority groups when doing so helps them stay in power, and U.S. judges rarely do more than reflect those coalition politics. Because Japanese politicians have not faced analogous potential gains from soliciting minority support, they gen-erally have not tried to protect minority groups. If protecting minorities cannot explain independent judiciaries, then the principal empirical question remains: When will majority party politicians delegate discretion over decisions with serious electoral implications to judges they cannot constrain, and how will they control their judges if they decide not to delegate?

We suggest an answer from the fundamental principles of the theory of repeated games. In a Prisoner's Dilemma, rational players who expect to play the game only once will not refrain from taking advantage of each other in their choices. If, however, they think their own cooperation will induce the other side to cooperate with them later, players who expect to play the game with each other indefinitely do have an incentive to cooperate.

So too with whether rational politicians will keep their hands off the courts. Fundamentally, whether they keep them independent—the analogue to the cooperative strategy in the Prisoner's Dilemma—depends on two things: whether they expect elections to continue indefinitely, and whether they expect to alternate with the other party in winning elections if elections do continue. Only where the ruling party expects there to be future elections and believes it has a good chance of being in and out of power will it favor independent courts. And if the ruling party does not wish to keep courts independent, the method it uses to control the courts will depend on the length of time it expects to survive before losing power.[1]

The party-alternation theory is easy to illustrate. First, in the United States, politicians expect the electoral system to continue, but no one gives either party high odds of controlling the government indefinitely. As a result, both parties have offered independent courts. Second, in modern Japan, politicians expect competitive elections to continue indefinitely, but until recently those in the ruling Liberal Democratic Party (LDP) rationally expected to win every time. As a result, they offered less independent courts. Because they expected to keep winning, however, they could use the leisurely control method of indirect influence over judicial promotions. Thereby, they retained the advantages of judicial independence in nonpolitical disputes.

Last, in imperial Japan, none of the politicians could expect his party to always win elections, but none could expect the electoral system itself to continue either. At any time, the military might intervene and end the elections or make them meaningless. As a result, the ruling politicians had short time horizons and hence allowed less independent courts. With no time to spare, when they intervened they used cruder methods than Japanese politicians today.

Before we begin, a word of explanation. We will speak of politicians choosing this and doing that with regard to policies and judges. Misleading as it may sometimes seem, we do so because fundamentally politicians must pay attention to voters. In a competitive electoral regime, they must pay them a lot of attention, and can usually be viewed as simply the tool of the electorate (with appropriate weight to voters who spend more of their time or money trying to elect particular politicians). Even in a less democratic regime such as Meiji Japan, they must pay some attention to the populace. Even there, after all, popular support was one element of their power.

---

1. This argument is modeled formally by Stephenson (2001), who draws attention to the importance of the parties' forward-lookingness and risk aversion and the judges' independent positions not being too extreme. Here, we do not rely on risk aversion, and we subsume judges' independent positions under the general cost of not monitoring judges closely. Stephenson also finds empirical support for the theory in regressions of judicial independence on electoral competition using national-level data.

Although constitutions are written by past politicians and influenced by past citizens, current politicians and voters retain them. Thus, when we speak of the choice of a Constitution by politicians, we refer both to the choice past politicians made under the influence of past voters, and to the choice of present politicians and voters not to try to change it. Japan's LDP did not write or adopt the modern Japanese Constitution or the parliamentary act that specified details of the judicial system. Indeed, when the Constitution and statute took effect it did not even exist. Once it came to power, however, the LDP did maintain the Constitution and the statute as part of the policy portfolio it offered Japanese voters. Even though the Constitution was hard to change, it would likely have faced far less opposition to changing the statute. Given that LDP politicians are the ones who make the decisions, as the agents of the voters, we phrase our discussion in terms of the choices they make.

We illustrate our party-alternation theory of comparative judicial independence through three examples: modern Japan (section I), the federal courts of the United States (section II), and imperial (1868–1945) Japan (section III). We discuss this theory in more detail in section IV, and in section V address the second of the comparative puzzles: why judiciaries are different from other bureaucracies.

I. Modern Japan

LDP politicians ruled Japan continuously from 1955 to 1993. They did not hold power this long by chance. In part, they held it by providing median voter policies, aided by the reluctance of opposition Socialists and Communists to moderate their ideologies. In part, too, they held it by rationally manipulating the institutional structure of government to their electoral advantage.

The modern Japanese Constitution vests the "whole judicial power" in the courts. It bans other judicial institutions (Art. 76[a]) and gives parties to administrative disputes the right to appeal to the courts (Art. 76[b]). It further declares that "judges shall be independent in the exercise of their conscience and shall be bound by the Constitution and the laws" (Art. 76[c]). Although the Cabinet does appoint judges to the Supreme Court and lower courts, it cannot fire them at will. Instead, only the Diet can fire them, and only through impeachment (Art. 78). To impeach, the Diet must find that a judge grossly violated the standards of the office, neglected the duties of the job, or dishonored the institution of the courts.[2] We include the relevant

---

2. Saibansho ho (Courts Act), Law No. 59 of April 16, 1947; Saibankan dangai ho (Judicial Impeachment Act), Law No. 137 of November 20, 1947, §3. Judges can also lose their job if declared "mentally or physically incompetent" by a court (Constitution, Art. 78).

provisions of the 1947 Japanese Constitution (along with the 1889 Japanese and 1789 U.S. Constitutions) in appendix A.

Although Japanese judges have not been as independent as their American peers,[3] the reason does not lie in any of the obvious institutional constraints.[4] The Japanese Diet seldom impeaches judges. From 1948 to 1989, its Judicial Impeachment Committee received 5,700 impeachment complaints but ruled against the judge only twelve times.[5] As noted in chapter 1, Japanese voters have never expelled a Supreme Court justice in a retention vote, and the Japanese Cabinet rarely refuses to rehire a judge at the end of a ten-year term.

Instead, LDP leaders controlled judges more subtly and indirectly through the job assignment process we study in this book. They controlled assignments through the court's administrative office, the Supreme Court Secretariat. In turn, they controlled the Secretariat through the series of strategic moves explained earlier. First, they appointed only loyal LDP partisans to the Supreme Court, which formally controls the Secretariat. Second, to ensure that their Supreme Court appointees did not change their views while in office, they appointed them late in life. As a result, Japanese Supreme Court justices served a mean of only six years before retiring at age seventy (ZSKS 1990: 468–70). Third, LDP leaders regularly appointed to the Supreme Court a career judge who had headed the Secretariat. At all times, therefore, they had on the Court a loyal partisan who knew in detail how the administrative offices worked. Although this assignment system was a creature of statute (not the Constitution), it was a statutory system the LDP could readily have changed—but that it chose instead to retain.

LDP leaders used this control over the Secretariat to reward judges in part according to whether they decided politically important cases the way the LDP politicians and voters wanted. Through the Secretariat, they institutionalized a system in which judges who decided controversial cases in accord with the preferences of the party (and who otherwise did good work) went to important positions in Tokyo. Others went to the branch offices. Through this control over

3. For some empirical evidence that American federal judges may not act quite as independently as we have often thought, see Cohen 1992, 1991; Spiller and Gely 1992; Toma 1991; De Figueiredo and Tiller 1996.

4. To be sure, this does not make the institutional structure irrelevant. If judges know that the Diet can impeach them, that the Cabinet may refuse to rehire them, or that voters can expel them, they may ignore majority preferences less. If so, then in equilibrium, politicians and voters would not often exercise the institutional control anyway. Judges would not ignore majority preferences, and voters and politicians would not punish them.

5. ZSKS 1990. On the frequency of impeachments in the United States, see Culver and Cruikshanks 1982.

job assignments the LDP influenced judges, indirectly to be sure, by promoting some and by not promoting others.

II. United States

A. Twentieth Century

In contrast, American federal politicians implicitly follow a strict hands-off-the-courts rule. Unless a judge is insane, rankly incompetent, or crooked, they let him sit in court and draw the standard salary. Whether he implements the majority party's ideology or anything else, they let him be.

Federal politicians in the United States may try to shape judicial ideology at the stage of a judge's initial appointment, but not later, and sometimes not even at appointment. Over the decades, some politicians have weighted ideology heavily, others more lightly. Few, however, have ignored it altogether, and few have picked more than a trivial number of judges from the rival party (Freund 1988).

Nonetheless, the implicit hands-off-the-courts rule is strong enough that sometimes observers criticize even attempts to influence the judiciary at the appointment stage. When Ronald Reagan nominated Robert Bork to the Supreme Court, some Democrats claimed he violated an implicit agreement to appoint only centrist jurists. When Bill Clinton named Lani Guinier to a position in the attorney general's office, many Republicans argued the same. And when the Senate hesitates to approve an appointment because of ideology, the president's supporters cry foul. The Democrats' successful campaign to block Bork gave rise to the derogatory term "borking," even though it was merely a publicity campaign to influence senators' approval votes.

The implicit hands-off-the-courts rule is deeply held, as Franklin Roosevelt discovered. When the Supreme Court rejected his New Deal, he proposed to enlarge the Court. Nothing in the Constitution required that it have nine justices. Indeed, politicians had manipulated its size to political ends before.[6] When serving as U.S. attorney general in 1913 as part of a Democratic Administration that followed a long string of Republican presidents, one of the Court's hostile judges—James McReynolds—had himself authored a report favoring a court-packing scheme much like Roosevelt's (Manchester 1973: 183). And increasing the size of the lower courts was, everyone seemed to think and still thinks, perfectly fair game (see De Figueiredo and Tiller 1996). By enlarging the Court to fifteen and appointing committed New Dealers to

6. See the discussion of the 1801 Judiciary Act, below, and the instances cited in Choper 1974: 850–52; Mason 1937: 667–68.

it, Roosevelt planned to build the Court majority he needed to implement the programs for which he won his electoral landslide (Currie 1990: 235–36; Leuchtenburg 1966).

Even Roosevelt's friends balked. Not only were judicial careers off limits to American politicians, apparently the number of Supreme Court justices was off-limits too. Roosevelt may have won by a landslide in 1936, but in politics, as in much of life, turnabout is fair play. What the congressional Democrats could do to the Republicans, someone else—perhaps the Republicans, perhaps President Roosevelt—could do to them. The Democratic congressmen knew that they would eventually lose office, either to a revived Republican Party (as actually happened) or to a different faction of the Democratic Party.[7] If they set a precedent for manipulating Court size now, it could haunt them later. That, many of them did not want. Rather than renege on the implicit hands-off rule now, they opted to risk Roosevelt's entire program.

B. Early Nineteenth Century

By the standards of the early republic, Roosevelt's scheme was meek. Politicians a century earlier had not followed any hands-off-the-courts rule. Before the Revolution, the Crown had sometimes controlled judicial careers (Surrency 1967). After the Revolution, voters in many states did the same. Some states made judges elected officials and kept them on a short leash with one-year terms. Others gave control to the politicians, and let their judges hold office only at the pleasure of the legislature (Ellis 1971).

Not only were state court judges subject to loss of their jobs, federal courts were fair game too. Consider the shift from Federalist to Republican rule after the first partisan election for president.[8] In 1800, Thomas Jefferson beat John Adams in a bitter election, and Adams was not amused. With but two weeks left in his term, he engineered the 1801 Judiciary Act (2 Stat. 89). Through it, he expanded the judiciary and packed it with party loyalists (Turner 1961). Along with stacking the courts, he also cut the size of the Supreme Court. It had been six. Adams cut it to five, effective on the next retirement. Thereby, he would prevent Jefferson from appointing anyone to the Court until two justices quit.

7. In 1937 Roosevelt's Democrats controlled over 75 percent of each house of Congress. In 1936 the Republicans had lost 5 million presidential votes since their heavy defeat in 1932, the first Depression election, and Roosevelt had won the presidential electoral college 523 to 8, joking, "I knew I should have gone to Maine and Vermont. . . . " (Manchester 1973: 174). Yet by 1946 the Republicans had regained Congress, and in 1952, the presidency.

8. The Republican Party of Jefferson eventually changed its name and is today's Democratic Party. The present-day Republican Party was only founded in the 1850s.

On taking office, Jefferson retaliated in kind. First, he fired Adams's non-judicial appointees. Then he fired the new judges. Given Article III of the U.S. Constitution, he could not do so directly, of course. If Adams's Congress had passed the 1801 Judiciary Act, however, Jefferson's Congress could repeal it. Repeal it his Congress did (2 Stat. 132, 1802). In the process, it threw the judges appointed under the 1801 Act out of their jobs. By the Constitution, they held their office during "good Behavior." Yet their office itself was a creature of Congress, and what Congress could create, Congress could abolish. It abolished their offices, and the judges were judges without postings—whether on good behavior or bad. Lest John Marshall's Federalist Supreme Court rule the ploy unconstitutional, Congress recessed the Court for fourteen months.[9]

By the time the Supreme Court finally faced the issue, even the Federalist justices had lost their nerve. They declined to hold the 1802 Act unconstitutional (*Stuart v. Laird*, 5 U.S. (I Cranch) 299 [1803]). Discretion may have saved them their jobs, for many Republicans were ready to go further. Some wanted to amend the Constitution and appoint judges to serve at the pleasure of Congress. Others wanted to abolish the courts altogether and rely on the state courts (Ellis 1971: 21).

Moderation prevailed. The Republicans never amended the Constitution to control the judges, and no one ever abolished judges' jobs again. Indeed, when Congress abolished the Commerce Court at the turn of the century, it simply kept the judges on the payroll (*Donegan v. Dyson*, 269 U.S. 49 [1925]). By Roosevelt's time, this moderation had become the modern hands-off-the-courts rule. Even Supreme Court size was now sacred—but as a matter of custom, not of constitutional text.

C. JUDICIAL MIGHT-HAVE-BEENS

As we have seen, in America the constitutional text is not always a good guide to constitutional practice. The Constitution allows Congress to abolish judicial offices, limit jurisdiction, change Supreme Court size, and reject presidential appointments, but the extent to which these practices have been used has varied widely over time. Japanese and American politicians treat judges differently, but not because of any differences in the constitutional text. If

---

9. Even at the time, not all observers thought that the judges whose postings were abolished should lose their salary. See Story (1833: vol. 3, 494) (on the 1802 Act: "if its constitutionality can be successfully vindicated, [it] prostrates in the dust the independence of all inferior judges"); Haskins and Johnson (1981: vol. 2, 171–72). More recently, at least some Supreme Court justices have argued that abolishing the courts would simply create salaried judges without courts. See, e.g., Glidden v. Zdanok, 370 U.S. 530, 544–47 (1962) (Harlan, J.).

they chose, Japanese politicians could insulate judges from political control. At least by the text of the Constitution, American politicians could intervene LDP-style in the courts.

Start with the Japanese Constitution. It does not forbid the Japanese government from passing implementation laws setting up a system very like the American one. The chief constraint on the lower courts is Article 80, which provides that the "judges of the inferior courts shall be appointed by the Cabinet from a list of persons nominated by the Supreme Court. All such judges shall hold office for a term of ten (10) years with privilege of reappointment, provided that they shall be retired upon the attainment of the age as fixed by law."

Thus, to appoint lower-court judges, the Supreme Court and Cabinet must agree on appointments, rather than the president and Senate as in the United States. But the Diet could pass an implementation law setting a retirement age of one hundred and establishing separate posts for trial courts and appellate courts, and it could specify that judges are not to be transferred from their initial posts without going through the appointment process again. Combined with the present-day custom of almost-automatic reappointment, the result would be much like the current U.S. federal system. Thus, the constitutional text does not mandate the current system in Japan; it could be changed by the politicians if they wanted.

Look now to the U.S. Constitution. Once a judge takes office, the president cannot freely fire him or dock his pay (U.S. Const. art. III, § 1). Suppose John Doe becomes president and appoints eminent University of Chicago Professor I. Jones to the local Seventh Circuit Court of Appeals in downtown Chicago, conveniently near his home. Neither Doe nor any of his successors could fire Jones without evidence of serious fault (U.S. Const. art. III, § 1; Shartel 1930; Block 1970). Neither could anyone reduce his pay. That is all the U.S. Constitution says on point, and the Japanese Constitution says much the same thing. Politicians in both countries could impeach judges whose decisions they disliked; in practice, in neither country do they impeach except for such things as criminal offenses.

Where the two systems diverge is not in their Constitutions, but in the laws that the legislatures pass to implement the day-to-day aspects of a judicial system—what judges do, and where they do it. By the text of the Constitution, politicians could change these laws as easily and often as they change the tax code. In Japan, they could change the judicial administration law to imitate the U.S. system if they wished. Similarly, in America our hypothetical President Doe need not be very creative to penalize Judge Jones. Even under the existing statute, he can transfer him. For example, suppose the president has the chief justice on his side. If he can make a plausible showing of need, he can order Jones to show up "temporarily" for work in Omaha (28 U.S.C. § 291).

Or suppose President Doe, like Roosevelt and the LDP, has a majority of his party in the legislative branch. He decides the Seventh Circuit is a hotbed of unreconstructed radicals. To punish the judges, he could merge the Seventh Circuit into the adjoining Eighth (28 U.S.C. § 48), forcing the Chicagoans to appear for work in either St. Louis, Kansas City, Omaha, or St. Paul. Or maybe all four, in rotation. The Supreme Court itself once held that Congress could order the justices to ride circuit (*Stuart v. Laird,* 5 U.S. [I Cranch] 299 [1803]). By comparison, sending Chicago judges to Omaha seems mild.

More comprehensively, if President Doe's allies controlled Congress they could import virtually the entire Japanese system on a turnkey basis. They would first abolish the statutory circuit designations (28 U.S.C. § 48; Posner 1985: 25). All judges would then serve on one national circuit. Either directly or through the chief justice, Doe could now transfer judges at will. Like the LDP leaders, he would reward the faithful with glamorous posts. He would dispatch the renegades to the outback.

Indeed, Doe could do more. The president now appoints judges as either district or circuit judges (28 U.S.C. §§ 44, 133). With a modest statutory change, he could appoint all judges as "federal judges." Depending on their performance, he could move them on or off appellate panels. Similarly, all district judges now earn the same pay, and so do the circuit judges. With a little change, he could establish a salary range, start everyone with a low salary, and reward the faithful with bigger and more frequent raises.

The text of the U.S. Constitution prevents none of this. Before 1891, the president appointed only two tiers of federal judges: district judges and Supreme Court justices (Act of Mar. 3, 1891, ch. 517, 28 Stat. 826; Posner 1985: 23–24). As recently as 1875, district judges received a salary from a pay range (Posner 1985: 43). And when the Congress abolished the short-lived Commerce Court (Act of Oct. 22, 1913, 38 Stat. 208, 219), existing Commerce Court judges became judges without a court. Like Japanese judges, they sat wherever the Supreme Court chief justice told them to sit (*Donegan v. Dyson,* 269 U.S. 49 [1925]).

Although modern Japanese judges enjoy less political independence than federal judges, the difference has nothing to do with the constitutional text. The Japanese Constitution does not require the ruling party to intervene in the courts; the U.S. Constitution does not prevent Congress and the president from intervening in the courts. Before considering further why modern Japanese and

American politicians do adopt different approaches (in section IV), consider first the approach that Japanese politicians took before World War II.

III. Imperial Japan

A. INTRODUCTION

The 1889 Japanese Constitution[10] seemed to give judges less independence than the modern Constitution. After all, the imperial judges were under the Ministry of Justice rather than a formally independent Supreme Court. Nonetheless, actual practice differed little. Before World War II, as after, political leaders could use the judicial career structure to influence the way judges decided cases.

B. JUDICIAL STRUCTURE

The 1889 Constitution (Art. 58[b]; see Arts. 59–61) set the basic institutional contours of judicial independence: "no judge shall be dismissed from work except through a criminal conviction or disciplinary disposition." The 1890 Judicial Organization Act (1890 Act)[11] specified the detail for this constitutional mandate. Although it placed courts squarely within the Ministry of Justice (1890 Act, § 135), it insulated judges from control in several ways.[12]

First, the 1890 Act prohibited the minister of justice from transferring a judge against his will (1890 Act, § 73). Second, it let him order a judge to retire only if the judge no longer had the physical or mental capacity to perform his work and he obtained the approval of the en banc High Court or Supreme Court (1890 Act, § 74). Third, it let him discipline a judge only if the judge had misbehaved egregiously, and only through proceedings before panels of either the High Court or the Supreme Court.[13] Last, because the Act did not specify a mandatory retirement age, it effectively gave judges life tenure. Thus, the imperial judge had all the protections of the modern judge, and more besides.

This institutional framework made it hard for government leaders to manipulate the judiciary. Notwithstanding that difficulty, the oligarchs of late-nineteenth-century Japan soon decided to do an end run around this

10. Dai-Nippon teikoku kempo (The Constitution of the Great Japanese Empire), promulgated Feb. 1, 1889.

11. Saibansho kosei ho (Judicial Organization Act), Law No. 6 of Feb. 10, 1890. Further details on the status of judges were determined by the Hanji kenji ken nado hokyurei (Order Regarding the Compensation of Judges and Prosecutors, etc.), Chokurei No. 17 of Feb. 14, 1894.

12. Why the oligarchs then in power did this is not clear, though it probably had to do with renegotiating the consular jurisdiction imposed by Western governments under the treaties in effect at the time.

13. The judge would then face penalties ranging from pay cuts to impeachment. Hanji chukai ho (Judicial Disciplinary Act), Law No. 68 of Aug. 20, 1890, §§ 2–9.

framework, as we will shortly describe. Thirty-some years later, the professional politicians who followed them to power would do the same.

C. Oligarchic Manipulation

At the turn of the twentieth century, a clique of unelected oligarchs held power in Japan. Formally, they held power by virtue of their access to the emperor. Substantively, they held it by virtue of their control over the military. Already by the mid-1890s, these men had intervened in the judiciary.

The oligarchs intervened primarily for technical reasons, not political ones. They had created the judicial system itself in 1872, even before the Constitution.[14] During the first two decades, they had hired as judges men with very little legal education. They had little choice, for legally trained men were not available. By the 1890s, the new university system gave them a large cadre of judicial candidates with sophisticated legal training. Accordingly, if the oligarchs could remove the sitting untrained judges, they could replace them with newcomers far better educated. Therefore, during the nineteen months from July 1893 to March 1894 and August 1898 to May 1899, they told 158 judges to retire.[15]

The institutional framework did not make this a straightforward task. If the minister of justice asked a judge to retire, or even to move to an obscure provincial court, the judge could properly refuse. If the minister then wanted to force the judge to retire, he had to submit the matter to the High Court or Supreme Court with accusations of incapacity or misconduct. He had no assurance, however, that the courts would decide matters the way he wanted. In any case, the publicity would be undesirable, and the ex-judges would likely themselves resist because of the associated stigma.

So to induce judges not to contest his order, the minister of justice bribed them. He did this by promoting them to more prestigious courts at higher pay in exchange for their agreeing to retire quickly and quietly thereafter. This not only gave them the face-saving chance to resign from a higher court and after a recent promotion had indicated the government's regard for their talent, it also boosted their pension. Under the rules then in effect, a judge's pension depended on his total years of service and his final pay.[16] If he earned his final

14. See Shiho shokumu teisei (Rules regarding Judicial Functions), Dajokan unnumbered Tatsu of Aug. 3, 1872. The Supreme Court (Daishin'in) was created by the Daishin'in sho saibansho shokusei shotei (Rules and Duties of the Supreme Court and Other Courts), Dajokan Fukoku No. 91 of May 24, 1875.

15. Ramseyer and Rosenbluth 1995: ch. 6. The capacity of the courts at the time was about twelve hundred judges. See Chokurei No. 17 of Feb. 14, 1894 (1,220 judges); Chokurei No. 122 of June 20, 1898 (1,195 judges).

16. See Kanshi onkyu ho (Government Employee Pension Act), Law No. 43 of June 21, 1890, §5.

high salary for a day, he earned a highly paid judge's pension for the rest of his life.

The minister of justice bribed judges with pensions on a wide scale. During the last months of 1898 and early months of 1899, he even appointed fifteen judges to the twenty-nine-member Supreme Court.[17] Court packing? No. The new judges served terms of one day to three weeks each. The minister agreed to name them to the Court; they agreed to quit; and everyone seems to have kept his bargain. The judiciary was rejuvenated, and if perhaps there remained some less competent old judges who had refused the bribes, they were few enough not to reduce the effectiveness of the system at delivering legal decisions to the public.

D. POLITICAL MANIPULATION
1. Shift of Control

Over the next several decades, control of the Cabinet gradually shifted from the aging Meiji oligarchs to a new breed of professional politicians in the Diet. In 1889, shortly after the promulgation of the Constitution, Prime Minister Kuroda made it clear that constitutional government did not mean government at the behest of voters. In a famous speech he laid out his theory of "transcendental government." Not just the judiciary, but also the executive branch would be independent, free from the grubby hands of the politicians: "The government must always take a fixed course. It must stand above and outside the political parties and cleave to the path of supreme fairness and supreme justice" (Sashihara, Meiji Seishi, p. 1931, as reported in Mitani 1988: 57). If judicial independence from voters is a good thing, runs the logic, why not executive independence? With the military and the other oligarchs on his side, nobody argued with Kuroda in 1889.

By the 1920s, power had shifted. The transition was gradual, but 1924 marked a turning point. After two years of Cabinets that contained not a single member of the House of Representatives, the politicians rebelled. The leaders of the major parties announced their dissatisfaction, formed a coalition, and won the next general election. The Cabinet of peers resigned and was replaced by a politician-dominated Cabinet. From that time until 1932, Japan clearly had an executive branch responsive to the electorate. The oligarchs were gone, and the politicians were in control. Ominously, an independent military waited in the wings, no longer under the personal control of the people running the

---

17. Kusunoki 1989: 282–93. For the size of the Supreme Court, see Hanji kenji ken nado hokyurei, note 11 above, § 2.

Table 7.1 Major Personnel Changes within the Ministry of Justice

	Kato	Tanaka	Hamaguchi	Inukai
Prime Minister:				
Cabinet Formation:	8/2/25	4/20/27	7/2/29	12/13/31
Party:	Kenseikai	Seiyukai	Minseito	Seiyukai

A. Major posts[a] (months till a replacement)

	Kato	Tanaka	Hamaguchi	Inukai
Adm. vice minister	—	1 month	—	1 month
Par. vice minister	1 month	1 month	1 month	1 month
Chief, Criminal Bureau	1 month	—	—	—
Chief, Civil Bureau	—	—	—	—
Chief prosecutor, S. Ct.	—	—	—	—
Asst. prosecutor, S. Ct.	—	1 month	—	—
Chief justice, S. Ct.	—	4 months	—	1 month

B. Subsidiary posts[b] (reassignments within two months and the next twelve months)

	Kato	Tanaka	Hamaguchi	Inukai
Chief prosecutor, High Ct. (7 posts)	0, 0	0, 4	3, 1	2, 0
Chief prosecutor, D. Ct. (51 posts)	1, 16	3, 17	1, 9	12, 12
Section chief, S. Ct. (8 posts)	0, 0	0, 1	0, 0	0, 1
Chief judge, High Ct. (7 posts)	1, 0	0, 1	0, 0	1, 0
Chief judge, D. Ct. (51 posts)	3, 19	0, 14	3, 12	2, 14

SOURCE: Calculated on the basis of data in Hata 1981; shiho sho 1939.
NOTE: The Wakatsuki Cabinets are omitted because they followed Cabinets of the same party (the Kenseikai in 1926 and the Minseito in 1931).
[a]Months from Cabinet change to personnel change, if within one year; blank if there was no personnel change.
[b]Number of reassignments within two months, followed by number of additional reassignments within shorter of (i) subsequent ten months and (ii) period of time until change in party controlling Cabinet.

government. In the judicial sphere, the politicians inherited from the oligarchs an institutional legacy that complicated their ability to constrain judges.

2. Intervention

At an aggregate level, the data on senior appointments in the Ministry of Justice in panel A of table 7.1 show a curious pattern of political involvement beginning in 1925, the year of the first Cabinet after the grand coalition of 1924 fell apart. It continues until 1931, the year before the military commandeered the government. Panel A shows the number of months from a Cabinet change to personnel change, if any personnel change occurred within a year after the Cabinet change. The parliamentary vice minister was immediately changed every time—that post is meant to be occupied by a politician. The equally high-ranked administrative vice minister of justice was replaced only by Prime Ministers Giichi Tanaka and Tsuyoshi Inukai. No prime minister ever replaced either the Civil Bureau chief or the chief prosecutor.

Panel B shows statistics for somewhat lower-ranked officials, and compares how many posts were reassigned in the first two months of the new Cabinet with how many were reassigned in the subsequent ten months. Except for Inukai's

Table 7.2 Judicial Forced Retirements during the Four Months
before and after Cabinet Changes

	Before	After
A. No. of judges assigned to S. Ct.		
Kato (August 2, 1925, Kenseikai)	5	3
Tanaka (April 20, 1927, Seiyukai)	1	2
Hamaguchi (July 2, 1929, Minseito)	0	2
Inukai (December 13, 1931, Seiyukai)	3	13
B. No. of judges forceably retired		
Kato (August 2, 1925, Kenseikai)	16	8
Tanaka (April 20, 1927, Seiyukai)	13	15
Hamaguchi (July 2, 1929, Minseito)	9	10
Inukai (December 13, 1931, Seiyukai)	7	29

SOURCE: Compiled from *Kanpo,* the daily official government gazette (various issues).
NOTE: "Forced retirement" refers to judges officially ordered to retire—those for whom the notice "taishoku wo meizu" appeared in *Kanpo.*
    The Wakatsuki Cabinets are omitted because they followed Cabinets of the same party.

replacement of twelve chief District Court prosecutors (of which more later), no new Cabinet ever replaced more than three officials in the ranks covered by panel B within two months. Adding ten extra months increases the turnover considerably, but even then less than half the officials are replaced—and remember that parties during this period stayed in power for only about two years. Compare this with the United States, where despite the inevitable disruption in government business it creates, a new administration of a different party replaces en masse not just the higher-ranking officials, but the U.S. attorneys, the equivalent of the chief prosecutors of the District Courts.

To the U.S. observer, the turnover in judges in panel B of table 7.1 may look misleadingly high. Although judges were not replaced immediately after the new Cabinet gained control, within a year an average of 16.25 of the 51 chief judges of District Courts were replaced. Is this a large number? Not really. If a typical term in a particular posting was three years, as it was postwar, the number would be seventeen even without any political intervention.

Table 7.2 takes a different approach. Focusing just on judges, it shows the number of (A) appointments to the Supreme Court and (B) forced retirements of judges generally. It shows the number of each of these in the four months of a Cabinet of a new party and the four months immediately preceding the Cabinet change. Notice first that until 1931 none of the three prime ministers who replaced a prime minister of a different party either appointed more supporters to the top of the judiciary (the Supreme Court) or fired more at the bottom (through forced retirements) than their predecessors had done in the preceding four months. Hypothetically, the incoming party could have fired the preceding Cabinets' appointments, and reappointed the judges who had been forced to retire. This they seem not to have done. On reconfiguring his Cabinet in 1925, Kato did not fire any more judges than he had in the months before. Tanaka and Hamaguchi fired a few more, but the difference barely shows.

According to these tables, politicians did not replace a previous administration's judges with their own. Rather, they kept judicial personnel largely unchanged. By U.S. standards, firing about one judge per month seems extreme, but at that rate it would take a long time to turn over the entire judiciary.[18] That the firings were not concentrated in the months after a new party took power suggests that the firings may have been relatively nonpartisan.

Although they suggest that partisan politics may not have been a major force in the judiciary, tables 7.1 and 7.2 do understate the extent that politicians manipulated the courts. This happened even before the politicians established consistent control of the executive branch. Back in 1913, the Seiyukai had controlled both the Cabinet and the Diet. That April it set out to reshape the personnel of the courts. It first amended the Judicial Organization Act to ease its job.[19] Under the revised act, the minister of justice could transfer judges against their will by a simple majority vote in either the High Court or the Supreme Court. Through a similar vote, he could place as many as 232 judges and prosecutors on inactive status. From April to June, the minister retired 98 judges and prosecutors, placed 131 on inactive status, and transferred 443 (Nomura 1966: vol. 3, 382).

When the Seiyukai regained the Diet and Cabinet several years later, it instituted mandatory judicial retirement (Law No. 6 of May 17, 1921). By doing so, it automatically purged many of the men appointed by the oligarchs and could now install its own. One such victim was Chief Justice Yokota Kuniomi, who as administrative vice minister of justice in 1898 had carried out the oligarch's purge. Tit for tat—but this time without a compensating bribe.

The Seiyukai thus did intervene in the Ministry of Justice in the years before the events in tables 7.1 and 7.2. During the dozen years after 1913, it controlled the Cabinet only about half of the time. Although the remaining years might

18. Although the firings were too infrequent to affect significantly the pool of judges, they could have had incentive effects, showing what would happen to judges who overstepped the boundaries of what the party in power would tolerate. The effectiveness of this incentive, however, was limited by the ability of the succeeding party to reappoint the fired judge after the next government turnover.

19. Law No. 6 of Apr. 5, 1913; Law No. 7 of Apr. 5, 1913. Law No. 6 in fact provided that the transfer provision applied "when necessary for trial business." Because the Judicial Organization Act already allowed the minister of justice to transfer judges when it was necessary to fill a vacancy (1890 Act, § 73 proviso), ordinary canons of statutory interpretation suggest this was a looser requirement.

have given the rival Kenseikai party time to appoint its own sympathizers to the Ministry, it did not. Instead, it wasted almost half its term in office with a minister of justice, Yukio Ozaki, who had little interest in personnel issues ("Yamaoka" 1925; "Shiho" 1925).

The Kenseikai was not altogether passive, however. Consider the career of Mannosuke Yamaoka. On finishing college in 1899, Yamaoka worked as a prosecutor's apprentice and then as a Tokyo judge. After a stint in Germany, he returned to Japan in 1910 as a prosecutor. By 1914, he had endeared himself to a Seiyukai-affiliated senior bureaucrat. With that patronage, he moved into a series of important posts, and by 1925 headed the Criminal Bureau. Then, under a Kenseikai Cabinet, the minister of justice summarily placed him on inactive status (Hosojima 1964: 45–95; "Shiho" 1925). Legal commentators complained that politicians were politicizing the judiciary, but Yamaoka was graceful in his response:

> I do think I've been impartial,... but if you look at the Ministry of Justice from the Kenseikai's perspective, you'll see it's just about completely stacked with Seiyukai people. It's true that Mr. Ozaki was Minister of Justice for a while under the [1914] Okuma Cabinet, but he stayed almost totally aloof from these things. As a result, there's hardly any trace of the Kenseikai there. ("Shiho" 1925)

Whatever modest independence the judiciary had, it lost completely when Seiyukai party leader Inukai became prime minister in 1931—he of the twelve prosecutors replaced within two months in panel B of table 7.1. Because the military usurped the government in 1932, Inukai was the last prime minister to take office as a party politician. He dominated the courts straightforwardly.[20] Even before he took office, some observers predicted he would make massive changes (3352 Horitsu shimbun 17 [1931]). He did indeed. Within four months of taking office on 13 December 1931, he appointed thirteen justices to the twenty-nine-member Supreme Court and fired twenty-nine lower-court judges (table 7.2). A day later (on April 14, 1932), he announced yet another massive series of personnel changes. The legal press called it "The Great Judicial Office Shuffle." In one day, he transferred 213 judges and prosecutors (3396 Horitsu shimbun 19 [1932]).

All told, the independent judiciary had a spotty record in imperial Japan. Under the oligarchs, it lacked independence—though with good effect on its professional quality. Under the politicians, some prime ministers were strong

---

20. The claim by Mitani (1980: 18–19) that the judiciary remained independent from the political parties misses some of what happened in the 1920s and almost all of what happened in 1931.

enough and interested enough to try to change the personnel of the judicial branch. Although others were not, by the end of party rule, judges clearly lacked independence. That end came in 1932. On May 15, several naval cadets assassinated Prime Minister Inukai. An admiral replaced him, and set in motion the military control that would carry the country into World War II.

IV. A Theory of Judicial Independence

A. INTRODUCTION

It is a tale of three courts: a relatively independent American federal judiciary, a relatively nonindependent modern Japanese judiciary, and an even less independent imperial Japanese judiciary. These differences do not derive from *constitutional* texts (they do derive from statutory texts, but statutes are—at least formally—easy to change). Neither do they derive from any obviously stronger American taste for independent courts. After all, many Japanese observers react to judicial career manipulation with the same consternation that many Americans would show, and many Americans wish they could force their judges to show more restraint.

Nor do modern theories of judicial independence explain the differences. To date, most scholars have tried to explain why rational politicians find it advantageous to use independent courts, rather than why some politicians find it advantageous while others do not. In perhaps the most innovative article on point, William Landes and Richard Posner (1975) advanced independent courts as a way for politicians to make long-term bargains with their constituents. Without independent courts, they argued, politicians would have an incentive to cheat on any deals their predecessors made—or, indeed, on any they made themselves. Constituents would then reward politicians less for passing advantageous statutes, knowing that courts could nullify the statutes at the politicians' direction.

Indeed, the problem would exist even in a one-party state. Politician X might wish to take contributions in exchange for passing law Y. If he can instruct bureaucrats to disregard law Y and act as if it had never been passed, however, no forward-looking contributor will pay him for its passage. The government could not even obtain supplies by procurement contracts without paying a hefty risk premium. If the court were always on the government's side, the supplier would lose any contract dispute.

Independent judges, Landes and Posner suggested, mitigate this problem. Precisely because of their independence, they are willing to enforce legislative deals. By stopping successor parties from reneging on their predecessors' deals, and by preventing even the original parties to the deal from reneging, the judges will help all legislators extract the money or power for which they sold their deals to the voting public. Douglass North and Barry Weingast (1989) seem to find evidence for this theory in seventeenth-century England.

Placed in a broader theoretical framework, the Landes–Posner theory fits within what Oliver Williamson (1993; Moe 1991) and others have since described as purposefully inefficient bureaucracies. "Incumbent politicians who create and design bureaus are aware that the opposition can be expected to win and take control in the future," explains Williamson. "A farsighted majority party will therefore design some degree of (apparent) inefficiency into the agency at the outset—the effect of which will be to frustrate the efforts of successor administrations to reshape the purpose served by the agency" (1993: 121).

Mathew McCubbins and Thomas Schwartz (1984) advance a hypothesis with a different twist—one we introduced in chapter 5 in connection with tax disputes. They argue that independent judges help politicians monitor the people they appoint to bureaucratic posts. Monitoring bureaucrats routinely would entail resources politicians would like to use elsewhere. Politicians instead keep bureaucrats in line by giving constituents a right to sue them in independent courts. In this theory, courts are kept independent of politicians because otherwise politicians would find it hard to use them to monitor the bureaucrats.

Absent other considerations, both the Landes–Posner and the McCubbins–Schwartz theories imply that competitive electoral markets should lead to one equilibrium outcome: independent courts. Perhaps politicians who keep courts independent will more successfully raise money (Landes–Posner), or perhaps they will more successfully monitor their bureaucrats (McCubbins–Schwartz). In either case, politicians who keep courts independent would compete more successfully in electoral markets than those who do not. A forward-looking politician will establish independent courts as the first item on his agenda. Even if some politicians were less aware of their own interests, independent courts would arise over time as the evolutionary pressure of electoral competition drove politicians who could not keep their deals into extinction.

But this is not true. Not all regimes have independent judges. This might be because of the types of cases judges are deciding or the electoral framework within which politicians compete. We discussed types of cases in chapters 4–6. We turn now to the possibility that differences in judicial monitoring might result from different electoral exigencies. In the U.S.–Japanese comparison, those exigencies are twofold:

1. the long-term electoral dominance of the LDP in postwar Japan compared to the erratic electoral performance of American political parties; and

2. the long-term likelihood of continued democratic elections in the United States and postwar Japan, compared to the short-term time horizons in imperial Japan.

B. THE PARTY-ALTERNATION THEORY OF COMPARATIVE INDEPENDENCE

1. The Electoral Logic

Although modern Japanese elections are highly competitive affairs, for nearly forty years the LDP consistently won them.[21] Partly by shifting its policies to follow the shifting median voter (recall the discussion of reapportionment in section II.C of chapter 4) and partly by using its control over government to give constituents generous private goods, the LDP dominated the political marketplace (see generally Ramseyer and Rosenbluth 1997: chs. 2–5). By contrast, American parties win erratically. As a result, LDP leaders could reasonably expect that they would continue to control the government indefinitely.[22] No American leader of either party could expect such a thing.

If politicians face significant odds of losing their majority position, they may rationally try to reduce the downside risk from being in the minority party. In part, they can do this by insulating the judicial system from political control. Suppose that by virtue of institutional design or some other means, the incumbent party has little control over judges and cannot rely on them to help win elections. That party will be less likely to win the next election, but will also have a better chance to return to power later after losing. American politicians seem to have chosen this option.

LDP leaders had less reason to insulate their judges from election pressures. Because they could realistically expect to stay in power indefinitely, they placed little value on being able to return to power more easily if they lost it. Consequently, LDP leaders could rationally elect to monitor judges instead, and thereby obtain greater control over policy. Although they increased the cost of losing an election, they apparently accepted this, since they were less likely to lose.

At stake is an intertemporal calculus. American political leaders have increased their control over the future judiciary by reducing their control over

21. Individual Japanese incumbents, as opposed to the LDP as a party, faced a higher risk of losing office than incumbents in either Britain, West Germany (as it was), or the United States. See Calder 1988: 68. This was perhaps due to the multiple-member districts used during the period of our study.

22. This conclusion is not affected by the LDP's loss in the summer of 1993. The point is not that the LDP's odds of winning were always 100 percent, but rather that they were extremely high. Very few observers predicted the 1993 LDP loss; but it had always had some small probability of losing an election.

the present one. They freely make political appointments, routinely naming party loyalists. By insulating these judges, once appointed, from political control, they increase the impact that these same appointments will have after they lose office. By politicizing appointments but depoliticizing control, they augment their influence during periods when they are out of power. All this, of course, comes at the cost of reducing their influence over policy while in power. Because political leaders in the United States must run the country with numerous independent judges appointed by their predecessors, they necessarily have less impact over policy while in office.

LDP politicians apparently adopted the opposite tactic: they increased their control over judges in the present by decreasing the extent to which that control lingers into the future.[23] By giving the party in power control over judges, they increased the electoral stakes. As long as they stayed in power, they kept tight control over policy. Once they lost an election, they sacrificed more power than a losing American party would sacrifice. Because LDP leaders rationally expected not to lose, they rationally took the risk.

The American equilibrium rests on nothing more than mutual cooperation. American politicians do not adopt LDP tactics. Yet they avoid them only by implicitly agreeing to use cooperative strategies in what they all recognize as a game closely resembling an indefinitely repeated Prisoner's Dilemma (Kreps et al. 1982). In such repeated games, however, implicit cooperation is fragile at best. Parties to indefinitely repeated Prisoner's Dilemmas do not necessarily cooperate. At least theoretically, they may do anything at all, depending on self-fulfilling expectations of varying degrees of trust (Rasmusen 2001: 92; Fudenberg and Maskin 1986; Buckley and Rasmusen 2000). They might agree to insulate their courts. Then again, they might not.

Yet one thing is certain, and that is that rational politicians will not cooperate if they cannot expect their rivals to do the same. The battle over the 1801 Judiciary Act illustrates the problem. Under the new Constitution, the transition in 1801 was the first. At the time, the Federalists had no idea what shape a Republican government would take. Given the French bloodbath and Jefferson's Francophilia, they could easily fear the worst. Even if Jefferson did not bring out the guillotine, the size of his victory, the extension of the franchise to poorer, non-Federalist voters, and the likely admission of new states in the non-Federalist west all portended a long period of Republican rule. Indeed,

23. Restated, American politicians politicize appointments but depoliticize control. Japanese politicians politicize control and therefore need not politicize appointments as strongly. A judge's personal preferences do not matter as much if he can be deterred from excercising them or transferred if he does.

such a forecast would have been accurate; the Federalists disintegrated and the Republicans held the presidency until they split into factions and a Whig won some forty years later.

In this turbulent world, to exercise self-restraint out of a hope that the Republicans might reciprocate struck many Federalists as insane. Given that the Federalists showed no self-restraint, neither were the Republicans inclined to restrain themselves. Only as the decades passed and the parties alternated in power regularly did cooperation (and greater judicial independence) eventually evolve.

The contrast between the demise of the Federalists and the later demise of the Whigs in America is instructive. The Whig Party disintegrated in the 1850s because of the tension between its pro-slavery and anti-slavery factions, yet it did not try to interfere with judicial independence in its final years. Partly this was because the most controversial issue before the courts, slavery, was the one on which the Whig leaders could not agree. Partly, however, this was because despite the disintegration of the Whig Party, the Whig politicians themselves had a brighter future. They expected to continue in politics under some new party label, with a good chance of regaining power. And, indeed, a coalition of ex-Whigs and dissatisfied Democrats formed an anti-slavery party, the new Republican Party, which captured the presidency within ten years.

It is significant that the greatest breakdown in the American consensus on the judiciary occurred when the two-party system was at its weakest. This is shown not just by the events of 1801, but by those of 1937. Following the Democrats' smashing presidential and congressional victory of 1936, Roosevelt tried to pack the Supreme Court. That he failed, at least in the court-packing plan itself, is less important than that he tried.

Although two parties alternated in power in imperial Japan, by 1931 they also intervened in the courts. Here, the explanation lies in the fear of a military takeover. Parties to a repeated Prisoner's Dilemma will often defect if they expect the game to end soon (Selten 1978). The higher the odds that it will end, the higher the odds they will defect. By the late 1920s, few in Japan expected democracy to continue forever. The military had almost entirely removed itself from civilian control. Abroad, it was aggressively expanding onto the Asian continent, conducting a foreign policy at odds with that of the elected government. Domestically, it was beginning to threaten a coup. Democracy was on borrowed time, and anyone who followed Japanese politics knew it. For just that reason, rational politicians increasingly adopted endgame tactics.

If all this be true, then whether a coalition of rational voters will provide independent courts depends primarily on electoral probabilities. At root, it involves three possibilities.

1. *Alternating-Party Regime.* Coalition X is in power but expects to alternate in power with Coalition Y indefinitely (the modern American parties). The two coalitions may rationally have an understanding that whoever is in power will keep judges independent, though nothing in game theory says that is the only possible understanding. Just as easily, it may be that the two coalitions engage in cutthroat competition with a politicized judiciary, to their mutual detriment but with no easy way out.

2. *Dominant-Party Regime.* Coalition X is in power and expects to stay in power indefinitely (the postwar LDP). Coalition X will manipulate the courts in politically sensitive cases. It would earn the greatest return from a hand-off-the-courts strategy only if it expected to be out of power periodically. If it does not expect to lose power, it has less incentive not to monitor and discipline its judges, both for reasons of pure politics and of efficient court administration.

3. *End-Period.* Coalition X is in power but fears it may lose power soon and will never regain it later, regardless of whether the judiciary remains independent after its defeat (the prewar Japanese parties, or the American Federalists). Some other Coalition Y—the military in Japan, the Republicans in the United States—is about to take X's place indefinitely. Coalition X has no reason to hold back from manipulating the courts to make the best of its present situation and perhaps delay its terminal loss of power.

2. Independence by Type of Dispute
(a) Nonelectoral Disputes

The idea behind the behavior we expect in all three regimes is that inefficient behavior is the only equilibrium outcome in a repeated Prisoner's Dilemma with shortsighted players, but efficient behavior can be the outcome if players are farsighted. Crucially, even within a given regime the equilibrium level of judicial independence will depend on the type of dispute at issue. On issues not involving directly electoral questions, the LDP does maintain courts with independence. It does so because it wants a reputation for keeping its commitments and for having courts that decide impartially between private parties regardless of their political clout. Keeping commitments and deciding impartially are efficient outcomes, given the goals of inducing people to rely on those commitments and to engage in business dealings that depend on the law for such matters as contract enforcement. The LDP would acquire a short-term benefit from bringing the judiciary under tighter control, but sacrifice other benefits in future years.

Let us denote the value of the short-term benefit from interfering with the judiciary, as viewed from the present by the decisionmaker, as S; and the long-term cost as L. Conditions that favor the decisionmaker keeping judges independent are that

1. L is positive (nonindependence must have some cost),
2. L is large relative to S (the benefit of independence is larger than the cost),
3. the decisionmaker has a long time horizon (long enough to make L large).

Consider the sort of crude interference in the courts represented by the forced retirements in prewar Japan. For the LDP, with its professional politicians and sound prospects for staying in power, the cost L to such interference would be very large. It would diminish its ability credibly to promise voters that it would keep its current promises in future years. For the political parties in imperial Japan in 1931, with the threat of military takeover looming, L was not so large, and the more profitable course was to take the short-term benefit S.

(b) Electorally Sensitive Disputes

The logic above depends on L being large relative to S, and the relative magnitude of L and S will vary by the type of dispute involved. Although L does depend on the time horizon used by the decisionmaker, that is not the only thing that matters. Underlying the discussion of the previous paragraph was the assumption that L was positive—that there were indeed long-term benefits to the decisionmaker from holding back on seizing the short-term benefit S.

Our Japanese data illustrate the importance of the type of dispute at issue. On certain kinds of issues—the constitutionality of the military, injunctions against the national government, and issues involving electioneering—we found that Japanese judges deviated from the LDP line at their peril. By contrast, they faced no such peril for criminal or tax cases or for injunctions against local governments. Our explanation is that L is small or negative for the first set of issues but large for the second set. The LDP would seem to derive no long-term benefit from being forced to adhere to the more impractical clauses of the Constitution the Allied Occupation gave Japan some years before the LDP was formed. Neither does it gain from letting judges intervene in the executive branch by issuing injunctions against its decisions, or in maintaining a reputation for fair play against electoral rivals. Its rivals were unlikely ever to be able to pay the LDP back in kind, especially if the LDP interfered with the rules of the game. Thus, when it came to the electorally most sensitive issues, L was zero or small and the LDP faced no trade-off between the short run and the long run.

Parties in an alternating-party regime make similar calculations, but reach different outcomes. There, the ruling party does have to worry about upsetting an implicit deal not to coerce judges. The result of upsetting the deal would be an equilibrium in which both parties rigged elections to give themselves an extra margin, and in which statutory and constitutional interpretation flipped back and forth depending on who was in power. Quite possibly, this long-term loss L would outweigh the short-term advantage S, and the ruling party would adhere to the implicit deal.

3. Risk Aversion

This logic is strengthened by a party's aversion to risk, but risk aversion is not a necessary part of the argument. Suppose that if a ruling party controls the courts tightly, it can hurt the opposition party by amount Z and help itself by that same amount. The only reason not to control the courts tightly would then be strong aversion to the risk of sometimes receiving Z and sometimes losing Z depending on chance and the electorate. We say "strong" because the risk aversion must overcome the advantage of tight control, that the party we are considering is currently in power and so is guaranteed some period of time when it is the lucky recipient of Z. If the party's risk aversion is weak, these symmetric gains and losses will make the short-term cost of restraint S greater than the long-term benefit L.

A situation in which the gain of Z to the controlling party is equal to the loss to the opposition is not, however, a Prisoner's Dilemma. The Prisoner's Dilemma is a dilemma because the gain to the player taking the "defect" action is less than the loss to the other player. Here, that takes the form of the gain to the ruling party of tight control over judges being some amount G that is less than the loss Z to the opposition. If, for example, tight control allows the ruling party to use violence against the opposition party, the gain G might be less than the loss Z, and the ruling party would be willing to forgo G now in order to avoid an equal amount of time paying Z later. To relate this more directly to the previous chapters: the ruling party would be unwilling to use the courts to make communicating with the voters more costly for the opposition—as by restricting door-to-door canvassing—if it expected to be in opposition itself and the gain G from the restriction was less than the cost Z to the opposition party.

4. Independence by Type of Intervention

The party-alternation theory not only predicts when politicians will intervene in courts, but how they will intervene when they do. On the one hand, whether alternating in power or secure in power, politicians with long-term perspectives will want to be able to make commitments and to monitor bureaucrats (Landes and Posner 1975; McCubbins and Schwartz 1984). Yet the two groups of politicians will face incentives that differ in two respects. First, a party that alternates in power has less motivation for making the bureaucracy and court administration effective. Part of the benefit, after all, will go to the next party in power and help it carry out its own policies.

Second, a party that alternates in power cannot make as effective use of promotion policies. If judges have postings of fixed terms, the party may not be in power by the time an offending judge is up for his next posting. Even if the party is in power at an opportune time, it only controls the postings while it is in power, and the other party can reverse its decisions when assuming control. Moreover, a party only temporarily in power will find it hard to delegate the implementation of judicial promotions to an administrative secretariat. There is a fixed cost to creating a loyal secretariat, and time is required to test the loyalty of its individual members. In Japan, the LDP could foresee enough years in power for it to be worthwhile to shape a dependable secretariat and rely on it to keep the judiciary in line. Any party that replaced the LDP would have to intervene more directly in the judiciary and could not safely delegate the task to the experienced bureaucrats.

These differences directly influence the strategies that the politicians in the two regimes will adopt. Under the dominant-party regime, if politicians do intervene, they may choose methods that are more direct. Potentially, for example, they may choose to fire judges outright rather than to control personnel policies. They did not do so in postwar Japan, but our theory suggests it might have been a potential equilibrium if they had. So too in end-period regimes, since politicians in those regimes likewise have little time in which to influence the judiciary before they lose power. In prewar Japan and at various times in American history, they did just that.

C. European Courts and State Courts in the United States
1. European Countries

What of court systems other than the three we have been discussing? We can make predictions according to the theory, even though testing them would require additional institutional and empirical investigation.

For bureaucratic court systems similar to Japan's, the outcome of political influence via posting should resemble the Japanese outcome if the country's ruling party expects to stay in power indefinitely. Italy during the Christian Democrat years of the 1960s and 1970s is perhaps in this category.[24] In a country with the same court system but ruling parties that alternate in power, the prediction is weaker. Perhaps the parties will vitiate the effect of bureaucratic organization by implicitly agreeing with each other not to intervene at all; perhaps they will use the cruder tactics of 1920s Japan, or simply use judicial promotions and transfers less effectively than in modern Japan. Germany during the 1950s to the 1980s, when Social Democrats and Christian Democrats alternated in power, might fit the latter category.

In many countries the picture is further complicated by the frequency of coalition governments, which would to some extent differ as to what they wanted judges to do. Japan's LDP is in some respects like a coalition, in that its factions compete against each other for influence; but the LDP factions do not differ much in policy preferences. Certainly, they do not differ in their support for the Self-Defence Force or for laws that would continue to make electioneering difficult for minor parties, issues we have used in our regressions in this book.

2. State Courts

Prediction becomes more difficult for systems that are neither like the Japanese system, with entry by examination, nearly life tenure, and promotion by a Secretariat, or like the U.S. federal system, with entry by political appointment, life tenure, and little chance of promotion. Most of the state courts in the United States fit neither category. In each state, there are federal courts to adjudicate federal laws and to adjudicate disputes between citizens of different states, but there are also state courts that handle virtually everything else. The U.S. president appoints federal judges, with the consent of the U.S. Senate, but he has no role in appointing state judges. Rather, each state decides for itself how it selects state judges, and they have chosen from a wide variety of ways.

Consider just state supreme court judges (lower-court judges are often chosen differently). The initial selection is sometimes by partisan election,

24. It seems that courts in Italy were politicized, but not under tight Christian Democrat control. The Christian Democrats almost always governed in coalitions and never obtained a majority of votes. Judicial promotions were strictly by seniority, resulting in weaker judicial incentives than in Japan and slow processing of cases. Until the 1960s, conservative older judges controlled court administration, but in that decade factions of the Right and the Left were clearly identifiable within the judiciary, and many judges became openly activist. Spotts and Wieser 1986: ch. 8. The topic is ripe for further research.

sometimes by nonpartisan election (where the judges are not identified by party on the ballot), sometimes by appointment by the governor (sometimes from a set of nominees by a committee of lawyers), and sometimes by legislative appointment. Once in office, their terms vary from six years to life. In some states, to retain their jobs judges must win reelection or reappointment, and in some an appointed judge must win a retention election in which voters vote for or against him but without any other candidate on the ballot.

Why states have such a variety of features and terms of office is a fascinating question. Even the theoretical predictions of our repeated-game model for which states will choose which methods are somewhat unclear. For one thing, a distinction must be made between selection and retention. It is often said that elected state judges are not independent because they owe their position to the voters. Being elected by the voters directly, however, makes a judge no less independent than does appointment by the president. In both cases, the judge is not chosen randomly or by passing an examination: someone has done the selecting on the basis of both the judge's views and his abilities. Once selected, the judge does not lack independence merely because someone else chose him. Even if he made campaign promises, they are not binding.

Rather, what raises the dimensions of judicial independence at issue in this book is what happens in the future to someone currently a judge. If the president could refuse to renew a judge at the end of a ten-year term, that would limit the judge's independence. Similarly, if the electorate could refuse to reelect a judge at the end of a ten-year term, that would limit the judge's independence. On the other hand, a judge restricted by law to one term is much more likely to be independent—he has nothing to lose by making controversial decisions.

What matters, then, is the length of a judge's term in a particular post, his promotion possibilities, and what determines whether he retains his post for a succeeding term. It is not that elected judges are less independent (at least as we use the term), but that judges who are forced to face reelection must worry about their futures. An effective way to insulate judges from outside influence would be to pass term limits forbidding them to be reappointed or reelected, but no state has done this.

Note, however, that an independent judge can still be politically responsive. Suppose judges are limited to a single, nonrenewable two-year term, after which new judges are elected. Those judges will be independent, but if the voters want to use the judiciary to reverse a law, they can do so within two years by electing new judges chosen for their desire, independent of personal gain, to reverse the law. The judges are independent to be sure, but they are still politically responsive and will not help politicians commit in the way suggested by Landes and Posner.

Another difficulty in fitting the different states' methods into our theory involves the distinction between independence from the politicians and independence from the voters. In our earlier analysis this did not matter. The LDP was the majority party because it advocated the policies supported by a broad swath of the voters. As a result, the majority of voters and the LDP had roughly similar preferences about judicial behavior. Both would have hoped judges would make electioneering hard for minor parties, and both would have wanted them to stop fringe-left local politicians. Similarly, in the United States when the president appoints and the Senate confirms judges, they are reflecting the desires of their constituents. In the American states, however, electing judges makes sense only if there is a divergence between the interests of the governor and the electorate.

3. Bundling Voter Choice

There is a difference between electing a governor who appoints judges, the system in some U.S. states, and choosing a governor and judges in the same election but by checking different boxes on a ballot. When judges are appointed, the voter must make a bundled choice: he cannot vote for the Republican governor and the Democrat judge. The same goes for retention. If the governor has the power to reappoint a judge, then the voters have bundled that power together with other gubernatorial powers. In voting for a governor, they are also voting for judges' being retained on the basis of how much they please the governor.

What determines how a state bundles the voters' choice? This question of course applies more widely than just to judges and governors. For example, voters could form a democracy in which they vote for just one executive, who would appoint everyone else in the executive branch. Alternatively, they could form a democracy where they vote for every employee separately, all the way down to whoever takes out the trash. The basic trade-off is between minimizing the information the voter needs to decide how to vote, which is accomplished by having fewer elected offices, and reducing the power of the executive, achieved by having more elected offices.

Voters would like the executive to have more power if he will use it to carry out the policies for which they elect him. They face the problem, however, that once elected he may use the power for personal ends—for example, acquiring wealth, helping friends, or advancing his private political preferences.

Unbundling power helps solve that problem by diversifying the voters' portfolio of policy providers, and by introducing "checks and balances"—the ability of different officials to monitor each other without fear of being fired, and in some cases the need for several to agree before new laws can take effect. Thus, having judges elected separately from governors means that if the governor fails to carry out the laws that he writes, the judges can on occasion force him to do so; and if he embezzles from the state treasury and shows up in court, he will be convicted.

4. Parallel Empirical Research

F. Andrew Hanssen (2001) has made an admirable start at untangling the institutional structure of the state courts. Using regressions, he finds that partisan elections are associated with the strength of the ruling party. The use of the "merit plan," in which politicians (usually the governor) appoint judges from a list compiled by a nonpartisan nominating commission and the judge keeps his job if he wins an uncontested retention election, is inversely associated with the strength of the ruling party.

Hanssen's results accord with our alternating-parties theory. Focus on the retention method in each case. The futures of judges who must face the voters in partisan elections are certainly dependent on the voters, but they are also dependent on the politicians who influence party endorsements, so partisan elections make for less independent judges. Judges under the merit plan are more independent. They must win appointment by finding favor with the nominating commission and the politician who makes the actual appointment, to be sure, but what matters more is the retention method. Since it is a nonpartisan election, without opposing candidates, it is very difficult to unseat such a judge, and politicians cannot intervene in the election by promoting rival candidates or withholding endorsements. Thus, Hanssen's results support the theory that where rival parties alternate in power they may agree to insulate the judiciary from pressure by whichever party happens to be in power.

Why are U.S. federal judges appointed for life terms rather than having to face retention elections? Part of the answer is historical. For whatever reason, amending the U.S. Constitution has been much more difficult than amending state constitutions, so unless the voters thought retention elections were clearly superior, it would not be worth the cost of changing the institution. More practically, however, one of the main functions of the federal court system is to protect the national welfare from state interference. If U.S. district judges were subject to retention votes from the people of their districts, it would be hard for them to make rulings that were in accord with the national majority of voters but opposed by the local district majority. It would be impractical, however, to hold retention elections in which every citizen of the United States voted for every judge. Only at the Supreme Court level would such a system potentially be useful.

V. Judges and Bureaucrats

A. THE ISSUE

A further comparative puzzle is why politicians treat judges differently from other bureaucrats. Most government employees are more like judges in imperial Japan than like judges in either modern Japan or the United States. They are subject to the direct commands of the politicians, who can order them to change their decisions in particular cases. And the politicians can control promotions. The bureaucrats may object that the politicians' orders are illegal, of course, but their recourse is the same as that of any citizen: go to the courts. After all, the politicians are their bosses.

B. MODERN JAPANESE BUREAUCRATS

The modern Japanese bureaucracy contains a fast track giving bureaucrats careers very similar to those of judges. The Level 1 Entrance Examination for the National Civil Service is ordinarily taken by students in their last year of college. In 1993, of 35,887 test-takers, 1,863 passed, a rate of 5.2 percent (Ikuta 1995: 36). There were 1,012 entry positions, and the bureaus had already chosen many of the students they wanted, based on college performance, before they passed the exam. Like judges, the successful test-takers were disproportionately from Tokyo and Kyoto Universities, and the Tokyo undergraduate program in law is known as the place to be for an aspiring elite bureaucrat.

Once the new graduate finds a job, he ordinarily works his way up the ladder within that particular ministry. Nonelite bureaucrats and those hired for their technical skills are regularly evaluated, but the fast-trackers are subject only to informal, unwritten evaluation (Ikuta 1995: 57). The most successful young bureaucrat will rise from officer to senior officer to unit chief to assistant director to division director, deputy director-general, director-general, and administrative vice minister.

Most elite bureaucrats will not make it to vice minister. Instead, they will retire in their early or mid-fifties to take jobs in the private sector or quasi-government agencies (a process known as "descent from heaven"). Like judges, elite bureaucrats are well paid—a director-general earns 1,230,000 yen per year (about $100,000)—but not nearly as well paid as their university peers who enter the private sector straight out of college.[25]

Thus, elite bureaucrats are much the same kind of people as elite judges, which is more than a cut above the ordinary Japanese politician in educational background and intellectual ability. Some observers conclude that they are out of the control of the politicians, and that the bureaucrats determine government policy in Japan. Johnson (1982: 20–21), for example, once claimed that the bureaucrats in the Ministry of International Trade and Industry "make most major decisions, draft virtually all legislation, control the national budget, and [are] the source of all major policy innovations in the system." James Q. Wilson observed that "in Japan, the bureaucracy is the government" (1989: 308). Tadahide Ikuta said that ministers rarely if ever reject promotions put forward by the Ministry officials, and concludes: "The cabinet is practically a rubberstamp for nominees appointed by an agency's bureaucrats" (1995: 12). Karel Van Wolferen (1989: 190) admitted that politicians had some leverage, but denied that they had any impact:

> Even if a minister uses all his remaining powers, it will not enable him in practice to redirect Japanese policy in any noticeable manner. A minister may have influence over a ministry in the sense that he can promote or fire officials, and exert leverage in the allocation of resources to benefit his supporters and constituency. But this is different from wielding strong political power over a bureaucracy. Except when it is part of a longstanding campaign to assert control over education, for example, a minister's "policy-making" is generally too limited to deserve the name at all.

In fact, however, bureaucrats do respond to the desires of politicians. Ramseyer and Rosenbluth (1997: ch. 7) show that bureaucratic policymaking promotes the electoral objectives of the LDP. McCubbins and Thies (1997) find that even shifts in the power of the different factions within the LDP result in changes in budget priorities. McCubbins and Noble (1995) show that the LDP keeps tabs on the political implications of what bureaucrats do and takes care

25. Tadahide Ikuta (1995) is a good general guide to the civil service, as written by an experienced Japanese journalist. The National Personnel Authority's website, "Introduction to the Japanese Civil Service System," http://www.jinji.admix.go.jp/english/intro.htm (July 10, 2001), in both English and Japanese, provides details of procedures, ranks, and salaries, as well as data on such matters as age at separation from the civil service. Two other sources that contain entertaining anecdotes are Schlesinger 1997, which focuses on politicians, and the somewhat naïve Miyamoto 1995.

to control the policy agenda. And Yung Park (1986: 61–77) explains in detail how politicians, particularly those in the LDP party committees ("tribes") created to monitor individual ministries, intervene in personnel policies in particular.

Even writers who repeat the conventional wisdom that the bureaucrats are independent give evidence that this is not so. Van Wolferen (1989: 151, 177) tells us that Construction Ministry officials spend much of their time talking with politicians who want roads and such projects in their districts; that LDP members who intervene on behalf of city or prefectural governments for nationally funded projects routinely were kicked back 2 percent of the project's value; and that the Tanaka political machine was able to leverage its commission for building contracts or regulatory changes to 3 percent of the value. The politician may not even need to ask. Shortly after Takeshita became prime minister, almost all the building requests from his home prefecture of Shimane won approval, which is highly unusual. The governor of Shimane thanked the Construction Ministry for what he called a "congratulatory gift" to the new prime minister (ibid.: 156).

Ikuta recounts similar stories in his book on Japanese officialdom. Allowing contractors about to bid on a public project to meet and decide who will get which parts of the project and at what price is obviously fraudulent. But high profits on construction projects are quite useful to politicians so long as contractors are appropriately grateful. As a result, prosecutions lagged (Ikuta 1995: 168). Legislation is indeed written by bureaucrats, proposed by the Ministries, and routinely passed by the Diet. Yet even after it has been modified within its originating Ministry, it must pass through the Cabinet Legislation Bureau, and "[n]o agency reportedly has ever had a Cabinet order proposal forwarded to a Cabinet meeting in its original form" (ibid.: 75).

The anecdotes are legion. One new agriculture minister started his job with a speech to his bureaucrats (Park, 1986: 66, as cited in Ramseyer and Rosenbluth, 1997: 111):

> It is said that art is long and life is short. You must think that "agriculture lasts long and the minister's life is short." You fellows don't last long either. My term is at most one year, but I can fire you through evaluations of your work performance. The truth is that "agriculture is long and the bureaucrat's life is short."

When asked why his ministry drafted futile statutes to rescue a textile industry doomed by international competition, a Ministry of International Trade and Industry (MITI) bureaucrat explained: "We know the industry won't last. We've known that for years. But in the meantime these textile firms use people who vote LDP. The party's got to be able to show them that it cares. So we do our part. We give the politicians a new statute to show the textile people every year" (Ramseyer and Rosenbluth, 1997: 121).

Similarly, MITI drafted the Large Stores Act in 1973 by a distinctly political logic. The statute authorized regulation to encourage the appropriate development of the retail industry, paying attention to the protection of consumer interests and guaranteeing the business opportunities of smaller retailers.[26] After earlier regulation failed to do the trick, it came up with regulations that effectively required supermarkets to buy out the local retailers before they started building. During the four years after 1979, supermarket construction fell from 576 a year to 125 (Ramseyer and Rosenbluth 1997: 129–30). Small business support of the LDP was likely not coincidental; lack of protection of consumer interests was tangential.

Ministry of Finance officials failed to consolidate the banking industry for a similar political reason. They had hoped to consolidate the banking industry ever since the Allied Occupation. Toward that end, they proposed statutes and jawboned to try to ease out the smaller and weaker banks that are most likely to cause headaches for regulators. But they consistently failed to get their bills passed, and the targeted banks, supporters of and supported by the LDP, found little to worry about (Rosenbluth 1989, summarized in Ramseyer and Rosenbluth 1997: 126).

Finally, when Ichiro Kono became minister of construction in 1962, he chose his own top officials. To the bureaucrats, he explained: "I don't give a damn what you have done before I came here. Stay if you want to work with me. Leave if you do not want to cooperate or are not competent for the job." Resignations ensued (Ikuta 1995: 107).

Although we offer these anecdotes as part of our argument, we have not tried to replicate the statistical tests we used for judges on Japanese bureaucrats. Judicial decisions are a very special sort of bureaucratic decision: public, sharp, attributable to a single panel of judges, and not circulated for comment before they are made. The end-product of other bureaucratic decisionmaking can be equally sharp and public—the road is built in Shimane or it is not—but it is much harder for an outsider to know whether a bureaucrat's initial decision

26. Daikibo kouritenpo ni okeru kourigyo no jigyo katsudo no chosei ni kansuru horitsu (Law concerning the Adjustment of Retail Business Operations in Large Retail Stores), Law No. 109 of 1973.

was reversed within the organization by other bureaucrats or politicians and to determine who is responsible for the ultimate decision.[27]

C. U.S. BUREAUCRATS

Studies of U.S. bureaucrats have shown them to respond to the same kinds of pressures as politicians.[28] Granted, the top politicians rarely intervene in the bureaus directly. The general pattern is that the president (or governor) appoints heads of bureaus and one or two layers of subordinates from outside the career bureaucracy. The vast majority of the personnel are then civil service employees, immune from political firing. Congress and the state legislatures have even less control, merely setting budgets and with the right, at most, to embarrass bureaucrats with public questioning. Yet the bureaucrats seem responsive not just to the president, but to members of Congress as well, and must perform an intricate dance when the chief executive and congressional representatives are of different parties.

The reason for the combination of a lack of crude political intervention and bureaucratic responsiveness in the United States follows the logic of the master–butler relationship we described in chapter 1 in our discussion of the *Remains of the Day:* politicians do not need to intervene if bureaucrats anticipate what they want. Knowing that politicians can intervene if necessary with outright reversal, reduced budgets, unpleasant job assignments, and promotion blocks, bureaucrats administer according to the political preferences of the party in power—and the politicians have no reason to intervene.

D. PREWAR JAPANESE BUREAUCRATS

Scholars and popular writers have paid less attention to the bureaucracy in imperial Japan than the bureaucracy in either modern Japan or the United States. Yet given the rhetoric of the times—"transcendental government,"

27. It is perhaps worth mentioning one class of anecdote that seems to illustrate bureaucratic independence: the public prosecutor bureaucrats who pursue corruption cases against politicians. The most famous of these, the prosecution of former Prime Minister Tanaka for bribery by Lockheed, illustrates when prosecutors are likely to bring these cases. As Ikuta explains it (1995: 124-27), at the time of the arrest in 1976, Tanaka's rival within the LDP, Takeo Miki, was prime minister, and the justice minister was Osamu Inaba, of yet another rival faction. For many in the party, Tanaka was expendable. Although phenomenally popular in his own district, the corrupt machine he controlled was increasingly alienating voters across the country. To many party leaders, prosecuting Tanaka was a price worth paying for preserving the party's general electoral success.

28. The empirical evidence is overwhelming. Among the many studies is Calvert, Moran, and Weingast 1987, which looks at the responses of American bureaucrats to changes in the way politicians run the relevant congressional committees. Others include Bagnoli and McKee 1991; Coate, Higgins, and McChesney 1990; and Weingast and Moran 1983.

Table 7.3 Personnel Changes in the Ministry of Home Affairs

A. Mid- and Senior-Level Personnel Turnover

Year	Cabinet Shift	Turnover
1921	S to S	13
1922	S to N	51*
1923	N to N	48
1924	N to N and N to K	80*
1925	None	38
1926	K to K	46
1927	K to S	73*
1928	None	39
1929	S to M	77*
1930	None	27
1931	M to S	116*

B. Governorship Turnover (out of forty-five governors)

Cabinet Date	Prime Minister	Party	Turnover
June 11, 1924	Kato	K	27*
June 30, 1926	Wakatsuki	K	0
April 20, 1927	Tanaka	S	40*
July 2, 1929	Hamaguchi	M	35*
April 14, 1931	Wakatsuki	M	6
December 13, 1931	Inukai	S	41*

SOURCE: Calculated from data in Hata 1981.

NOTE: S is a Seiyukai Cabinet, N is a nonparty Cabinet, K is a Kenseikai Cabinet, and M is a Minseito Cabinet. Asterisks follow the numbers associated with changes in party.

In panel A, turnover is the number of changes at the level of section chief (*kacho*) or higher during the calendar year. In panel B, turnover is the number of new governors appointed within one month after the change in Cabinet.

independent of politicians—the imperial bureaucracy is especially interesting. Despite the rhetoric, by the 1920s elected politicians controlled both the Cabinet and the bureaus. Table 7.3 illustrates the ties between staff turnover and political control in two areas of the bureaucracy. Take panel A of table 7.3: changes in personnel at the Ministry of Home Affairs at the posts of section chief or higher each year. During the five years when the party controlling the Cabinet changed, an average of 79.4 people changed office. In the six years when the party did not change, an average of 35.2 people changed office. Whenever a Cabinet succeeded a rival party Cabinet, mid- and senior-level turnover doubled.

Similarly, take panel B of table 7.3: changes in the governorships. These posts too were under the Ministry of Home Affairs. On the two occasions when a Cabinet succeeded another Cabinet from the same party, the new Cabinet replaced almost no governors. When a Cabinet succeeded a rival party Cabinet, it immediately replaced almost all the governors.

Why did the prewar Japanese politicians manipulate the bureaus earlier and more aggressively than the courts? In one sense, the puzzle is no greater than why it is that postwar Japanese and U.S. politicians exercise tighter control over the bureaus than the courts. Yet the dominant political philosophy of the time purported to protect both, while the politicians were quicker to manipulate the bureaus.

One explanation lies in electoral advantage. By the 1920s, party politicians realized that they were in an endgame. The military increasingly controlled the course of national policy. Given their limited future, politicians abandoned any cooperative strategies they might have played earlier. Once they had decided to renege, they had to decide where to focus their resources.

In imperial Japan, the bureau with the most immediate electoral implications was the Ministry of Home Affairs. The Home Ministry, not the Ministry of Justice, controlled the police, and the police supervised electoral campaigns. Through the police, the party in power could harass its opponents. Five days before the 1928 general election, the police had already filed electoral law charges against 638 people, and almost all were opposition party supporters (*Tokyo Asahi Shimbun*, 15 February 1928). "The police only reported the actions of the parties out of power," onetime prime minister Takashi Hara (1965: 93, entry for 28 March 1915) once observed. They largely "left the government party alone to do as it pleased."

In elections, courts mattered less directly. As a result, party politicians did not begin to manipulate them until they had learned how to manipulate the more immediately relevant institutions. They had, after all, only recently taken control of the government. Before they could manipulate any government institution, they needed first to learn how it worked. Accordingly, they focused their resources first on the institutions with the greatest electoral impact. They turned to the courts only later.

E. Judges and Bureaucrats Compared
1. Introduction

It seems that in all three regimes we have been discussing—imperial Japan, modern Japan, and the United States—politicians controlled bureaucrats, even though the degree of judicial independence varied among the three regimes. Why would politicians in modern Japan and the United States wish to maintain institutions that control bureaucrats more tightly than judges? In modern Japan, the LDP gave considerable (though not complete) independence to judges, and could thereby provide voters with commitments to carry out the policies for which they were elected. Under the system in place, judges face politically skewed incentives only indirectly via promotions and transfers, and only if they take non-LDP positions in a limited category of cases of particular interest to LDP politicians. In alternating-party regimes such as the United States, the two parties can choose to adhere to an equilibrium in which the party in power refrains from changing the institutions of the judiciary to reduce its independence. They refrain, presumably, because each fears the rival party might otherwise use the courts against it if it were to win the next election. But why not apply this logic to the bureaucracy too? Why not grant bureaucrats a similar independence, whether in Japan or the United States?

2. Monitoring Incentives

To answer this question, return to our theory of judicial independence. Under this theory, politicians will keep judges independent only when the short-term benefit S of political interference is less than the long-term cost L. There is certainly a short-term advantage S to the ruling party from controlling bureaucrats. But is there a long-term cost L to depriving them of independence?

For judges, the two leading explanations for why politicians preserve judicial independence are the Landes–Posner theory of judges as promise-enforcers, and the McCubbins–Schwartz theory of judges as bureaucrat-monitors. Neither of these applies to the bureaucracy. If there were no independent judiciary, by the Landes–Posner theory politicians would find it desirable to have independent bureaucrats to enforce promises. But if a group of bureaucrats were carved off and given independence for this purpose, this in effect would be to create an independent judiciary.

The McCubbins–Schwartz theory applies even less. If bureaucrats were made independent, then voters would have no forum in which to complain about nonperforming bureaucrats; so this theory cannot justify their independence either. Both theories suggest that politicians starting with just a non-independent bureaucracy would like to carve off a certain part of it and make it into an independent judiciary. Neither suggests they would want the whole bureaucracy independent.

Too, we must remember the straightforward reasons for keeping bureaucrats under the control of politicians that made it necessary to explain the independence of the judiciary in the first place. The voters elect politicians as their agents to produce and enforce policies and services. Independent bureaucrats would thwart this in two ways. First, they could substitute their personal policy preferences for those of the voters. Without the power to control the bureaucracy, politicians would find themselves unable potentially to deliver the policies and services the voters wanted. Second, the bureaucrats would lack incentives to administer either new or old policies effectively. Without the threat of personnel policy, why should a bureaucrat work hard? To be sure, someone must control promotions even in an independent bureaucracy. Given bureaucratic independence, however, the top bureaucrat would lack the incentives to monitor his subordinates.

As a result, politicians have good reason to keep control over bureaucrats. Any organization that hires people at a young age and keeps them for most of their working lives will need incentives. In such a world, promotions constitute the obvious "carrot." Absent sufficient carrots, workers in the organization will lack the incentive to work hard or effectively. Yet if the organization will differentially promote workers, someone must choose the workers it will reward. By placing democratically elected politicians in control over that choice, voters merely help to ensure that the bureaucrats will work hard to deliver the policies and services for which they elected the politicians.

Even aside from the promise-enforcing and bureaucrat-monitoring functions of judges, the type of work that bureaucrats do makes direct control of them more important for everyday administrative efficiency. Where judges make public decisions attributable at least to a three-judge panel, bureaucrats make closed-door decisions with diffuse responsibility. Even distant observers can detect misbehavior in a court proceeding. Detecting bureaucratic misbehavior requires observing the decision process as it unfolds behind the ministry doors. Bureaucratic decisionmaking is thus more of an example of the "teams" problem studied by Holmstrom (1982), in which individual efforts generate a group output and individual members can hide their shirking.

Perhaps the most important difference between what judges do and what other officials do is that the task of carrying out policies requires effort. By contrast, judges do not have to exert any more effort to carry out a policy than to block it—perhaps less, since blocking a policy usually requires more explanation. Unless bureaucrats exert effort, voters will not receive the programs and services they want politicians to deliver. For judges, politicians have correspondingly less reason to give strong incentives to work hard.

3. Monitoring Institutions

Even if politicians might find it advantageous to control bureaucrats, can they? Politicians are outnumbered: there are far more unelected officials than elected ones. Moreover, most of the elected officials are in the legislative branch and in no position to exercise day-to-day authority even if they had it. It is no wonder that Japanese bureaucrats draft most legislation and make most decisions, for politicians are too few to do the job. They may also be too dull. Other than the former bureaucrats, politicians tend to be men and women who attended second- and third-tier universities, and who probably failed the Level 1 civil service entrance examination, if they bothered to take it at all.

To monitor bureaucrats, politicians sample the decisions they make and evaluate the results they obtain. Like executives in large corporations, they set policy goals and then delegate authority to subordinates, often more technically adept, whose future careers they control. Ramseyer and Rosenbluth (1997: ch. 6) details how politicians have done this in Japan, a means whose sophistication was raised to its zenith by former prime minister and high-school dropout Kakuei Tanaka. As Tanaka himself put it:

> Government officials are human computers; politicians set directions for them. . . . At first you fight with the official, who typically responds with "Why should I listen to you?" You then tell the official, "It's government by party rule. When you become director-general, you will have use for me." The official then will think about it, and come to his senses. The official will then come to you. (Quoted in Ikuta 1995: 109)

A politician needs at least two things to run a bureaucracy: incentives to offer bureaucrats, and information about what they are doing. Politicians control incentives by controlling career advancement opportunities and budgets. In Japan, "descent from heaven" jobs provide another. Typically, observers see these jobs as putting the bureaucracy under the control of the private sector. This neglects the fact that some of the usefulness of ex-bureaucrats derives from their contacts with their old bureau and the politicians who oversee them. If they have pleased the politicians, they may have contacts that prove valuable in some situations; if they have displeased the politicians, it may be safer not to hire them—at least in a country like Japan, where the offended party will continue to be in power. This is of course most true when the postretirement job is in a quasi-governmental organization or is election to the Diet, a not uncommon second career for elite bureaucrats.[29]

Politicians obtain information they need to monitor bureaucrats both through the ex-bureaucrats in the Diet and through current bureaucrats looking for promotions or postretirement jobs. Information is a valuable commodity in bureaucracies, and if the politician has something with which to buy it—favor and promotions—he will find bureaucrats willing to sell it. The transactions are not so crude, of course, but where gains from trade exist, we would expect trade to occur.

---

29. An exception that proves the rule is the difficulty the Socialists had in their nine-month-long administration in 1947. Ministry of Finance official Takeo Fukuda could not find the funds for a sensitive program for the Socialists, but was more successful a few months later for the conservative government that succeeded them. He later resigned to become a leading LDP politician (Van Wolferen, 1989: 189). A government whose duration is expected to be short will have difficulty in using bureaucrats for partisan purposes.

Even without information about bureaucratic disobedience volunteered by other bureaucrats eager to please, a politician would not be totally in the dark. Hierarchies are set up in organizations so that the leaders can limit their personal effort to monitoring their immediate subordinates. In this case, the politician can delegate monitoring to his immediate subordinates in the bureaucracy, letting them know what kinds of policies he wants to see, or even relying on their own experience to tell them what politicians want. They, in turn, delegate monitoring to their own subordinates, using their own influence over promotions. For the politician, such a strategy is particularly feasible because it is the top bureaucrats whose promotions he can most easily influence and who, being older, are nearing the time when they hope to move into high-profile postretirement jobs.

Politicians also obtain information from other politicians and voters. McCubbins and Schwartz (1984) explain how drastically this reduces the need for direct monitoring. Rather than examine every decision the bureaucrats make, the politician can wait for complaints from people whose interests he shares—his voters and politicians from his party. This is how even junior politicians outside a ministry obtain influence. If the bureaucrat rejects the junior politician's request, he can appeal to the senior politician with formal authority over the bureaucrat, who will then investigate the decision.

In modern Japan, the LDP's party oversight committees exist to aid this process. Backbenchers join committees that watch individual ministries carefully. If the backbenchers are unhappy with the shape legislation is taking, they let the minister and prime minister know. If all the politicians agree, the bureaucrats responsible can be told to change what they are doing. Otherwise, the discussion becomes an element in the intricate process by which backbenchers choose prime ministers and prime ministers choose ministers.

Thus, politicians will find it both desirable and feasible to control bureaucrats, and if their control is tight enough, we will never observe bureaucrats doing anything the majority politicians dislike. Indeed, we will often see bureaucrats anticipating the desires of those politicians, making proposals that the politicians like but would never have thought of on their own. Such bureaucratic initiative is a sign of effective control, not lack of control. The bureaucrats will be accountable to the politicians, and the politicians to the voters.[30] It is only when bureaucrats are unsure of what politicians want (as in transitions

---

30. For a book-length treatment of comparative government institutions as solutions to this kind of agency problem, see Cooter (2000). His more abstract treatment draws out other implications: for example, that if there is sufficiently high probability that mere bad luck will make bureaucratic behavior come to light, the politician will give the bureaucrat wider discretion *ex ante* (ibid.: 86).

from one party to another, when the party changes policies suddenly, or when there is dissension within a party) that we will observe bureaucrats making decisions the majority party does not want.

4. Unbundling Revisited

An alternative way for voters to control bureaucrats would be for them to elect bureaucrats directly. Why have any middleman between the voter and his public servant? We earlier discussed unbundling the electoral package of governor and supreme court judges in U.S. states. Why not similarly unbundle the package of governor and administrators, voting separately for each office, all the way down to the janitor who cleans the governor's office? This seems absurd—and is absurd, but why? The response that immediately comes to mind—that there is a practical difficulty in voting for hundreds of offices—is not the main problem. It is not hard to set up a voting machine so that voters can vote for a straight party ticket with the exception of particular offices they care about. This saves the typical voter from having to puzzle over whom to support for local coroner or state comptroller. It also points to one problem with voting for minor officials: the swing votes will come from those voters who take a special interest in that official, and those are the ones whose interests he will tend to favor. As a result, direct elections favor voters with strong private interests at stake, even as they lower the general welfare.[31]

The trade-off we discussed in connection with elected judges was that voting for the unbundled package of judge and governor requires the voter to become informed about more candidates, but it also reduces the power of the governor, which diversifies the risk to voters and reduces the governor's possibilities for opportunism. This trade-off also applies to unbundling the governor and executive officials.

A different reason to package governor and lower officials together, which applies better to executive officials than to judges, is to avoid divided responsibility. If voters elect bureaucrats and governors separately, then after a project fails the governor can point the voters toward the official, while the official will suggest that the governor is to blame. Since voters will suspect both, they both will share the penalty, and this gives neither one the efficient incentive to

31. Having the governor appoint the official does not completely solve the problem. It remains the case that those voters who are particularly affected by the official will be the ones whose vote for governor will turn on his appointment of that official. If the governor knows this, his appointment will be influenced by the desire of the special interest. Having the governor in between, however, hinders the special interest from making so easy use of its votes, because it must obtain access to the governor, who is busy with many other lobbying requests, to let him know of its members' interest in that official.

put forth his best effort. This is yet another example of the "teams" problem alluded to earlier (Holmstrom 1982). If, on the other hand, only the governor is elected and the bureaucracy is not independent, the voters will always blame the governor: either he made the mistake himself, or he failed by not properly controlling the lower official.

Both of these reasons point to a paradox: when too many officials are accountable at the ballot box, none is as accountable as when only one is up for election. Voters simply incur too high a cost to track all officials. They do better, as a result, if they delegate their authority to one, and monitor him scrupulously. *Do* put all your eggs in one basket, as the response to the proverb goes, but watch it fiercely.[32]

Perhaps this discussion of electing bureaucrats seems too theoretical, too far from the practice of any real-world country. American readers should realize that it is not. In a federalist system such as that of the United States, voters do not usually elect both an executive and his subordinates. Yet in most states, they do face separate elections for governor and other high state officials like the secretary of state and attorney general.

Moreover, American voters face multiple hierarchies across jurisdictions. Many a voter will vote for a president of his country, a governor of his state, a commissioner of his county, and a mayor of his city. Some services, such as crime prevention and detection, he obtains from all four levels. Others he obtains from some levels but not others. Only the federal government runs an army, sometimes only the county runs the library, and usually only the state runs universities and only the city dispenses liquor licenses. Voters need to track the talents of four separate executives, not to mention the legislative bodies associated with them.

The reason for this hierarchical structure probably goes to product differentiation: different localities want different services, so voters promote their

32. A different set of reasons for unbundling offices is based on improving the efficiency of the electoral process rather than efficient administration. Multiple elected offices allow more politicians to demonstrate and hone their talents for appealing to the voters; running for attorney general or secretary of state is a way to test the waters for a run for governor. Campaigning to voters directly is more costly than appealing for a job to the governor, however, so it is not useful to have too large a number of offices elected. A related reason for unbundling is that it may make coalition formation more efficient. Given the uncertainty about what voters want and how effective members of the coalition are at appealing to voters, a coalition may find it can provide a better package to the voter by allowing voters to pick and choose among candidates than by presenting them with a bundle in which they must take the good with the bad.

The standard reference on career paths of elected officials in the United States is Schlesinger 1966. Most political science research on careers has been about legislators and U.S. presidents. For one exception, a study of mayors, see Murphy 1980.

own welfare by unbundling liquor licensing in Bloomington, Indiana from liquor licensing in Cambridge, Massachusetts. But this logic does not explain the situation in Japan, where school textbooks are an issue for the prime minister,[33] nor does it explain why countries other than Japan and the United States sometimes maintain even more centralized and bundled governments. Indeed, viewing just the Japanese case, one might explain the bundling there as the *result* of regional differences: if majority voters think that majorities in atypical localities such as left-wing Kyoto would use federalism to promote atypical policies there, they would vote against regional unbundling. And, in any case, we are left wondering why centrally elected officials could not administer heterogenous local rules, instead of having to elect local officials for local rules. The question of which bureaucrats are bundled is both practical and interesting—but too complex for us fully to address here.[34]

5. Civil Service Rules

One detail of the puzzle remains. We have seen that it is useful for politicians to be able to discipline bureaucrats and that, as in private corporations, politicians use hierarchies to monitor their subordinates. In private corporations, however, the board of directors allows the chief executive to fire his subordinates at will. Why, then, do governments adopt civil service rules that make firing hard even when they retain promotions and transfers as incentives?

The answer is not the conventional one that a civil service system eliminates political influence.[35] It does not, since politicians can still intervene directly

33. China and South Korea objected to the treatment of prewar Japanese wrongs in the textbooks approved for Japanese schools and this became a national Japanese issue. See, for example, Kiroku Hannai, "Textbook Criticism Right on Target," *The Japan Times Online,* 25 June 2001, http://www.japantimes.co.jp (viewed July 20, 2001).

34. The classic work on federalism from a public choice perspective is Riker 1964. For a more recent treatment by a leading economist, see Cooter 2000: chs. 5 and 6. It is clear that sometimes it is desirable to have local regulations because local conditions differ. The harder question is why a central government administering heterogeneous local rules is not better than a variety of local governments.

35. Johnson and Libecap (1994: 9, 170), for example, argue that civil service protection is most important for higher officials, to avoid politicization, and least important for lower officials, because it encourages slack effort (they ascribe civil service for lower officials to unionization, the source of inefficient practices even in the private sector). Our argument is the opposite: that civil service protection has little importance for higher officials anyway, whose careers still depend on politicians and whose decisions can be more easily reversed, and is important to keep lower officials from being replaced after every election by party loyalists needing jobs. We admit that civil service protection induces slack effort, a cost to be set against the benefit of lower turnover. The best regime might be a norm in the alternating-parties game that a few lower officials could be fired (to enforce discipline) but not too many. This is hard to maintain as the equilibrium of a game, since it is not a bright-line strategy, easily observed.

to change decisions and can still affect personnel policy, even if they cannot take away a bureaucrat's salary. As we have explained, voters would not want to eliminate political influence anyway, since doing so would prevent their representatives from delivering the policies they want.

Rather, the usefulness of a civil service system is that it forces the politicians to use the bureaucracy solely to deliver services rather than to reward supporters. This is particularly important because giving supporters jobs is generally an inefficient way to channel wealth to them. Someone who wants a reward for political support is unlikely to have the talents and skills appropriate to the bureaucratic post available. A ward election committee chairman may be fine as a general manager, but the bureaucracy needs accountants and computer programmers too. To be sure, the politicians will not put incompetents in all the posts, since they must deliver services to voters as well as please special supporters. The presence of political deadwood will nonetheless degrade the quality of services and raise their cost.

Political change compounds the inefficiency of patronage. If such changes lead to turnover in jobs (more of a problem in an alternating-party regime like the United States than in a dominant-party regime like Japan), the politically appointed bureaucrats will never learn their jobs properly. Instead, they will remain perpetually in end periods of repeated games. Expecting to move on soon anyway, they will remain perpetually untrustworthy.

For all these reasons, it makes sense for voters to support politicians who agree to install a civil service system that restricts the amount of patronage available. In an alternating-party regime, the politicians might favor a civil service even without voter pressure. After all, not only does patronage lower efficiency generally, it potentially benefits the other party when electoral fortunes change.

VI. Conclusion

There once was a senior professor, the story runs, who always attended his collegues' funerals. Otherwise, he explained, they might skip his. He saw it as a repeated Prisoner's Dilemma, and in indefinitely repeated Prisoner's Dilemmas, every outcome is an equilibrium—sort of. At least, so runs the famous Folk Theorem of game theory. And it is this theorem, we suggest, that explains the independence of U.S. federal judges compared to their Japanese peers.

For judicial independence is not primarily a matter of constitutional text. Both the modern Japanese and the modern American constitutions purport to insulate judges from political leaders. Yet modern American politicians insulate their judges, while Japanese politicians do not. American politicians appoint party loyalists, but once they appoint them they intervene no further. Japanese politicians maintain a politically skewed incentive structure that helps to ensure that their judges stay loyal in the electorally most sensitive (but only most sensitive) cases. American politicians could restructure their courts to enable them to maintain a Japanese-style structure. Notwithstanding, they do not.

Instead, whether politicians maintain a politically skewed court system seems a function of electoral exigency. Although both American and Japanese political leaders must compete in electoral markets, LDP leaders competed far more successfully than the leaders of either the Democratic or the Republican Parties. As a result, LDP leaders had better odds of retaining control. Having better odds, they faced lower risk-adjusted costs to nonindependent judiciaries. With lower costs, they opted for judges who seem in significant ways not to have been independent.

Independent courts represent a cooperative equilibrium to a game that closely resembles an indefinitely repeated Prisoner's Dilemma. As such, they represent one outcome—but not a unique one. In indefinitely repeated Prisoner's Dilemmas, a wide range of outcomes can be equilibria. Only if a repeated Prisoner's Dilemma is about to end do the outcomes become more predictable. Where one party expects to win elections consistently, it may well decide not to keep courts independent. Where both parties expect the electoral market to end soon, they will not keep courts independent. Landes and Posner nicely captured the electoral logic behind the American judicial system. In doing so, however, they captured a special case—a result peculiar to electoral markets where all parties perform erratically. Here, we generalize the theory to a broader range of competitive electoral markets.

The theory would seem to apply to bureaucrats as well as judges, yet bureaucrats lack independence in all three regimes that we consider (modern Japan, prewar Japan, and the United States), regardless of the degree of interparty competition or the approach of an end period. We conclude that this is because the benefits of independence—the enforcing of promises made by the politicians and the monitoring of bureaucrats—are benefits that can be gained by making only a small number of government personnel independent, and the costs—reduced accountability to the electorate in policy decisions and reduced incentives for quality effort—are lower for the tasks that judges perform.

Potentially, the fifty American states present a more systematic test of the theory. The various states maintain courts with a wide range of institutional independence. In some states, politicians and voters keep close control over judicial careers; in others, they offer judges an independence akin to that of federal judges. Over the past century, the fifty states have also presented electoral markets with a wide range of political variability. In some states, one party maintained a lock on power for decades; elsewhere, the parties alternated regularly in office. The theory we have proposed suggests that states with alternating parties may or may not maintain independent courts, but that states where one party regularly wins elections will be less likely to maintain independent courts.

We have not performed that systematic test. Instead, we offer here a more modest argument, one with three archetypal examples. In the modern United States, neither party controls either the legislature or the presidency. The parties maintain a strict hands-off-the-courts rule. In postwar Japan, one party dominated the electoral market. It consistently offered courts that seem to have lacked independence on crucial dimensions. In prewar Japan, both parties knew that the military would likely usurp government soon. They too eventually offered nonindependent courts. Despite most of what is taught in law schools, judicial independence has had less to do with constitutional texts. It has had more to do with elections.

8

Conclusions

The best of times, the worst of times. . . . For all the platitudes we heap on judicial independence, we do face troubling times for American courts. The trouble has been brewing for decades, of course. But the extortionate suits to shut down the gun and tobacco industries should make obvious even to us in the academy what most voters have known for years: that U.S. judges sometimes use their independence to indulge their personal policy preferences and impose on the country policies that voters oppose, and that we academics like judges to be independent of politicians because judges are more likely to share our preferences than are politicians. At root, some of our paeans to independent judiciaries seem paeans to judges who listen to us.

Whether normative or positive, the puzzle to judicial independence is not in the independence of judges from parties to private disputes. No one advocates letting judges take bribes in private suits. And electoral markets in modern democracies give majority politicians strong incentives to ensure that judges stay honest in such suits anyway. Neither is the puzzle the independence of judges from bureaucrats in mundane administrative suits. Here too, politicians usually earn electoral returns by offering voters an unbiased forum in which to challenge bureaucratic decisions.

Instead, the normative and positive puzzles concern independence in basic political decisions. When, if ever, should sitting politicians let judges decide politically charged issues on their own? Is the world really a better place, for example, if a judge can decide independently to route rents to favored groups of voters? Is it a better place if he can decide independently to shut down industries he does not like? Or, on the other side, is it a better place if politicians cannot use independent judges to tie their own hands and enforce the bargains they made?

But table the "should." When *will* sitting politicians let judges decide basic politically charged issues independently? On questions of policy with electoral consequences, politicians are specialists. Absent more, why would they improve their electoral odds by delegating discretion over those issues to agents they cannot control? Is it enough to argue that independent judges help politicians commit in advance to long-term, rent-extracting bargains? Or is more at stake? The real puzzle is not why politicians in some countries keep control over judges on issues of policy. It is why politicians in others apparently do not.

At least in Japan, politicians do maintain control. We began by asking whether a judge's political affiliation affects his career prospects. It does. We then asked whether the opinions he writes affect his career too. Using first a broad composite index of opinions that went contrary to government positions, we located evidence that judges who write such opinions suffer a career hit.

Not all opinions that contradict government positions present the same electoral implications, of course. So from this beginning we asked which opinions matter most to judicial careers. We found that politically charged opinions matter enormously. If an opinion presents policy issues of major electoral consequence, Japanese politicians do not defer to judges. Instead, they use general rules of standing and jurisdiction to remove many such disputes from the courts. They then use politically biased career incentives to ensure that judges who handle the remaining cases dispose of them in the way the politicians prefer.

Of course, most cases to which the government is a party do not present political questions. Rather, they involve routine decisions made by mid- and lower-level bureaucrats. Like bureaucrats anywhere, Japanese bureaucrats sometimes ignore government policy and sometimes simply shirk. As a result, politicians can profitably offer voters access to independent, unbiased courts as a way to keep bureaucrats in line. And in Japan they do.

Prosecutors are bureaucrats too, and like other bureaucrats can err or shirk. Japanese budgetary considerations suggest that they will usually be too overworked to prosecute any but the most obviously guilty defendants. If so, then honest judges will usually convict. And they do. Still, the logic to monitoring bureaucrats applies to prosecutors as well, and suggests that judges who acquit should not suffer in their careers. We found that unless they acquit in ways that violate basic components of majority party policy or involve serious legal error, they do not.

We take our data from the period before 1993. One of the key institutional features highlighted in chapter 1 was the dominance of the Liberal Democratic

Party (LDP), a dominance that may have ended in 1993. The LDP is still the major player on the political scene in Japan, but it can no longer expect to stay in power continuously. This apparent change is crucial, and presents predictable consequences (even if, at the time of writing, we still lack the data to test them). More specifically, the lower the ruling party's (whether the LDP's or any other's) chances of winning the next election, the likelier it will be to propose measures that extend its hold on the judiciary in the future but reduce its control over it currently. Such measures might include appointment of young Supreme Court justices, the creation of a special constitutional court, the elimination of mandatory retirement, or even an attempt to amend the Constitution more clearly to support LDP policies. Rhetorically, however, the government will do all this with fervent praise for judicial independence.

In contrast to their Japanese peers, U.S. politicians do seem to let federal judges make policy independently. The key to this strategy lies, we suggest, in the dynamics of indefinitely repeated games. Although politicians in countries that keep courts off limits lower their ability to earn political points while in office, they limit their losses while out of office. Precisely because independent courts reduce the returns to electoral wins, they also reduce the harm from electoral losses. The cost of this is a judiciary that sometimes does what neither the majority party nor the majority of voters wants, but politicians may well find this a cost worth bearing. In Japan, the LDP for decades faced high odds of staying in power—and had little reason to cut its potential losses from an electoral disaster. By contrast, at the national level the principal American parties regularly alternate in office. Consequently, if politicians were to benefit from a policy of keeping hands off the courts anywhere, they were more likely to benefit in the United States than in Japan.

And so it has been. For better or for worse, federal politicians did adopt such a policy in the United States. They did not adopt it in Japan.

Appendix A

Excerpts from the Constitutional Texts

Chapter V: The Diet

Article 64: The Diet shall set up an impeachment court from among the members of both Houses for the purposes of trying those judges against whom removal proceedings have been instituted. 2) Matters relating to impeachment shall be provided for by law.

Chapter VI: Judiciary

Article 76: The whole judicial power is vested in a Supreme Court and in such inferior courts as are established by law. 2) No extraordinary tribunal shall be established, nor shall any organ or agency of the Executive be given final judicial power. 3) All judges shall be independent in the exercise of their conscience and shall be bound only by this Constitution and the laws.

Article 77: The Supreme Court is vested with the rule-making power under which it determines the rules of procedure and of practice, and of matters relating to attorneys, the internal discipline of the courts and the administration of judicial affairs. 2) Public procurators shall be subject to the rule-making power of the Supreme Court. 3) The Supreme Court may delegate the power to make rules for inferior courts to such courts.

Article 78: Judges shall not be removed except by public impeachment unless judicially declared mentally or physically incompetent to perform official duties. No disciplinary action against judges shall be administered by any executive organ or agency.

Article 79: The Supreme Court shall consist of a Chief Judge and such number of judges as may be determined by law; all such judges excepting the Chief Judge shall be appointed by the Cabinet. 2) The appointment of the judges of the Supreme Court shall be reviewed by the people at the first general election of members of the House of Representatives following their appointment, and shall be reviewed again at the first general election of members of the House of Representatives after a lapse of ten (10) years, and in the same manner thereafter.

Article 80: The judges of the inferior courts shall be appointed by the Cabinet from a list of persons nominated by the Supreme Court. All such judges shall hold office for a term of ten (10) years with privilege of reappointment, provided that they shall be retired upon the attainment of the age as fixed by law. 2) The judges of the inferior courts shall receive, at regular stated intervals, adequate compensation which shall not be decreased during their terms of office.

Article 81: The Supreme Court is the court of last resort with power to determine the constitutionality of any law, order, regulation or official act.

Article 82: Trials shall be conducted and judgment declared publicly. 2) Where a court unanimously determines publicity to be dangerous to public order or morals, a trial may be conducted privately, but trials of political offenses, offenses involving the press, or cases wherein the rights of people as guaranteed in Chapter III of this Constitution are in question shall always be conducted publicly.

JAPAN: THE 1889 MEIJI CONSTITUTION
Chapter V. The Judicature

Article 57: The Judicature shall be exercised by the Courts of Law according to law, in the name of the Emperor. (2) The organization of the Courts of Law shall be determined by law.

Article 58: The judges shall be appointed from among those who possess proper qualifications according to law. (2) No judge shall be deprived of his position, unless by way of criminal sentence or disciplinary punishment. (3) Rules for disciplinary punishment shall be determined by law.

Article 59: Trials and judgments of a Court shall be conducted publicly. When, however, there exists any fear, that such publicity may be prejudicial to peace and order, or to the maintenance of public morality, the public trial may be suspended by provisions of law or by the decision of the Court of Law.

Article 60: All matters that fall within the competency of a special Court, shall be specially provided for by law.

Article 61: No suit at law, which relates to rights alleged to have been infringed by the illegal measures of the administrative authorities, and which shall come within the competency of the Court of Administrative Litigation specially established by law, shall be taken cognizance of by Court of Law.[1]

1. Available at http://uiarchive.uiuc.edu/mirrors/ftp/ibiblio.unc.edu/pub/docs/books/gutenberg/etext96/cjold10.txt (July 23, 2001).

UNITED STATES: THE 1789 CONSTITUTION
Article I

Section 2: The House of Representatives shall choose their Speaker and other Officers; and shall have the sole Power of Impeachment.

Section 3: The Senate shall have the sole Power to try all Impeachments. When sitting for that Purpose, they shall be on Oath or Affirmation. When the President of the United States is tried, the Chief Justice shall preside: And no Person shall be convicted without the Concurrence of two thirds of the Members present.

Judgment in Cases of Impeachment shall not extend further than to removal from Office, and disqualification to hold and enjoy any Office of honor, Trust or Profit under the United States: but the Party convicted shall nevertheless be liable and subject to Indictment, Trial, Judgment and Punishment, according to Law.

Article III

Section 1: The judicial Power of the United States shall be vested in one supreme Court, and in such inferior Courts as the Congress may from time to time ordain and establish. The Judges, both of the supreme and inferior Courts, shall hold their Offices during good Behaviour, and shall, at stated Times, receive for their Services a Compensation, which shall not be diminished during their Continuance in Office.

Section 2: The judicial Power shall extend to all Cases, in Law and Equity, arising under this Constitution, the Laws of the United States, and Treaties made, or which shall be made, under their Authority;—to all Cases affecting Ambassadors, other public Ministers and Consuls;—to all Cases of admiralty and maritime Jurisdiction;—to Controversies to which the United States shall be a Party;—to Controversies between two or more States;—between a State and Citizens of another State [modified by Amendment XI];—between Citizens of different States;—between Citizens of the same State claiming Lands under Grants of different States, and between a State, or the Citizens thereof, and foreign States, Citizens or Subjects.

In all Cases affecting Ambassadors, other public Ministers and Consuls, and those in which a State shall be Party, the supreme Court shall have original Jurisdiction. In all the other Cases before mentioned, the supreme Court shall have appellate Jurisdiction, both as to Law and Fact, with such Exceptions, and under such Regulations as the Congress shall make.

The Trial of all Crimes, except in Cases of Impeachment, shall be by Jury; and such Trial shall be held in the State where the said Crimes shall have been committed; but when not committed within any State, the Trial shall be at such Place or Places as the Congress may by Law have directed.

Section 3: Treason against the United States shall consist only in levying War against them, or in adhering to their Enemies, giving them Aid and Comfort. No

Person shall be convicted of Treason unless on the Testimony of two Witnesses to the same overt Act, or on Confession in open Court. The Congress shall have Power to declare the Punishment of Treason, but no Attainder of Treason shall work Corruption of Blood, or Forfeiture except during the Life of the Person attainted.

Appendix B

Data Used for *Time2Sok* Estimates

in Tables 2.5–2.7

For this test, we took as our starting point all judges hired between 1959 and 1968 (793 judges). We then made two important adjustments.[1] First, we dropped those judges who held nonjudicial postings (generally regarded as prestigious) in the two years before their first *sokatsu* posting. A judge in such a post could not have held *sokatsu* duties but might well have been at Step 3 already, having postponed the more mundane *sokatsu* career step. If we included the time-to-first-*sokatsu* figures for these fast-track judges in our database base we would exaggerate the time required for promotion.[2]

Of course, by dropping such judges entirely we bias our data in a different way.[3] Since these judges were among the more successful in their cohort, by dropping them we exaggerate our estimate of the true time to *sokatsu* for judges with their characteristics. In chapter 3, we show that YJL members did not receive these prestigious administrative responsibilities as often as their peers. As a result, by dropping these star judges we drop *non*-YJL judges disproportionately. We thereby understate the success of the non-YJL judges and concomitantly bias our data *against* finding anti-YJL discrimination.[4]

1. We also dropped judges who did not join the court within a year of graduating from the LRTI.
2. In those rare cases where a judge served as chief judge before serving as *sokatsu*, we treated his appointment as chief judge as his *sokatsu* posting. Such an appointment is unambiguously higher than a *sokatsu* post.
3. Nonetheless, we chose to drop the judges rather than to keep them in and include their time-to-first-*sokatsu*, even though both procedures biased the sample in the same direction, because dropping them entirely would make it hardest to find statistically significant evidence of discrimination.
4. A hypothetical may help to illustrate the bias problem. Suppose that 90 percent of non-YJL judges get fast-track administrative appointments and early pay raises, but no YJL judges do, that those administrative appointees all become *sokatsu* some years later, and that YJL judges indeed get their pay raises much later on average. If we retained the fast-trackers, we would conclude that being in the YJL *helped* in getting an early pay raise, since the YJL judges would make *sokatsu* much earlier on average. If we omitted the fast-trackers, we would be left with the YJL judges and just the worst 10 percent of the non-YJL judges, and we would find little if any difference in their rate of pay increase. Since it is not true that 90 percent of non-YJL judges are on the fast track, the bias is not so large, but it still exists.

177

Second, we had somehow to deal with judges who never obtained a *sokatsu* appointment. The true value of time-to-*sokatsu* for them is infinity, but using that value obviously would distort the analysis. Our first adjustment was to drop the group of 164 judges, 23.8 percent of whom were YJL members judges, who (i) never obtained a *sokatsu* appointment and (ii) quit or died *before* the mean time-to-*sokatsu* for the rest of the group, 20.41 years. Our second adjustment was that if a judge quit or died *after* 20.41 years without a *sokatsu* appointment,[5] we kept him in the data set but treated his death or resignation as his time of first *sokatsu* appointment. We applied this procedure to eighty-three judges, 33.7 percent of whom were YJL members.[6]

Although these last two adjustments also bias our data, they again bias it *against* finding anti-YJL discrimination. If a judge quit during the first twenty years of his career, the fact that he quit tells us little about how well he was doing. If he quit later, however, when many of his peers were serving as *sokatsu* but he was not, we can deduce that he was a relatively unsuccessful judge. By treating his resignation as equivalent to a *sokatsu* appointment, we overstate his professional success. Because he never received a *sokatsu* appointment, the length of his career will necessarily be shorter (or equal to) the length of time it would have taken him to reach *sokatsu* had he not quit. Interestingly, this group of unsuccessful judges included a disproportionately high fraction of YJL members (33.7 percent). By making this adjustment, therefore, we will tend to *under*estimate the time-to-first-*sokatsu* for YJL members.

In two cases, we did not have a judge's date of birth, and thus could not calculate *Flunks*. Accordingly, we used the mean for the group as a whole.

5. We include here those judges who still did not have a *sokatsu* appointment as of 1997, the last year for which the ZSKS includes data.

6. We computed the mean values of the variables for the 294 judges we dropped for the various reasons to get some idea of how they compare with the 501 judges we retained and whose descriptive statistics are shown in table 2.5. For the retained and dropped judges the values of *YJL* were .28 and .22; the values of *1st_Tokyo* were .10 and .24; the values of *Elite_College* were .32 and .38; and the values of *Flunks* were 4.83 and 4.84. Thus, the main difference is that the dropped judges include many more fast-trackers who started with Tokyo postings—as one would expect from our retention criterion. Heckman and Robb (1985) initiated a literature in labor econometrics on how to deal with people who exit a labor force nonrandomly, but we have not tried to use those techniques here.

Appendix C

Interpreting Ordered Probit Results

in Tables 3.3 and 3.4

TABLE 3.3

The discussion in chapter 3 focused on which variables were statistically significant, rather than on the values of the coefficients. Interpreting ordered probit coefficients requires some care. To find the predicted post or location for a judge, we combine the estimated table 3.3 coefficients and each judge's variable values, as with linear regression. We then use these terms to generate a "score" for each judge. As ordered probit also generates estimated "cutoff scores," we match each judge's "score" to the cutoffs in order to generate a predicted posting for each judge.

To explore how this works, consider Takeo Wada, the very last judge in our sample, who can fairly be called a typical judge based on observable measures. For regression B in table 3.3, the cutoff scores were −3.25, −2.57, and −2.05. Table C.1 shows that Judge Wada's location score is −3.52. Because −3.52 falls below the bottom cutoff of −3.25, the modal value of his predicted location is 0. If his score were −2.90, he would fall in the −3.25 to −2.57 range and have a predicted modal location of 1.

Since we have only an estimated score for each judge, our predictions do not take straightforward integer values. If we knew with certainty that Judge Wada's true location score was −3.52, we could predict with certainty a posting of 0. Because −3.52 is just an estimate, however, his true score might be higher or lower. With positive probability, his score might even be 0.5, for example, in which case his predicted posting would be 3 rather than 0. Accordingly, if Judge Wada's score is −3.52, our best prediction is not a posting of 0 but a weighted average of 0, 1, 2, and 3. Those weights will be our estimated probabilities of the true score lying in the four intervals of [−infinity, 3.25], [−3.25, −2.57], [−2.57, −2.05], and [−infinity, 2.05], found by using the standard error of the estimate. Our predicted career quality is the resulting weighted average.

For Judge Wada, with a score of −3.52, the expected value of his first location is 0.64. (The actual value for his first location was 0, so the residual is −0.64.) If the score rose from −3.52 to −3.10 because the judge began his career three years younger, the expected location would improve to 1.05 and the modal location would jump to 1. Thus

179

Table C.1 Interpreting First-Job Coefficients

Variable	Mean in Population (a)	Value for Judge Wada (b)	Posting Coefficient (c)	Contribution for Wada (b)*(c)	Location Coefficient (d)	Contribution for Wada (b)*(d)
Male	.91	1	−.56	−.56	.35	.35
Flunks	29.85	29	−.12*	−3.48	−.14	−4.06
Tokyo_U	.20	0	−1.8	0	1.37*	0
Kyoto_U	.04	0	−.72	0	.71*	0
Chuo_U	.20	1	−.54	−.54	.11	.11
No_University	.47	0	−.49	0	.18	0
YJL	.27	0	−.07	0	−.01	0
Total score	—	—	—	−4.46	—	−3.52

NOTE: The cut points for regression 3.3A are −5.69 and 1.19. The cut points for regression 3.3B are −3.25, −2.57, and −2.05.
* Statistically significant at the 10 percent level.

the coefficient on age is not only statistically significant, but is large enough that a reasonable change in its value leads to a real change in the predicted job location.

This discussion can also be used to see the relative importance of the different variables. If the judge were three years older, his score would fall by 0.42, as just discussed. If the judge were female, her score would fall by 0.35. Both of these are realistic magnitudes of change within the population, implying that sex and age are of roughly the same importance.

Interpreting the posting regression is similar, but it has less interesting results. Judge Wada has an expected first posting of 0.90 and a modal location of 1. (His actual posting value was 3.) If the score were to rise from −4.46 to −4.10 because the judge began his career three years younger, the expected location would improve to .98, and the modal location would remain at 1. As this shows, the posting regression has less predictive power than the location regression. It takes a much bigger improvement in characteristics to get a sizable improvement in predicted career. Not only are the coefficients in the first posting regression mostly statistically insignificant, they are also "economically insignificant."

TABLE 3.4

Interpreting the regression coefficients in table 3.4 requires the same procedure as with the regressions for the first job. Again we will use Judge Wada. As with table 3.3, we ask how a realistic change in the value of a variable would affect the score. Converting from male to female, the score would fall by 0.22, as shown in table C.2. If the judge were three years older, his score would fall by 0.21. Both of these are realistic magnitudes of change within the population, and so one might conclude that sex and age are of approximately equal importance. The location score gives the judge an expected location of 0.94 and a modal location of 0. (The actual value for this judge was 1.) If we add 0.22 to increase the score from −1.11 to −0.89, the expected location would improve to 1.17 and the modal location would jump to 1.

Table C.2 Interpreting Career Coefficients

Variable	Population Mean (a)	Value for Judge Wada (b)	Posting Coefficient (c)	Contribution for Wada (b)*(c)	Location Coefficient (d)	Contribution for Wada (b)*(d)
Male	.91	1	.33	.33	.22	.22
Flunks	29.85	29	−.03	−.87	−.073*	−2.12
Tokyo_U	.20	0	.03	0	.18	0
Kyoto_U	.04	0	.20	0	.15	0
Chuo_U	.20	1	.19	.19	.48	.48
No_University	.47	0	−.07	0	−.04	0
1st_Location = 1	.22	0	.33*	0	.36*	0
1st_Location = 2	.13	0	−.14	0	.30	0
1st_Location = 3	.18	0	.79*	0	1.13*	0
Opinions_yr	1.75	1.55	.19*	.29	.20*	.31
YJL	.27	0	−.28*	0	.16	0
Total score	—	—	—	−.03	—	−1.11

NOTE: The cut points for regression 3.4A are −1.29, −.77, and .92. The cut points for regression 3.4B are −.94, −.61, and .25.

* Statistically significant at the 10 percent level.

Indeed, it seems that in the location regression the variables that are statistically significant all have coefficients that are also of meaningful size, although some other variables (like sex) that are statistically insignificant also have large coefficients. Most interesting, perhaps, is the very large coefficient of 1.13 on *1st_Location* = 3. It contributes 1.13 to the judge's score if his first posting was in Tokyo, a very strong effect in terms of getting later Tokyo jobs. Note that this is not just the effect of inertia. The location variable here is based on the number of years spent in a location, but almost all judges rotate out of Tokyo at some point even if they begin there.

The posting regression's coefficients for the variables that were also statistically significant in the location regression—*1st_Location* = 1, *1st_Location* = 3, and *Opinons/Yr*—are of the same order of magnitude. Starting age has a coefficient size about half that in the location regression, so its size is reasonably large, but the error is greater, and so it is not statistically significant in the posting regression. *YJL* has the reasonably large coefficient of −0.28 and is statistically significant, but the error distribution in the posting regression is flat enough that the coefficient of 0.28 does not have a strong effect on the predicted posting. The posting score of −0.03 gives our benchmark, Judge Wada, an expected location of 1.84 and a modal posting of 2. (His actual value was 1.) If we convert him to a YJL member and subtract 0.28, his score falls from −0.03 to −0.31, the expected posting falls to 1.63, and the modal posting remains at 2. For the modal posting to fall to 1 would require a decrease in the score to −0.77, while to increase to 3 would require an increase to 0.92. What this tells us is that although the posting regression may be able to tell us what variables are statistically significant, its overall performance in predicting posting is poor—factors not in our regression equation are relatively more important than in the location regression.

Appendix D

A Formal Model of Prosecutorial Incentives

Our argument that an increased budget will reduce conviction rates does not apply under all circumstances, something formal modeling helps to show. Let us assume that the cost of any one case is trivial compared to the entire prosecutorial budget, so that we can model cases as points on a continuum. Potential cases will be indexed by θ, where θ varies from 0 to 1 in order of increasing ease of prosecution, so that the universe of possible cases has size 1. If the prosecutor decides to prosecute the easiest one-third of cases, he takes all the cases in the interval [2/3, 1].

We assume that prosecutors maximize the *number* of convictions they obtain, and that all cases involve the same crime. Even if, as seems likely, prosecutors also try to keep their conviction *rates* high, conviction rates can still decline with increasing prosecutorial budgets. Obviously, all cases do not involve the same crime, and in general prosecutors will face pressure to focus disproportionately on the more serious crimes. So long as they try to maximize convictions within each category of crime, however, conviction rates for each category will still decline with budget increases.

We denote the prosecutor's budget by B, the fixed cost of each case prosecuted by F (which we will assume is the same for each case), and the variable cost by e. A case of a given type will have a probability of conviction of $P(e,\theta)$.[1] Let us assume that $dP/de \geq 0$, $d^2P/de^2 \leq 0$, $dP/d\theta \geq 0$ and $d^2P/d\theta^2 \geq 0$. This says that the value of a case of a given type increases with prosecutorial effort, subject to diminishing returns, but it also allows for extra effort being unproductive ($P'=0$) or having neither increasing nor diminishing returns ($P''=0$). If two cases have equal expenditure, the easier case (with higher θ) has at least as great a chance of success, and perhaps a greater one, and

1. More generally, we could replace the probability of conviction P in the model with a value V that incorporates the probability of a conviction or a plea bargain, the length of the sentence, the importance of punishing the particular type of crime, and the chance of mistakenly prosecuting someone innocent. For present purposes, we are most interested in conviction rates; our model can be considered as a model of the conviction rate for a case with given sentence length, importance, and probability of mistake.

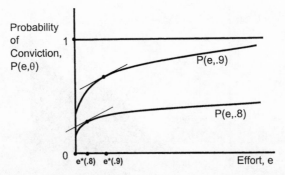

Figure D.1 How the probability of conviction varies with prosecutorial effort and case type

also has at least as great a marginal benefit of effort.[2] Figure D.1 shows how P might vary with e and θ.

We now come to the prosecutor's problem. He has two kinds of choices. First, he must decide which cases to prosecute. He will want to prosecute the easier cases first, which amounts to choosing a lower cutoff $\bar{\theta}$ for the interval of types $[\bar{\theta},1]$ that he prosecutes. Second, he needs to pick the $e(\theta)$ function that determines how much budget e he spends on each type θ of case. If the prosecutor chooses to equalize the marginal product of effort in two cases with $\theta = .8$ and $\theta = 1$, as in figure D.1, then he would choose $e(.8)$ and $e(1)$ to equalize the slopes of the $P(e; \theta)$ functions, which means that $e(1) > e(.8)$; that is, he will spend more on the stronger case. Figure D.2 shows one $e(\theta)$ function he might pick and the two dimensions in which he can change it—the extensive margin of reducing the cutoff (horizontal) and the intensive margin of increasing spending on existing cases (vertical).

The payoff function for the prosecutor is

$$\int_{\bar{\theta}}^{1} P(e(\theta), \theta)d\theta.$$

The budget constraint is

$$\int_{\bar{\theta}}^{1} [e(\theta) + F]d\theta \leq B.$$

2. These assumptions are plausible, but not invariably true. It might be, for example, that the prosecutor can secure a high probability of conviction in a certain case with very little effort, but that further effort is useless, whereas a different case requires more effort in general but has higher marginal product of effort too. Our assumptions rule out that kind of situation, in which the term "easier case" becomes highly ambiguous.

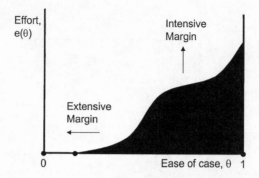

Figure D.2 The prosecutor's effort as a function of case type

The shaded area in figure D.2 represents the first part of this integral, the variable costs of prosecution.

The prosecutor's solution needs two kinds of optimality, both simple enough to be described without further mathematics.[3] First, the $e(\theta)$ function must be chosen so that the marginal product of effort must be the same for each case prosecuted. This is the optimal *intensive* margin of prosecution.

Second, the marginal product of effort for any case prosecuted must equal the average product of effort for the marginal case. This is the optimal *extensive* margin of prosecution.

Three things affect whether increasing the budget leads to a rise or a fall in the average probability of conviction: the size of the fixed cost of prosecuting a case, the rate at which returns to effort diminish, and the variability in ease of prosecution $dP/d\theta$.

First, the size of the fixed cost matters. If it is big, then the extra budget would best go to existing cases, and the average conviction rate will rise. If it is very small, then the prosecutor will prosecute all cases—another corner solution—and an increase in the budget will surely again increase the average probability of success. Thus, the average conviction rate increases with the budget if the fixed cost per case is either very large or very small.

Second, the speed at which the returns to effort diminish matters. Suppose the marginal return to effort does not change much as effort increases. Then as the budget increases, existing cases continue to provide almost as much marginal return to extra effort as they did before. Accordingly, most of the increased spending will go to those existing cases. The marginal case will not change much, but the effort on each existing case will increase, so the average conviction rate will go up. On the other hand, if there are diminishing returns to spending on existing cases, then if new budget dollars went to old cases, the marginal return to effort would fall sharply, to the point where it would be well below the average return to effort for new cases. Therefore, more of the

3. For a mathematical exposition, see Ramseyer and Rasmusen 1998.

new budget will go to new cases. The identity of the marginal case, $\bar{\theta}$, will decline and the average conviction rate will decline with it. Thus, the average conviction rate will decline with extra budget if the diminishing returns are large.

Third, it matters how rapidly the quality of cases declines, which is captured by the value of $dP/d\theta$. If $dP/d\theta$ is large, then as the prosecutor selects better cases his probabilities of conviction rise dramatically. Correspondingly, dipping deeper into the case pool will reduce his success rate. This means that the prosecutor will be reluctant to add new cases as his budget increases, and will use more of the extra money to improve his chances in the old cases.

Consider two extreme cases that illustrate these considerations.

Situation Alpha. Let all cases be identical in their $P(e, \theta)$ functions, so $dP/d\theta = 0$, with the fixed cost low relative to the budget. All cases are taken. Additional budget leads to increased spending on existing cases, and higher average success.

Situation Beta. Let all cases be identical in their $P(e, \theta)$ functions, so $dP/d\theta = 0$, with the fixed cost high. The marginal benefit of effort per case falls sharply, so P'' is very negative. Then, additional budget will lead to more cases, and a lower average success.

We believe Japan is more like *Situation Beta:* if a prosecutor were given a greater budget, he would tend to spend it on prosecuting more cases rather than in prosecuting his existing cases more intensely.

First, as explained above, in *Situation Alpha* the prosecutor takes all cases. We know, however, that in Japan prosecutors take only a very small fraction of cases. Most criminal cases they simply drop, unprosecuted.

Second, because prosecutors care about their reputations before judges, whether in Japan or in the United States, they avoid irritating judges with sloppy work. As a result, the fixed cost F will be nontrivial, and prosecutors will not file cases unless they can invest enough resources to make a plausible showing of guilt.

Third, in bench trial jurisdictions like Japan, the investments a prosecutor makes in a case should earn high returns initially (quickly raising the expected conviction rate from near zero to a comfortable probability), but run into sharply diminishing marginal returns thereafter. After investing enough effort in a case to make the basic showing, the U.S. prosecutor devotes much of the rest of his time to such tasks as *voir dire* in jury selection or showmanship before the jury. By contrast, Japanese prosecutors argue before professional judges. It is important for the prosecutor to present the facts and the law, but how he presents them—a task with enormous potential for polishing and artistry—matters less. That initial investment in presenting the facts, however, is all the more important, since before a jury a small investment in dramatic performance can sometimes cure a sloppy case with poor advance research.

References

Abe, Haruhiko. 1971. "Saibankan ron (A Theory of Judges)." 469 *Jurisuto* 194–98.

Abe, Teruya, and Masaaki Ikeda, eds. 1989. *Shinpan: Kenpo hanrei* (New Edition: Constitutional Cases). Tokyo: Yuhikaku.

Administrative Office of the U.S. Courts. 1995. *Judicial Business of the U.S. Courts.* Washington, D.C.: Administrative Office of the U.S. Courts.

American Bar Association. 1976. *Code of Judicial Conduct.* Chicago: American Bar Association.

Anderson, Gary, William Shughart, and Robert Tollison. 1989. "On the Incentive of Judges to Enforce Legislative Wealth Transfers." 32 *Journal of Law and Economics* 215–28 (April).

Atkins, Burton M., and William Zavoina. 1974. "Judicial Leadership on the Court of Appeals: A Probability Analysis of Panel Assignment in Race Relations Cases on the Fifth Circuit." 18 *American Journal of Political Science* 701–11 (November).

Auer, James E. 1993. "Article 9: Renunciation of War." In *Japanese Constitutional Law,* edited by Percy R. Luney Jr. and Kazuyuki Takahashi. Pp. 69–86. Tokyo: University of Tokyo Press.

Bagnoli, Mark, and Michael McKee. 1991. "Controlling the Game: Political Sponsors and Bureaus." 7 *Journal of Law, Economics, and Organization* 229–47 (Fall).

Becker, Gary S. 1968. "Crime and Punishment: An Economic Approach." 76 *Journal of Political Economy* 169–217 (March/April).

Beer, Lawrence W., and Hiroshi Itoh. 1996. "Introduction: Japan's Constitutional Law, 1945–1990." In *The Constitutional Case Law of Japan, 1970 through 1990,* edited by Lawrence W. Beer and Hiroshi Itoh. Pp. 3–66. Seattle: University of Washington Press.

Block, Stewart A. 1970. "The Limitations of Article 111 on the Proposed Judicial Removal Machinery: S. 1506." 118 *University of Pennsylvania Law Review* 1064–90 (June).

Buckley, Frank and Eric Rasmusen. 2000. "The Uneasy Case for the Flat Tax." 11 *Constitutional Political Economy* 295–318 (December).

Caldeira, Gregory A., and James L. Gibson. 1995. "The Legitimacy of the Court of Justice in the European Union: Models of Institutional Support." 89 *American Political Science Review* 356–76 (October).

Caldeira, Gregory A., John R. Wright, and Christopher J. W. Zorn. 1999. "Sophisticated Voting and Gate-Keeping in the Supreme Court." 15 *Journal of Law, Economics and Organization* 549–72 (October).

Calder, Kent E. 1988. *Crisis and Compensation: Public Policy and Political Stability in Japan.* Princeton: Princeton University Press.

Calvert, Randall Law, Mark J. Moran, and Barry R. Weingast. 1987. "Congressional Influence over Policy Making: The Case of the FTC." In *Congress: Structure and Policy,* edited by Mathew D. McCubbins and Terry Sullivan. Pp. 493–522. Cambridge: Cambridge University Press.

Calvert, Randall Law, Mathew D. McCubbins, and Barry R. Weingast. 1989. "A Theory of Political Control and Agency Discretion." 33 *American Journal of Political Science* 588–611 (August).

Cameron, Charles M., Albert D. Cover, and Jeffrey A. Segal. 1990. "Senate Voting on Supreme Court Nominees: A Neoinstitutional Model." 84 *American Political Science Review* 525–34 (June).

Cappelletti, Mauro. 1983. "Who Watches the Watchmen? A Comparative Study on Judicial Responsibility." 31 *American Journal of Comparative Law* 1–62 (Winter).

Castberg, A. Didrick. 1997. "Prosecutorial Independence In Japan." 16 *UCLA Pacific Basin Law Journal* 38–87 (Fall).

Choper, Jesse H. 1974. "The Supreme Court and the Political Branches: Democratic Theory and Practice." 122 *University of Pennsylvania Law Review* 810–58 (April).

Clark, David. 1988. "The Selection and Accountability of Judges in West Germany: Implementation of a Rechtstaat." 61 *Southern California Law Review* 1797–1847.

Coate, Malcolm B., Richard S. Higgins, and Fred S. McChesney. 1990. "Bureaucracy and Politics in FTC Merger Challenges." 33 *Journal of Law and Economics* 463–82 (October).

Cohen, Mark A. 1991. "Explaining Judicial Behavior or What's 'Unconstitutional' about the Sentencing Commission." 7 *Journal of Law, Economics and Organization* 183–99 (Spring).

———. 1992. "The Motives of Judges: Empirical Evidence from Antitrust Sentencing." 12 *International Review of Law and Economics* 13–30 (March).

Cooter, Robert. 1983. "The Objectives of Private and Public Judges." 41 *Public Choice* 107–32.

———. 2000. *The Strategic Constitution.* Princeton: Princeton University Press.

Cooter, Robert, and Thomas Ginsburg. 1996. "Comparative Judicial Discretion: An Empirical Test of Economic Models." 16 *International Review of Law and Economics* 295–313 (September).

Culver, John H., and Randal L. Cruikshanks. 1982. "Judicial Discipline at the Federal Level: A New Response to an Old Problem." In *The Analysis of Judicial Reform,* edited by Philip S. Dubois. Pp. 107–19. Lexington, Mass.: D. C. Heath.

Currie, David. 1990. *The Constitution in the Supreme Court: The Second Century, 1888– 1986.* Chicago: University of Chicago Press.

Daiichi hoki shuppan, K.K., ed. *Hanrei taikei* CD-ROM (A Systematic Case Law: CD-ROM). Tokyo: Daiichi hoki, biannual.

Davidow, Robert P. 1981. "Beyond Merit Selection: Judicial Careers through Merit Promotion." 12 *Texas Tech Law Review* 851–910.

De Figueiredo, John M., and Emerson H. Tiller. 1996. "Congressional Control of the Courts: A Theoretical and Empirical Analysis of Expansion of the Federal Judiciary." 39 *Journal of Law and Economics* 435–62 (October).

DeFrances, Carol, and Greg Steadman. 1998. "Prosecutors in State Courts, 1996." U.S. Department of Justice, Bureau of Justice Statistics Bulletin NCJ-170092 (July).

Dumbauld, Edward. 1987. Book Review, 81 *American Journal of International Law* 567–68 (April).

Easterbrook, Frank. 1982. "Ways of Criticizing the Court." 95 *Harvard Law Review* 802–32 (February).

———. 1983. "Criminal Justice as a Market System." 12 *Journal of Legal Studies* 289–332 (June).

Ellis, Richard E. 1971. *The Jeffersonian Crisis: Courts and Politics in the Young Republic.* New York: Oxford University Press.

Epp, Charles R. 1996. "Do Bills of Rights Matter? The Canadian Charter of Rights and Freedoms." 90 *American Political Science Review* 765–79 (December).

Ferejohn, John. 1995. "Law, Legislation, and Positive Political Theory." In *Modern Political Economy: Old Topics, New Directions,* edited by Jeffrey S. Banks and Eric A. Hanushek. Pp. 191–215. Cambridge: Cambridge University Press.

———. 1999. "Independent Judges, Dependent Judiciary: Explaining Judicial Independence." 72 *Southern California Law Review* 353–84 (January).

Foote, Daniel H. 1986. "Prosecutorial Discretion in Japan: A Response." 5 *UCLA Pacific Basin Law Journal* 96–106 (Spring/Fall).

———. 1992. "The Benevolent Paternalism of Japanese Criminal Justice." 80 *California Law Review* 317–90.

———. 1993. "From Japan's Death Row to Freedom." 1 *Pacific Rim Law and Policy Journal* 11–103.

———. 1993. "The Door that Never Opens? Capital Punishment and Post-Conviction Review of Death Sentences in the United States and Japan." 19 *Brooklyn Journal of International Law* 367–521.

Freund, Paul A. 1988. "Appointment of Justices: Some Historical Perspectives." 101 *Harvard Law Review* 1146–63 (April).

Frey, Bruno. 1997. *Not Just for the Money: An Economic Theory of Personal Motivation.* Cheltenham, U.K.: Edward Elgar Publishing.

Fudenberg, Drew, and Eric Maskin. 1986. "The Folk Theorem in Repeated Games with Discounting or with Incomplete Information." 54 *Econometrica* 533–54 (May).

Fukase, Chuichi. 1971. Tenkaiten ni tatsu mugunbi-hikaku heiwa shugi: 7 (Turning Point in Non-Military, Non-Nuclear Peace Principle: 7). Horitsu jiho, 48–61 (August).

George, B. J. 1984. "Discretionary Authority of Public Prosecutors in Japan." 17 *Law in Japan* 42–72.

Glaeser, Edward L., Daniel P. Kessler, and Anne Morrison Piehl. 2000. "What Do Prosecutors Maximize? An Analysis of the Federalization of Drug Crimes." 2 *American Law and Economics Review* 259–90 (Fall).

Goodman, Marcia E. 1986. "The Exercise and Control of Prosecutorial Discretion in Japan." 5 *UCLA Pacific Basin Law Journal* 16–95 (Spring/Fall).

Green, Stuart P. 1988. "Note, Private Challenges to Prosecutorial Inaction: A Model Declaratory Judgment Statute." 97 *Yale Law Journal* 488–507.

Haley, John Owen. 1991. *Authority without Power: Law and the Japanese Paradox.* New York: Oxford University Press.

———. 1998. *The Spirit of Japanese Law.* Athens: University of Georgia Press.

———. 1995. "Judicial Independence in Japan Revisited." 25 *Law in Japan* 1–18.

Hanssen, F. Andrew. 2001. "Is There a Politically Optimal Level of Judicial Independence?" Working paper, Department of Agricultural Economics and Economics, Montana State University, Bozeman, Montana.

Hara, Takashi. 1965. *Hara Takashi nikki* (Diary of Hara Takashi). Tokyo: Fukumura shoten.

Haskins, George Lee, and Herbert A. Johnson. 1981. *History of the Supreme Court of the United States.* New York: Macmillan.

Hata, Ikuhiko. 1981. *Senzenki Nihon kanryosei no seido, soshiki, jinji* (The System, Organization, and Personnel of the Pre-war Japanese Civil Service). Tokyo: Tokyo daigaku shuppankai.

Hayakawa, Takeo. 1971. "The Japanese Judiciary in the Whirlwind of Politics." 7 *Kobe University Law Review* 15–23.

Heckman, James, and Richard Robb. 1985. "Alternative Methods for Evaluating the Impact of Interventions: An Overview." 30 *Journal of Econometrics* 239–67 (October/ November).

Higgins, R.S., and Paul H. Rubin. 1980. "Judicial Discretion." 9 *Journal of Legal Studies* 129–38 (January).

Holmstrom, Bengt. 1982. "Moral Hazard in Teams." 13 *Bell Journal of Economics* 324–40 (Autumn).

Homusho, ed. 1996. *Hanzai hakusho* (White Paper on Crime). Tokyo: Okura sho.

Hosojima, Yoshimi. 1964. *Ningen Yamaoka Mannosuke den* (An Account of Yamaoka Mannosuke, the Man). Tokyo: Kodansha.

Hrebenar, Ronald J. 1986. *The Japanese Party System: From One-Party Rule to Coalition Government.* 1st ed. Boulder, Colo.: Westview Press.

Ikuta, Tadahide. 1995. *Kanryo: Japan's Hidden Government,* translated by Hideo Yanai. Tokyo: NHK Publishing.

Ishimatsu, Takeo. 1989. "Are Criminal Defendants in Japan Truly Receiving Trials by Judges?" translated by Daniel Foote. 22 *Law in Japan* 143–53.

Jescheck, Hans-Heinrich. 1970. "The Discretionary Powers of the Prosecuting Attorney in West Germany." 18 *American Journal of Comparative Law* 508–17.

Johnson, Chalmers. 1982. *MITI and the Japanese Miracle: The Growth of Industrial Policy 1925–1975.* Stanford: Stanford University Press.

Johnson, David Ted. 1996. *The Japanese Way of Justice: Prosecuting Crime in Japan.* Ph.D. diss., University of California, Berkeley.

Johnson, Elmer H. 1997. *Criminalization and Prisoners in Japan: Six Contrary Cohorts.* Carbondale: Southern Illinois University Press.

Johnson, Ronald N., and Gary D. Libecap. 1994. *The Federal Civil Service System and the Problem of Bureaucracy: The Economics and Politics of Institutional Change.* Cambridge, Mass.: National Bureau of Economic Research.

Kaneko, Hiroshi. 1992. *Sozei ho* (Tax Law). 4th ed. Tokyo: Yuhikaku.

Kaplan, Steven N. 1994. "Top Executive Rewards and Firm Performance: A Comparison of Japan and the United States." 102 *Journal of Political Economy* 510–46 (June).

Kaplan, Steven N., and Bernadette A. Minton. 1994. "Appointments of Outsiders to Japanese Boards: Determinants and Implications for Managers." 36 *Journal of Financial Economics* 225–58 (October).

Kaplan, Steven N., and J. Mark Ramseyer. 1996. "Those Japanese Firms with their Disdain for Shareholders: Another Fable for the Academy." 74 *Washington University Law Quarterly* 403–18 (Spring).

Kashimura, Shiro. 1991. "Rodo jiken ni okeru saibankan no keireki to hanketsu (The Opinions and Careers of Judges in Labor Cases)," 41 *Kobe hogaku zasshi* 206–325.

Kawashima, Takeyoshi. 1963. "Dispute Resolution in Contemporary Japan." In *Law in Japan: The Legal Order in a Changing Society,* edited by Arthur Taylor von Mehren. Cambridge, Mass.: Harvard University Press.

Keisatsu cho. 1996. *Keisatsu hakusho* (Police White Paper). Tokyo: Okura sho.

Kessler, Daniel, Thomas Meites, and Geoffrey Miller. 1996. "Explaining Deviations from the Fifty-Percent Rule: A Multimodal Approach to the Selection of Cases for Litigation." 25 *Journal of Legal Studies* 233–60 (January).

Kitamura, Ichiro. 1993. "The Judiciary in Contemporary Society: Japan." 25 *Case Western Reserve Journal of International Law* 263–91 (Spring).

Kreps, David, Paul Milgrom, John Roberts, and Robert Wilson. 1982. "Rational Cooperation in the Finitely Repeated Prisoners' Dilemma." 27 *Journal of Economic Theory* 245–52 (August).

Kusunoki, Seiichiro. 1989. *Meiji rikken sei to shiho kan* (The Meiji Constitution and Judicial Officers). Tokyo: Keio tsushin.

Landes, William M. 1971. "An Economic Analysis of the Courts." 14 *Journal Law and Economics* 61–107 (April).

Landes, William M., and Richard A. Posner. 1975. "The Independent Judiciary in an Interest-Group Perspective." 18 *Journal of Law and Economics* 875–901 (December).

Langbein, John. 1979. "Land without Plea Bargaining: How the Germans Do It." 78 *Michigan Law Review* 204–25 (December).

Leuchtenburg, William E. 1966. "The Origins of Franklin D. Roosevelt's 'Court-Packing' Plan." 1966 *Supreme Court Review* 347–400.

Manchester, William. 1973. *The Glory and the Dream: A Narrative History of the United States 1932–1972.* Boston: Little, Brown.

Mason, Alpheus Thomas. 1937. "Politics and the Supreme Court: President Roosevelt's Proposal." 85 *University of Pennsylvania Law Review* 659–77 (May).

Matsuo, Koya, and Masahito Inoue, eds. 1992. *Keiji sosho ho hanrei hyakusen* (The Code of Criminal Procedure: One Hundred Selected Cases). 6th ed. Tokyo: Yuhikaku.

Mayer, Cynthia. 1984. "Japan: Behind the Myth of Japanese Justice." *American Lawyer* 113 (July/August).

McCubbins, Mathew D., and Gregory W. Noble. 1995. "The Appearance of Power: Legislators, Bureaucrats, and the Budget Process in the United States and Japan." In *Structure and Policy in Japan and the United States,* edited by Peter Cowhey and Matthew McCubbins. Pp. 56–80. Cambridge: Cambridge University Press.

McCubbins, Mathew D., Roger G. Noll, and Barry R. Weingast, 1987. "Administrative Procedures as Instruments of Political Control." 3 *Journal of Law, Economics and Organization* 243–75 (Fall).

———. 1989. "Structure and Process, Politics and Policy: Administrative Arrangements and the Political Control of Agencies." 75 *Virginia Law Review* 431–82.

McCubbins, Mathew D., and Thomas Schwartz. 1984. "Congressional Oversight Overlooked: Police Patrols versus Fire Alarms." 28 *American Journal of Political Science* 165–79 (February).

McCubbins, Mathew D., and Michael Thies. 1997. "As a Matter of Factions: The Budgetary Implications of Shifting Factional Control in Japan's LDP." 22 *Legislative Studies Quarterly* 293–328 (August).

Meador, Daniel J. 1983. "German Appellate Judges: Career Patterns and American–English Comparisons." *Judicature* 16–27 (June–July).

Mitani, Taichiro. 1980. *Kindai Nihon no shihoken to seito* (The Modern Japanese Judiciary and Political Parties). Tokyo: Hanawa shobo.

———. 1988. "The Establishment of Party Cabinets, 1898–1932." In *The Twentieth Century.* Vol. 6 of *The Cambridge History of Japan,* edited by Peter Duus. Cambridge: Cambridge University Press.

Miyamoto, Masao. 1995. *Straightjacket Society: An Insider's Irreverent View of Bureaucratic Japan.* Tokyo: Kodansha International.

Miyazawa, Setsuo. 1991. "Administrative Control of Japanese Judges." In *Law and Technology in the Pacific Community,* edited by Philip S.C. Lewis. Boulder, Colo.: Westview Press.

Miyazawa, Setsuo. 1992. *Policing in Japan,* translated by F.G. Bennett Jr. Albany: SUNY Press.

Moe, Terry M. 1991. "Politics and the Theory of Organization." 7 *Journal of Law Economics and Organization* 106–29 (special issue).

Mohan roppo (Annotated Statutory Compilation). 1997. Tokyo: Sanseido.

Muller, Ingo. 1991. *Hitler's Justice: The Courts of the Third Reich.* Cambridge, Mass.: Harvard University Press.

Murphy, Russell D. 1980. "Whither the Mayors? A Note on Mayoral Careers." 42 *Journal of Politics* 277–90 (February).

Netto 46. 1995. *Saibankan ni narenai riyu* (The Reason They Cannot Become Judges). Tokyo: Aoki shoten.

Nihon minshu horitsuka kyokai, ed. 1990. *Zen saibankan keireki soran: kaitei shinban* (Biographical Information on All Judges: New Revised Edition). Tokyo: Konin sha (ZSKS).

Nihon minshu horitsuka kyokai, ed. 1998. *Zen saibankan keireki soran: Dai san ban* (Biographical Information on All Judges: 3d Edition). Tokyo: Konin sha (ZSKS).

Nomura, Jiro. 1981. *Japan's Judicial System.* About Japan Series 15. Tokyo: Foreign Press Center/Japan.

Nomura, Masao. 1966. *Hoso fuun roku* (Window into a Record of the Vicissitudes of the Law). Tokyo: Asahi shimbunsha.

North, Douglass C., and Barry R. Weingast. 1989. "Constitutions and Commitment: The Evolution of Institutions Governing Public Choice in Seventeenth-Century England." 49 *Journal of Economic History* 803–32 (December).

Okudaira, Yasuhiro. 1993. "Forty Years of the Constitution and Its Various Influences: Japanese, American and European." In *Japanese Constitutional Law,* edited by Percy R. Luney Jr. and Kazuyuki Takahashi. P. 20. Tokyo: University of Tokyo Press.

Park, Yung H. 1986. *Bureaucrats and Ministers in Contemporary Japanese Government.* Berkeley, Calif.: Institute of East Asian Studies.

Posner, Richard A. 1973. "An Economic Approach to Legal Procedure and Judicial Administration." 2 *Journal of Legal Studies* 399–458 (June).

———. 1985. *The Federal Courts: Crisis and Reform.* Cambridge, Mass.: Harvard University Press.

———. 1990. *The Problems of Jurisprudence.* Cambridge, Mass.: Harvard University Press.

———. 1993. "What Do Judges and Justices Maximize? (The Same Thing Everybody Else Does)." 3 *Supreme Court Economic Review* 1–42 (April).

———. 1998. *Economic Analysis of Law.* 5th ed. New York: Aspen.

Priest, George L., and Benjamin Klein. 1984. "The Selection of Disputes for Litigation." 13 *Journal of Legal Studies* 1–55 (January).

Ramseyer, J. Mark. 1989. "Kokuzeicho wa naze katsuka: 'Ho to keizaigaku' kara mita shoso ritsu (Why the National Tax Office Wins: Verdict Rates from a "Law and Economics" Perspective)." 934 *Jurisuto* 130–35.

———. 1990. *Ho to keizaigaku: Nihon ho no keizai bunseki* (Law and Economics: An Economic Analysis of Japanese Law). Tokyo: Kobundo.

———. 1994. "The Puzzling (In)dependence of Courts: A Comparative Approach." 23 *Journal of Legal Studies* 721–48 (June).

———. 1995. "Public Choice." In *Chicago Lectures in Law and Economics.* Pp. 101–12. New York: Foundation Press.

———. 1998. "Judicial Independence." In *The New Palgrave Dictionary of Economics and the Law.* Pp. 383–87. London: Macmillan.

———. 1999. "Rethinking Administrative Guidance." In *Finance, Development and Competition in Japan: Essays in Honor of Hugh Patrick,* edited by Masahiko Aoki and Gary Saxonhouse. Pp. 199–211. London: Oxford University Press.

Ramseyer, J. Mark, and Minoru Nakazato. 1989. "The Rational Litigant: Settlement Amounts and Verdict Rates in Japan." 18 *Journal of Legal Studies* 263–90 (June).

———. 1999. *Japanese Law: An Economic Approach.* Chicago: University of Chicago Press.

Ramseyer, J. Mark, and Eric B. Rasmusen. 1997. "Judicial Independence in a Civil Law Regime: The Evidence from Japan." 13 *Journal of Law, Economics and Organization* 259–86 (October).

————. 1998. "Why Is the Japanese Conviction Rate so High?" Discussion Paper No. 240. Harvard Law School John M. Olin Center for Law, Economics, and Business (October).

————. 1999. "Why the Japanese Taxpayer Always Loses." 72 *Southern California Law Review* 571–96. (January/March).

————. 2000. "Skewed Incentives: Paying for Politics as a Japanese Judge." 83 *Judicature* 190–95 (January/February).

————. 2001a. "Why Is the Japanese Conviction Rate So High?" 30 *Journal of Legal Studies* 53–88 (January).

————. 2001b. "Why Are Japanese Judges so Conservative in Politically Charged Cases?" 95 *American Political Science Review* 331–44 (June).

Ramseyer, J. Mark, and Frances McCall Rosenbluth. 1995. *The Politics of Oligarchy: Institutional Choice in Imperial Japan.* Cambridge: Cambridge University Press.

————. 1997. *Japan's Political Marketplace.* Rev. ed. Cambridge, Mass.: Harvard University Press.

Rasmusen, Eric B. 1994. "Judicial Legitimacy as a Repeated Game." 10 *Journal of Law, Economics and Organization* 62–83 (April).

————. 1995. "Predictable and Unpredictable Error in Tort Awards: The Effect of Plaintiff Self Selection and Signalling." 15 *International Review of Law and Economics* 323–45 (September).

————. 1997. "A Theory of Trustees, and Other Thoughts." In *Public Debt and Its Finance in a Model of a Macroeconomic Policy Game: Papers Presented at a Workshop held in Antalya, Turkey on October 10–11, 1997,* edited by Tahire Akder, http://Php.Indiana.edu/~erasmuse/papers/98.BOOK.trustees.NEW.pdf.

————. 1998. "*Mezzanatto* and the Economics of Self Incrimination." 19 *Cardozo Law Review* 1541–84 (May).

————. 2001. *Games and Information: An Introduction to Game Theory.* 3rd ed. Oxford: Basil Blackwell.

Riker, William. 1964. *Federalism: Origins, Operation, Significance.* Boston: Little, Brown.

Rosenberg, Gerald N. 1992. "Judicial Independence and the Reality of Political Power." 54 *Review of Politics* 369–98.

Rosenbluth, Frances McCall. 1989. *Financial Politics in Contemporary Japan.* Ithaca, N.Y.: Cornell University Press.

Saiko saiban sho. 1994. *Shiho tokei nempo* (Annual Report of Judicial Statistics). Tokyo: Hoso kai.

Sakaguchi, Tokuo. 1988. "Saibankan ni taisuru ninchi yakushoku 'sabetsu' ni tsuite (Regarding the "Discrimination" against Judges in Location and Official Responsibilities)." 5 [*Osaka bengoshi kai*] *Shiho mondai taisaku nyusu* 4.

Salzberger, Eli, and Paul Fenn. 1993. "A Positive Analysis of the Separation of Powers, or: Why Do We Have an Independent Judiciary?" 13 *International Review of Law and Economics* 349–79 (December).

————. 1999. "Judicial Independence: Some Evidence from the English Court of Appeal." 42 *Journal of Law and Economics* 831–47 (October).

Saxonhouse, Gary R. 2002. "How to Explain Japan's Legal System." 3 *American Law and Economics Review* 376–90.

Schlesinger, Jacob M. 1997. *Shadow Shoguns: The Rise and Fall of Japan's Postwar Political Machine.* New York: Simon and Schuster.

Schlesinger, Joseph. 1966. *Ambition and Politics: Political Careers in the United States.* Chicago: Rand McNally.

Segal, Jeffrey A. 1997. "Separation-of-Powers Games in the Positive Theory of Congress and Courts." 91 *American Political Science Review* 28–44 (March).

Selten, Reinhard. 1978. "The Chainstore Paradox." 9 *Theory and Decision* 127–59 (April).

Shartel, Burke. 1930. "Federal Judges—Appointment, Supervision, and Removal—Some Possibilities under the Constitution." 28 *Michigan Law Review* 870–909.

Shetreet, Shimon, ed. 1982. *Jerusalem Conference on Minimum Standards of Judicial Independence.* Dordrecht: Martinus Nijhoff.

Shetreet, Shimon, and Jules Deschenes, eds. 1985. *Judicial Independence: The Contemporary Debate.* Dordrecht: Martinus Nijhoff.

Shiho sho, ed. 1939. *Shiho enkakushi* (A Documentary History of the Judiciary). Republished, Tokyo: Hosokai, 1960.

"Shiho sho keiji kyoku cho kyushoku mondai (The Problem of the Inactive Status for the Bureau Chief of the Ministry of Justice Criminal Bureau)." 1925. 2438 *Horitsu shimbun* 19–20.

Shiso undo kenkyu sho, ed. 1969. *Osorubeki saiban* (Fearsome Trials). Tokyo: Zenbo sha.

Songer, Donald R., Jeffrey A. Segal, and Charles M. Cameron. 1994. "The Hierarchy of Justice: Testing a Principal–Agent Model of Supreme Court–Circuit Court Interactions." 38 *American Journal of Political Science* 673–96 (August).

Spiller, Pablo T., and Rafael Gely. 1992. "Congressional Control or Judicial Independence: The Determinants of U.S. Supreme Court Labor-Relations Decisions, 1949–1988." 23 *RAND Journal of Economics* 463–92 (Winter).

Spiller, Pablo T., and Matthew Law Spitzer. 1992. "Judicial Choice of Legal Doctrines." 8 *Journal of Law, Economics and Organization* 8–46 (March).

Spotts, Frederic, and Theodor Wieser. 1986. *Italy, a Difficult Democracy: A Survey of Italian Politics.* Cambridge: Cambridge University Press.

Stephenson, Matthew. 2001. "When the Devil Turns: The Political Foundations of Independent Judicial Review." Unpublished paper, Department of Government, Harvard University, Cambridge, Mass.

Story, Joseph. 1833. *Commentaries on the Constitution of the United States.* Boston: Hilliard, Gray.

Surrency, Erwin C. 1967. "The Courts in the American Colonies." 11 *American Journal of Legal History* 347–76.

Toma, Eugenia Froedge. 1991. "Congressional Influence and the Supreme Court: The Budget as a Signalling Device." 20 *Journal of Legal Studies* 131–46 (January).

Tomatsu, Hidenori. 1993. "Equal Protection of the Law." In *Japanese Constitutional Law,* edited by Percy R. Luney Jr. and Kazuyuki Takahashi. Tokyo: University of Tokyo Press.

Tsukahara, Eiji. 1991. "Saibankan keireki to saiban kodo (The Relationship between a Judge's Career and His Opinions)." 43 *Ho shakai gaku* 46–54.

Turner, Kathryn. 1961. "The Midnight Judges." 109 *University of Pennsylvania Law Review* 494–523 (February).

U.S. Dept. of Commerce. 1996. *Statistical Abstract of the United States.* Washington, D.C.: U.S. Department of Commerce.

U.S. Dept. of Justice. 1996. *Bulletin—Prosecutors in State Courts, 1994.* (NCJ-151656).

U.S. Dept. of Justice. 1997. *Bulletin—Felony Sentences in State Courts.* (NCJ-163391).

Ushiomi, Toshitaka. 1971. "Shiho gyosei no kempoteki kankaku (The Constitutional Sense of Judicial Administration)." *Hogaku seminaa* 2–5 (June).

Van Wolferen, Karel. 1989. *The Enigma of Japanese Power.* New York: Knopf.

Volcansek, Mary L. 1982. "The Effects of Judicial-Selection Reform: What We Know and What We Don't Know." In *The Analysis of Judicial Reform,* edited by Philip S. Dubois. Pp. 79–91. Lexington, Mass.: D.C. Heath.

Waldfogel, Joel. 1995. "The Selection Hypothesis and the Relationship between Trial and Plaintiff Victory." 103 *Journal of Political Economy* 229–60 (April).

Walsh, Carl. 1995. "Optimal Contracts for Central Bankers." 85 *American Economic Review* 150–67 (March).

Watanabe, Yasuo, Setsuo Miyazawa, Shigeo Kisa, Shosaburo Yoshino, and Tetsu Sato. 1997. *Tekisuto bukku gendai shiho* (Textbook: The Modern Judiciary). 3rd ed. Tokyo: Nihon hyoron sha.

Weingast, Barry R., and Mark J. Moran. 1983. "Bureaucratic Discretion or Congressional Control? Regulatory Policymaking by the FTC." 91 *Journal of Political Economy* 765–800 (October).

West, Mark D. 1992. "Note: Prosecution Review Commissions: Japan's Answer to the Problem of Prosecutorial Discretion." 92 *Columbia Law Review* 684–723 (April).

Williamson, Oliver E. 1993. "Transaction Cost Economics and Organization Theory." 2 *Industrial and Corporate Change* 107–56.

Wilson, James Q. 1989. *Bureaucracy: What Government Agencies Do and Why They Do It.* New York: Basic Books.

Witt, Elder. 1990. *Congressional Quarterly's Guide to the U.S. Supreme Court.* 2d ed. Washington, D.C.: Congressional Quarterly.

"Yamaoka keiji kyoku cho kyushoku ni kanshite (Regarding the Inactive Status of Criminal Bureau Chief Yamaoka)." 1925. 2438 *Horitsu shimbun* 20.

Zadankai. 1971. "Saibankan wa dokuritsu shite iruka (Are Judges Independent)?" *Hogaku seminaa* 57–73 (special issue).

ZSKS. See Nihon minshu.

Index

Abe, Haruhiko, 21, 24, 27
Abe, Teruya, 77
Adams, John, 128
adjusted R^2, 30
administrative assignments, relative prestige of, 12–14
administrative cases, 49, 62, 73–76, 82–95
affirmances by higher court. *See individual regression results*
alternating-parties regime, 144
anti-government opinions (composite index), 48–57
appellate review. *See individual regression results*
appointment of judges, 9–10, 15, 141–42, 166–67, 171
apportionment. *See* malapportionment
Auer, James E., 65

Bagnoli, Mark, 156n. 28
Becker, Gary S., 103n. 11
Beer, Lawrence W., 65
Block, Stewart A., 130
branch offices, relative prestige of, 7, 11–15, 21–23, 25. *See also individual regression results*
Buckley, Frank, 142
bundling, 150, 163–65
bureaucracy, in imperial Japan, 156–58
bureaucratic independence, 10, 17–18, 73, 85–86, 123, 152–68

cabinet, 9. *See also* appointment of judges
Calvert, Randall Law, 17, 156n. 28
campaign restrictions, 20–22, 58–60, 116

canvassing, door-to-door. *See* campaign restrictions
censored data, 35
chief judge, role of, 24. *See also individual regression results*
China, and Japanese textbooks, 165n. 33
Choper, Jesse H., 127
civil service protection, 165–66
Coate, Malcolm B., 156n. 28
coefficients, in regressions, 28
Cohen, Mark A., 126nn. 1, 3
Commerce Court, 129–31
Commercial Code litigation, 76–81
Communist Party, 21, 24, 58, 69, 119
comparative studies of judicial independence, ix, 2–4, 122–68
confessions, 98–101
Constitution of Japan (1889), 126, 132–39, 174
Constitution of Japan (1947), 2, 13, 15, 19, 21–22, 48–50, 62–73, 76–81, 125–26, 145, 166, 173–74
Constitution of the United States, 126–32, 166, 175–76
Construction Ministry, 154–55
control variables, in regressions, 28
conviction rates, 96–101, 108–9, 113, 119n. 31, 121
Cooter, Robert, 162n. 30, 165n. 34
corruption in the courts, 2–3, 122, 154, 169
court-packing incident, 127–28, 143
courts, in imperial Japan, 132–39
Courts Act, 7–9, 15, 113n. 27, 125n. 2
crime rates, 105–7, 119–21
criminal cases, 49, 96–121
Cruikshanks, Randal L., 126
cultural differences, 54

197